Lessons in Leadership from the White House to Your House

This book argues that we can learn a great deal about leadership from the experiences of eight US presidents who have served in the White House since Watergate. The eight presidents considered here differed widely in their family backgrounds, wealth, education, age, prior political experiences, and motivations for power. But they all made the same promise—to "faithfully execute the Office of President of the US and ... preserve, protect, and defend the Constitution of the United States"—and they all faced considerable challenges in fulfilling that promise.

While all eight presidents had policy successes and failures, the author argues that we gain real insight on their leadership acumen by analyzing the deeper structures of leadership effectiveness that all leaders need to address: vision, execution, management, and decision-making. The book assesses the performance of each president along these four dimensions of leadership and extends lessons learned to leaders in other sectors.

Michael Eric Siegel is an award-winning adjunct professor of Government at The Johns Hopkins University. He is also the author of *The President as Leader* (Routledge, 2018). He has written at least 20 articles in professional journals and published four op-eds in the Baltimore Sun. From 1987 until 2021, Dr. Siegel served as a Senior Education Specialist at the Federal Judicial Center in Washington, DC.

Lessons in Leadership from the White House to Your House

Michael Eric Siegel

Routledge
Taylor & Francis Group

NEW YORK AND LONDON

Designed cover image: Getty Images/miralex

First published 2023
by Routledge
605 Third Avenue, New York, NY 10158

and by Routledge
4 Park Square, Milton Park, Abingdon, Oxon, OX14 4RN

Routledge is an imprint of the Taylor & Francis Group, an informa business

British Library of Congress Cataloging-in-Publication Data
A catalogue record for this book is available from the British Library

ISBN: 978-1-032-25833-1 (hbk)
ISBN: 978-1-032-25831-7 (pbk)
ISBN: 978-1-003-28522-9 (ebk)

DOI: 10.4324/9781003285229

Typeset in Bembo
by KnowledgeWorks Global Ltd.

CONTENTS

PREFACE

We all need effective leadership and leaders for our continued vitality, prosperity, and well-being. We also need effective leadership to "preserve and protect" democratic institutions and a constitutional republic. Yet, we treat the idea with great timidity and caution, as if effective leadership is mysterious and beyond our comprehension, let alone our normal experience. Consider the following two, almost identical statements about subjects explored in this book: leadership in general and presidential leadership in particular.

In terms of leadership in general, the widely revered presidential historian, Professor James MacGregor Burns, in his classic book on leadership quipped, "Leadership is one of the most widely observed and least understood phenomena on earth."[1] And regarding presidential leadership, the well-respected University of Texas historian, Jeremi Suri, writing almost 30 years after Burns, said, "The U.S. presidency is the most talked about and least understood office in the world."[2]

There is good reason for skepticism about our comprehension of leadership, especially as expressed in the White House. Nevertheless, this book argues that presidential leadership, and leadership generally, are not as ineffable as Burns and Suri make them out to be. The author submits that by reviewing the leadership experiences of eight US presidents since Watergate, who differed widely in their backgrounds, age, educational levels, wealth, political experiences, and motivation for power, we can learn a great deal about leadership effectiveness. In addition, the author believes that using four specific leadership criteria—vision, execution, management, and decision-making—will help readers understand the relevance of presidential experiences along these dimensions of leadership to other sectors. All leaders must excel in the four identified areas of leadership.

To suggest that the vast, almost impossibly challenging responsibilities of US presidents can be boiled down to four variables is a bold and, some would argue, futile assertion. There are so many challenges and heavy responsibilities, so much uncertainty. This is true, and yet the office was designed for human beings, not for superheroes. Of course, the original constitutional design of the presidency barely resembles the modern presidency; so much has transpired, and the 45 men who served as president (there have been 46 presidencies, but only 45 presidents, as Grover Cleveland served twice). The men who have served, and the circumstances they faced, have had a strong influence on the nature of the presidency. In addition, the 45 presidents have possessed strengths and weaknesses, achieved great successes, and experienced dismal failures. All who are currently leaders or aspire to leadership can learn from the presidents as leaders.

The author argues that the analysis of contemporary presidential leadership should begin with presidents who served at least one full term since Watergate. Why? Because the office of the presidency and the "playing field" on which presidents operate changed in fundamental ways since Watergate. The office that Jimmy Carter entered in 1977 was a vastly different one than the one Nixon resigned from in 1974, and changes have continued since that time. Congress is more aggressive in its duty of overseeing the executive, especially in the realm of foreign policy; the public has become more cynical, less trusting of government, especially the presidency; the judiciary strengthened its resolve to protect the constitution and the rule of law; and the media, including the social media, have increased their coverage of the presidency, incessantly searching for every possible act of leadership ineptitude, error, or malfeasance.

Other leadership environments have also changed. There is less automatic faith in leaders, less tolerance for traditional organizational hierarchies, more scrutiny of leader's behaviors, more access to information through the Internet, and greater suspicion of the "Establishment."

With these and other contextual forces, presidents, as well as other leaders, must resort to a strategic approach to leadership. The author posits that the mastery of four components of leadership will give presidents and other leaders the guidelines they need to lead with purpose and impact in the 21st century and to overcome the considerable obstacles they face in the exercise of power. The book considers the leadership strategies and styles of eight presidents since Watergate along the following four leadership components:

a. Policy, or vision—the president's purpose, goals, and aspirations, the future they envision.
b. Politics, or strategy—the president's efficacy in translating vision into reality through maintaining control of an agenda and effective persuasion and negotiation.
c. Structure, or management—the president as chief executive who deftly manages the White House and executive branch, most likely with a capable chief of staff.

d. Process, or decision-making—the president's ability to create the condi-
    tions for effective decision-making, comfort in making tough decisions,
    and willingness to monitor the consequences of their decisions.

The core argument of the book is that leadership effectiveness in the White
House demands that presidents stay focused on a compelling vision for their
administration, despite temporary setbacks or failures; surround themselves
with talented people—professionals, not friends—and give them the freedom
to conduct negotiations with Congress and other critical stakeholders: remain
keenly attuned to the details of effectively managing the White House and a
sprawling executive branch of some 3 million people; and carefully ensure the
conditions for effective decision-making, including encouraging dissenting
opinions, identifying appropriate venues, relying on facts and evidence, not
emotion or impulse, and strategically announcing decisions made.

The book argues that the success and vitality of American Government in
the 21st century and beyond are inextricably tied to the leadership acumen of
the men and women in the White House. As well, the author extends the leadership "lessons" from the White House to the leadership challenges of other
sectors in society and argues that they also must find ways to excel at vision,
execution, management, and decision-making.

The author is deeply indebted to Ms. Susan Fuchs, a Bethesda, Maryland
senior paralegal specialist and to Mr. Howard Goldblatt, a retired Washington
DC government relations specialist and former congressional staffer, who
painstakingly reviewed every chapter and provided focused and meaningful
feedback. The author would also like to thank Ambassador Dennis Ross, a
respected national security adviser and Middle East specialist in several recent
presidential administrations, for two interviews conducted in Washington
DC. Special thanks also goes to Ms. Jennifer Knerr, former emeritus senior
editor of political science at Routledge, for her ongoing encouragement and
support.

Finally, the author expresses special appreciation to his daughter, Sophie,
who has remained active in politics, while also raising two children; son-in-
law Aaron, an award-winning police detective and wonderful father; and to
his two wonderful grandsons, Avi and Lon. May they be led by great men
and women. Finally, the author dedicates this book to the loving memory of
his late wife Anne, whose passion for the democratic process was obvious and
admirable. May her memory be for a blessing.

Notes

1 James MacGregor Burns, *Leadership*. New York, NY: Harper Torch Books,
  1978, 2.
2 Jeremi Suri, *The Impossible Presidency: The Rise and Fall of America's Highest Office*.
  New York, NY: Basic Books, 2017, Introduction, xviii.

1

INTRODUCTION

The Presidency from the
Constitution to the Biden Era

"The presidency," according to the University of Texas History Professor Jeremi Suri, "was the most original innovation of America's founding moment. The enduring strength of the office comes from its original lack of definition. It is an ever-changing role."[1] A careful review of the presidency created by the founders at the constitutional convention reinforces the veracity of Suri's observation; they created an office of unclear expectations, limited powers, and modest ambitions. That the role has changed constantly and dramatically over the past 233 years is also indisputable.

In creating the office of the presidency, the founders were attempting to address weaknesses and gaps in the first scheme of government, The Articles of Confederation, that guided the political affairs of the young nation from 1781 to 1789. The Articles, ratified during the war against Britain on March 1, 1781, placed almost all political power in the 13 states, and more specifically in the legislatures of those states. According to Professor Suri, the Articles encouraged "fragmentation and weakness," while a "strong dynamic society—free from British rule—required strong leadership that would unify the country."[2] There was no provision in the Articles for a national figure who could provide the needed unity and could also assume emergency powers when legislators failed to perform their duties.[3]

The Article of Confederation failed for several reasons:

- The Articles did not give the national government the power to tax, placing Congress in the awkward position of pleading for money from the states to pay war debts and administer the affairs of the new state.
- The Articles made no provision for an independent leadership position to coordinate the government (the president was merely the presiding officer of Congress).

DOI: 10.4324/9781003285229-1

- The Articles did not allow the national government to regulate inter-state and foreign commerce. (When John Adams proposed that the Confederation enter into a commercial treaty with Britain after the war, he was asked, "Would you like one treaty or thirteen, Mr. Adams?").
- There was no provision in the Articles for national defense, as noted specifically by delegate Edmund Randolph of Virginia.
- The Articles could not be amended without the consent of all the state legislatures, giving each state the power to veto and changes in the Confederation.[4]

As Supreme Court Justice Robert H. Jackson would observe 150 years later, "While the Declaration of Independence was directed against an excess of authority, the Constitution (following the Articles of Confederation) was directed against anarchy."[5] The 55 delegates who arrived in Philadelphia in 1787 embraced the notion that there was a need to develop a leadership position, an executive function, in the US government. As Professor Suri indicates, the founders were influenced on this matter by British thinkers who had also grappled with the idea of executive power, John Locke, David Hume, and Edmund Burke.[6]

When William III ascended to the English throne in 1689, after a parliament led revolution, philosopher John Locke suggested the separation of "legislative and executive" power and the substitution of the word "executive" for the word "royal." Locke's executive was still a royal, but his role was justified less by divine right and more by the governing functions he served in a society based on the public good.[7] Although the other British thinkers did not share Locke's approval of the revolt against an unjust king, they echoed his analysis of the monarch's public duties. Hume and Burke defined the king as a civil "executive" rather than a divine ruler. Edmund Burke offered the "most sustained discussion of executive power in early modern Europe."[8]

Burke criticized the French Revolution's emphasis on unlimited popular rule and argued that without a check on peoples' power, the revolution would descend into extremes of violence and destruction. He made an impassioned case for a powerful executive—royal or not—which he believed was essential for a well-ordered society.

Expressing ideas that would influence the founders as they designed the presidency, Burke described his ideal executive as follows:

> It is a trust, indeed that has much depending on its faithful and diligent performance, both in the person presiding in it and in all its subordinates.... It ought to be envisioned with dignity, authority, and consideration, and it ought to lead to glory. The office of executive is an office of exertion. It is not from impotence that we are to expect the tasks of power.[9]

The drafting of the US Constitution, in short, marked a major rethinking of good government by the founders, especially around executive power and national leadership. Later in this book, we will return to the theme of rethinking and refer to the important work of organizational development expert Adam Grant. Professor Grant, in 2021, argued that intelligence is frequently thought to be our ability to learn and to think, but in a turbulent world there's another set of cognitive skills that might matter more: "the ability to rethink and unlearn."[10]

The founders were operating in a period of considerable turmoil, and they were forced to rethink their ideas of leadership in the nascent American republic. Earlier, their anti-royal assumptions had led the founders to a "rejection of executive power as a whole."[11]

Now, as they wrote the Constitution, they wanted to add executive power to the architecture of government, but to do so in a delicate manner that would not threaten liberty or crush local representation. According to political scientist Gary L. Gregg, "Though we tend to take it for granted, to have an institution that would in some ways resemble a monarch and yet would be limited in its power and influence, and that would be elected periodically was something unheard of at the time."[12]

The concept of the "executive" political leader traveled across the Atlantic and strongly influenced the founders. Madison, Hamilton, and others began to use the term "executive" when referring to government leadership. According to Jeremi Suri, "Locke's executive power of 1689 became the American presidential executive of 1787."[13] Yet, the founders were still deeply suspicious of any scheme of government that would return a monarch at the helm of government, prompting Professor Louis Koenig to write that the presidency was created "by a group of men who had their fingers crossed!"[14]

After lengthy deliberations and debates, the founders decided to create a national executive, separate from Congress, with clearly prescribed duties for executing and defending national laws and the ability to offer a contingent veto (subject to a legislative override) on acts of Congress. The following is a summary of the executive article of the Constitution (Article II) and pertains to the conditions and terms of the office of the presidency, as well as the actual powers available to the president.

Section One of Article II spells out the *conditions and terms of office* as follows:

- The executive Power is vested in a President of the United States, and he will hold Office for a term of 4 years, along with the Vice President.
- Each state will appoint electors, in a manner determined by the legislature, and the number of electors will equal the number of Senators and Representatives that the state has in Congress. No Senator or Representative, however, may be an elector. The electors will choose the President and Vice President.

- Congress is to choose the actual day for the election.
- The eligibility criteria for election to the Presidency are that the candidate must be a natural born citizen of the United States, and 35 years of age.
- The Vice President will succeed the President in case of the Removal of the President from Office, or his death, Resignation, or Inability to discharge the Powers and Duties of the Office.
- The President's compensation (salary) may not be increased or diminished during his tenure.
- The President, before he enters office, must take an oath to "preserve, protect, and defend the Constitution of the United States" (oath of affirmation).[15]

Section Two of Article II outlines the *powers of the office* of the president as follows:

- Commander-in-chief. The President shall be the commander-in-chief of the Army and Navy of the United States, and of the militia of the several states when called into actual service of the United States. He may require the opinions of officers in each executive department of government. And he has the right to grant reprieves and pardons for offenses against the United States, except in Cases of Impeachment.
- Treaties and Appointment of Officers. The President has the power, with the advice and consent of the Senate, to make treaties (with two-thirds Senate concurrence) and to nominate and (with the advice and consent of the senate) appoint ambassadors, other public ministers and consuls, and judges of the Supreme Court.
- Appointments during recess of the Senate. The President has the power to fill vacancies that may occur during a Senate recess by granting Commissions that expire at the end of the next session.
- Recommendations to Congress—Convene and Adjourn Congress— Receive Ambassadors—Execute laws. The President will deliver "from time to time" information on the state of the Union and recommend measures he judges are "necessary and expedient;" he may, on extraordinary occasions, convene both houses, or either of them; receive Ambassadors; take care that the laws be "faithfully executed" and commission officers of the United States.
- Removal from Office. The President, Vice President, and all civil officers of the United States will be removed from office on impeachment for conviction of treason, bribery, or other high crimes and misdemeanors.[16]

Once the dust had settled, the commentary on the completed Constitution and presidential provisions began. At the Virginia ratifying convention, for instance, Governor Patrick Henry expressed the fears of some about the founders' creation of the presidency:

> This Constitution is said to have beautiful features but when I come to examine those features, Sir, they appear to me to be horribly frightful. Among other deformities it has an awful squinting; it squints toward monarchy, and does that not raise indignation in the breast of every American?[17]

On the other hand, Alexander Hamilton, in the Federalist No. 70, refuted the allegations of "monarchy," and suggested that "energy" in the executive branch is a leading characteristic of good government. He added:

> A feeble executive implies a feeble execution of the government. A feeble executive is but another phrase for bad execution; and a government ill executed, whatever it may be in theory, must be, in practice, a bad government.[18]

Whether or not the presidency, as created by the founders, had enough or too much power would be debated long after 1789. But there is no doubt that the office created in the late eighteenth century proved to be an imperfect guide for presidents who followed. The Constitution did not anticipate a civil war, two world wars, or a "cold war"; it did not anticipate a world saturated with nuclear weapons and other means of mass destruction; it could not envision a world transformed by global forces of transnational terrorism or environmental degradation; it did not fathom the Internet or cell phones. In this sense, as of this writing, it was the actions and decisions of the 45 men who served in the office, building upon the pronouncements of the founders and philosophical insights of their contemporaries, that primarily shaped the presidency.[19]

Clearly, the office of the presidency grew far beyond the vision of the founders. In many ways, the growth of presidential power was precipitated by the various crises confronting the nation, including the civil war, two world wars, the Great Depression, the cold war, the war on terror, and a global pandemic. To respond to these crises, presidents like Lincoln, Teddy and Franklin D. Roosevelt, Lyndon Johnson, Richard Nixon, and George W. Bush took considerable leeway in adding to the executive role and stretched that role far beyond the original construction. Lincoln, for example, took several unilateral steps during the civil war to save the union. According to *Boston Globe* reporter, Charlie Savage:

> Without a declaration of war, Lincoln enlarged the Army and Navy, blockaded Southern ports, spent money not appropriated by Congress, and arrested Northerners suspected of being Southern agents without giving them legal rights–all exceeding the authority of federal law and the Constitution.[20]

Lincoln acknowledged that his actions were outside the scope of permissible presidential powers, and when Congress was back in session, he asked for its authorization for his emergency actions, arguing they had been necessary to save the union.[21]

While Congress was inclined to abide by and even legitimize Lincoln's actions,[22] the Supreme Court was emphatic in ruling that his actions were to be viewed as an aberration, and not as a new definition of presidential power.[23] A year after the end of the civil war, the high court struck down a military tribunal Lincoln had established to prosecute northern criminal, in the case *of Ex parte Milligan*, as follows:

> The Constitution of the United States is a law for rulers and people, especially in war and peace, and covers with the shield of protection all classes of men at all times, and under all circumstances. No doctrine involving more pernicious consequences was ever invented by the wit of man than that any of its provisions can be suspended during any of the great exigencies of government. Such a doctrine leads directly to anarchy or despotism.[24]

During the tragic days of the Great Depression, when unemployment in the United States reached higher than 25 percent of the working population and 34 states had closed their banks, influential voices in the United States, including columnist Walter Lippmann, called on President Franklin Delano Roosevelt to assume dictatorial powers.[25] Although FDR declined the idea of "dictatorial" powers, he did not shy away from using a muscular approach to presidential leadership, including introducing far-reaching economic and reform packages in the first hundred days of his administration and establishing a commission on management (Brownlow Report), to provide more analytical and centralized control of the government by the White House.[26] He also attempted to pack the Supreme Court with justices who would be more sympathetic to his policy initiatives.

In 1940, FDR violated the Neutrality Act by ordering the transfer of 50 destroyers to Britain to help its war effort, in exchange for the right to lease sites for US naval bases. Attorney General Robert Jackson argued that despite the ostensibly illegality of the exchange of destroyers for bases, Roosevelt's actions were sanctioned by his role of commander-in-chief. And in March 1941, Congress passed the Lend-Lease Act, which effectively legalized Roosevelt's actions.[27]

During the cold war between the United States and the Soviet Union from 1945 to 1970, Congress added legislative measures to increase presidential power, thereby enabling the commander-in-chief to lead the "containment" effort against the Soviet Union. For example, Congress passed the National Security Act of 1947,[28] which enhanced the president's leadership in the formulation and execution of US foreign policy; the Act created a single defense secretary responsible for all defense planning and the military budget.

According to political scientists Crenson and Ginsberg, "By creating a more unified military chain of command and a single defense budget, the National Security Act diminished Congress' ability to intervene in military planning and increased the president's control over the armed services and national security policy."[29] The National Security Act also created the Central Intelligence Agency (CIA) and placed it under the direct supervision of the president. Presidents from 1947 to 1970 gladly accepted the elevated grants of power and used them with great enthusiasm, and little oversight, to fight the cold war.[30]

After the September 11, 2001, terrorist attack on the United States, Congress again empowered the presidency through legislative action. Within a week of September 11, Congress authorized President George W. Bush to "use all necessary and appropriate force against those nations, organizations, or persons he determines planned, authorized, committed, or aided the terrorist attacks."[31] Though the Authorization for Use of Military Force (AUMF) was not a declaration of war, President Bush interpreted it as activating a full panoply of powers for a wartime president, including the power to detain "enemy combatants." Claiming that the Taliban and al Qaeda fighters were not entitled to the full protection of the Geneva Convention, the Bush administration asserted an ability to hold detainees indefinitely, subject them to harsh interrogation methods, and try them in military tribunals instead of criminal courts.[32]

Nevertheless, the federal judiciary acted to limit the president's unbridled freedom of action; in a memorable quotation from the US Supreme Court case of *Hamdi v. Rumsfeld*, Justice Sandra Day O'Connor, writing for the majority, said, "A state of war is not a blank check for the president when it comes to the rights of the nation's citizens."[33] In the Hamdi case, the Court decided that while the government could hold US citizens in military custody, the Court would scrutinize the procedures used to determine whether someone was, in fact, an "unlawful combatant."[34]

Another reason for the growth of presidential power during the last 233 years was because of personal ambition, and even feelings of grandiosity, among some of the occupants of the White House.[35] For instance, President Richard Nixon, who wanted to be "the architect of his times,"[36] took presidential powers to new heights, asserting that he understood the interests of the US better than the public, the Congress, and the courts did. According to presidential historian Douglas Brinkley, in a 2022 review of a book on Watergate, said of Nixon, "Treating politics as a blood sport, he disregarded the protocols and proprieties of the executive branch, putting himself above the law."[37] Similar tendencies were apparent during the presidency of Donald J. Trump.

While the growth of presidential power during the civil war, Great Depression, cold war, and war on terror seems to have been uninterrupted by the other branches, Congress and the judiciary intervened periodically, as already indicated. During the late 1960s and early 1970s, Congress reacted decisively to the unchecked growth of the "imperial presidency," a term coined by historian Arthur Schlesinger to describe the accelerating growth of presidential power, especially during the Johnson and Nixon presidencies.[38] Even before the end of the Vietnam War, Congress passed legislation limiting the president's ability to unilaterally sustain a prolonged commitment of US troops in a foreign conflict without seeking congressional approval.[39] Furthermore, Congress passed the Congressional Budget and Control Act of 1974, which severely restricted the president's ability to "impound" Congressionally appropriated funds, which Nixon had attempted to do. The Budget Reform Act also gave Congress a larger role in the formulation of the federal budget by creating a House and Senate Budget Committee and the Congressional Budget Office.[40] Political scientist referred to this burst of congressional activity as the "resurgence" of Congress."[41] In the aftermath of Vietnam and Watergate, and later various White House scandals and the financial crisis of 2007–2008, Americans "gazed at the White House with more skepticism than adoration," as I have written elsewhere.[42] The presidency had been taken down a few notches. In 1980, former President Gerald Ford said, to general applause, "We have not an imperial presidency but an imperiled presidency."[43] Book titles, such as *The Tethered Presidency*, gave the impression of a

> beleaguered and pathetic fellow sitting forlornly in the Oval Office, assailed by unprecedentedly intractable problems, paralyzed by the constitutional separation of powers, hemmed in by congressional and bureaucratic constraints, pushed one way and another by exigent interest groups, seduced, betrayed, and abandoned by the mass media.[44]

Nevertheless, the expectations of presidential leadership and power remained embedded in the public mind. According to presidential scholar Fred Greenstein, "the president became the most visible landmark in the political landscape, virtually standing for the federal government in the minds of many Americans."[45]

In their 2008 textbook, *Presidential Power: Unchecked and Unbalanced*, Johns Hopkins University political scientists Matthew Crenson and Benjamin Ginsberg assert, "Today whatever the travails of particular presidents, it is the presidency that dominates American government and politics."[46] In 1952, a period of relative tranquility, Supreme Court Justice Robert Jackson described the magnitude of the president's responsibilities in a way that sounds similar to the executive power of Edmund Burke:

> the concentration of executive authority in a single head in whose choice the whole nation has a part, making him the focus of public hopes and expectations. In drama, magnitude and finality his decisions so far overshadow any others that almost alone he fills the public eye and ear.[47]

Perhaps the trials and tribulations of the presidents parallel the challenges of leaders in many other sectors as well. Many other leaders confront the realities of heightened high expectations and limited opportunities to deliver due to the limitations placed on contemporary leaders: suspicion of authority, proliferating information and knowledge sources, collapsing of traditional hierarchical forms of organization, and the growing attraction to "transformational" as opposed to "transactional" leadership.[48]

While there are many obstacles to effective leadership, this book argues that US presidents, as well as other leaders, can succeed in the exercise of power by addressing four components of leadership in a strategic manner. The four components of leadership were chosen based on the author's years of observation and research of presidential performance, his 33 years of service in the federal government, 35 years of university teaching, interviews with former presidential advisers, and a model of the "strategic presidency" elucidated in a book by two executive veterans of the Carter Administration, titled, *Memorandum for the President: A Strategic Approach to Domestic Affairs in the 1980's.*[49]

The authors of *Memorandum for the President*, Ben W. Heineman and Curtis Hessler, served in high level executive positions in the Carter administration (Departments of Health, Education, and Welfare (HEW), now called Health and Human Services (HHS), and the Department of the Treasury), identified four core elements of a "strategic" presidency, which they believed were absent from the Carter administration: clear choice of goals to pursue (policy), activation of political coalitions to support the goals (politics), a strategic approach to competently managing the federal government (structure), and an effective decision-making process (process).[50]

Using the Heineman-Hessler ideas as a foundation, the author developed the following four categories of leadership to analyze the performance of presidents Carter through Biden:

1. **Policy (vision):** envisioned future, goals, purpose, priorities, legacy
2. **Politics (strategy):** translating vision into reality, persuasion methods, negotiating with Congress, listening skills
3. **Structure (management):** internal organization, management of the White House and executive branch, role of the chief of staff
4. **Process (decision-making):** including dissenting voices, respectful dialogue, choice of venue

Here is the central argument of the book. Great position, including the presidency of the United States, sets up great potential for achievement but does not guarantee it. The obstacles to achievement are substantial and persistent, and the tools available to a president are limited by the Constitution and by many other factors. But a president can succeed if he (or she) masters four components of leadership, and these components have relevance beyond the White House. He must enunciate a clear, compelling vision (policy); develop an execution strategy that recognizes an inevitable need for negotiation, persuasion (politics), and compromise; utilize a strategic approach to management in the White House and executive branch that emphasizes competence and minimizes infighting (strategy); and ensure that the conditions for effective decision-making, including the careful explorations of dissenting opinions, are protected (process).

When a president (or any other leader) has a strong vision:

- He will be able to convey his policy objectives to the public, to Congress, to the executive branch of government, and to his own staff in a compelling manner. His purpose will be clear, and the president and his staff will work hard to maintain control over their agenda and resist the tendency toward drift or complacency.
- The leader will wisely conserve his energy to pursue his vision.

When a president (or any other leader) has a strategy of execution:

- He will comprehend the inevitability of opposition to his ideas and agenda.
- He will negotiate with critical stakeholders and focus his energy and attention on a limited number of goals at any one time.
- He will surround himself with capable and influential deputies, including a competent chief of staff, who will "sell" the president's agenda, while respecting objections to it by well-meaning opponents.

When a president (or any other leader) adopts a strategic management approach:

- He will recruit talented managers to help support the accomplishment of his agenda.
- He will ensure that staff have adequate access to the Oval Office and to presidential staff.
- He will prefer professionalism over friendships and find ways to stay on touch and support his management team.

When a president (or any other leader) ensures an effective decision-making process:

- He will encourage the expression of dissenting points of view and avoid decision-making flaws like groupthink or confirmation bias.
- He will insist that his advisers tell him what he needs to hear, not what he wants to hear.
- Although he will encourage an open exploration of options and alternatives, the leader will bring the deliberative process to closure and make a firm decision. But the leader will also stay attuned to the consequences of that decision.

The following chapters are organized by the four leadership variables, and each chapter includes:

- An assessment of presidential performance (Carter through Biden) in each leadership skill.
- Application of lessons learned by the president to other sectors.
- Takeaways for all leaders.

Here are the specific questions considered in each skill:

Policy (vision)

- Why am I running for office?
- What is my purpose?
- Where do I want to lead the nation to?
- What do I want to accomplish during the next 4 years?
- How will my administration make a difference in the lives of US citizens?
- What do I want my legacy to be?
- What is my vision of the office I seek?

Politics (strategy/execution)

- How will I implement or execute my vision, my agenda?
- Upon whom will I rely to communicate my message? How will I work with the press?
- Who will manage congressional relations?
- What strategy will I use to influence the opposition party, or members of my own party who have their own political agendas?
- How will I stay true to my agenda, fulfill campaign promises, and still have time to reflect and assess how I am doing?
- How many issues will I tackle at one time?

Structure (management)

- How will I organize the White House?
- What management structure/strategy will I utilize?
- Will I have a chief of staff?
- Will I have an open or closed operation?
- How will I manage the entire executive branch of government?
- What skills/backgrounds will I favor in staffing my White House and cabinet?
- How will I assure the alignment of the management with my policy agenda?

Process (decision-making)

- How will I make and announce decisions?
- Who will I include in the decision-making process?
- Will I deliberately encourage dissenting views?
- How will I manage strong disagreements among my advisers?
- How will I keep track of the consequences of my decisions?
- How will I apply "damage control" when needed?

Notes

1 Jeremi Suri, *The Impossible Presidency: The Rise and Fall of America's Highest Office.* New York, NY: Basic Books, 2017, 20.
2 Ibid, 9.
3 Ibid.
4 Ibid, 16; Kenneth Janda, Jeffrey M. Berry, and Jerry Goldman, *The Challenge of Democracy: The Essentials.* 6th ed. Boston, MA: Houghton-Mifflin, 1996, 64.
5 Robert H. Jackson, *The Struggle for Judicial Supremacy—A Study of a Crisis in American Power and Politics.* New York, NY: Alfred A. Knopf, 1991, 8.
6 Suri, *The Impossible Presidency*, 9–10.
7 Ibid, 10.
8 Ibid.
9 Ibid, 11.
10 Adam Grant, *Think Again: The Power of Knowing What We Don't Know.* New York, NY: Viking, 2021, 2.
11 Suri, *The Impossible Presidency*, 14.
12 Gary L. Gregg, *Thinking about the Presidency: Documents and Essays from the Founding to the Present.* New York, NY: Rowman and Littlefield, 2005, 5.
13 Suri, *The Impossible Presidency*, 13.
14 Louis Koenig, *The Chief Executive*, 6th ed. New York, NY: Harcourt, Brace, 1995, 1.
15 US Constitution, Section One, Article II.
16 US Constitution, Section Two, Article II.
17 Gregg, *Thinking about the Presidency*, 8.
18 Ibid.
19 Siegel, *The President as Leader*, 2nd ed., 5.
20 Charles Savage, *Takeover: The Return of the Imperial Presidency and the Subversion of American Democracy.* New York, NY: Little Brown, 2007, 17.
21 Siegel, *The President as Leader*, 2nd ed., 5–6.
22 Crenson and Ginsberg, *Presidential Power*, 17.
23 Savage, *Takeover*, 17.
24 Ibid.
25 Jonathan Alter, *The Defining Moment: FDR's Hundred Days and the Triumph of Hope.* New York, NY: Simon and Schuster, 2007, 5.
26 Donald R. Brand, "The President as Chief Administrator: James Landis and the Brownlow Report." *Political Science Quarterly*, 123 no. 1 (Spring 2008), 70.
27 Crenson and Ginsberg, *Presidential Power*, 224–225.
28 Pub L. 80-235, 1947.
29 Crenson and Ginsberg, *Presidential Power*, 248.
30 Siegel, *The President as Leader*, 2nd ed., 7.

31 Authorization for Use of Military Force Against Terrorism, Pub L. 107-40, 115 Stat 224 (2001).

32 Michael C. Dorf, "The Detention and Trial of Enemy Combatants: A Drama in Three Branches." *Political Science Quarterly*, 122 no. 1 (Spring 2007), 45.

33 *Hamdi v. Rumsfeld*, 542 US 507, 569 (2004).

34 Dorf, "The Detention and Trial of Enemy Combatants," 51.

35 Siegel, *The President as Leader*, 2nd ed., 7.

36 Richard Reeves, *President Nixon Alone in the White House*. New York, NY: Simon and Schuster, 2001, 14.

37 Douglas Brinkley, "The Scandal that Refuses Go away: Watergate Continues to Fascinate 50 Years after the Events that Brought Down a Present." *The New York Times Book Review*, February 20, 2022, 10.

38 Arthur M. Schlesinger, Jr., *The Imperial Presidency*. Boston, MA: Mariner Books, 2004.

39 War Powers Act of 19783. Pub L. 93-148 H.J. Res 542 (1973).

40 Congressional Budget Reform and Impoundment Control Act of 1974. Pub L 93-344, 88 Stat 297 (1974).

41 James L. Sundquist, *The Decline and Resurgence of Congress*. Washington, DC: The Brookings Institution Press, 1982.

42 Siegel, *The President as Leader*, 2nd ed., 10.

43 Savage, *Takeover*, 9.

44 Robert Dalleck, *Hail to the Chief: The Making and Unmaking of American Presidents*. New York, NY: Hyperion, 1996, x.

45 Fred I. Greenstein, *The Presidential Difference: Leadership Style from FDR to George Bush*. Princeton, NJ: Princeton University Press, 2004, 9.

46 Crenson and Ginsberg, *Presidential Power*, 9.

47 Robert H. Jackson, Opinion, *Youngstown Sheet & Tube v. Sawyer*. 343 U.DS. 579 (1952).

48 These descriptions of leadership styles were first enunciated by James MacGregor Burns, *Leadership*. New York, NY: Harper Perennial Modern Classics, 1st ed., 2010.

49 Ben W. Heineman, Jr. and Curtis A. Hessler, *Memorandum for the President: A Strategic Approach to Domestic Affairs in the 1980's*. New York, NY: Random House, 1980.

50 Ibid, Preface, xiii–xv.

2

POLICY (VISION)

Importance to Presidents and All Other Leaders

Having a strong vision of the nation's future is central to the effectiveness of US presidents, just as it is to the success of leaders in other public sector agencies, as well as in the private and non-profit organizations. The following questions are important for a presidential candidate to ask:

- Why am I running for office?
- What is my purpose?
- Where do I want to lead the nation?
- What do I want to accomplish during the next four years?
- How will my administration make a difference in the lives of US citizens?
- What do I want my legacy to be?
- What is my vision of the office I am seeking?

According to historian Arthur Schlesinger, Jr. "The first requirement of presidential leadership is to point the republic in one direction or another. This can be done only if the man in the White House possesses, or is possessed by, a vision of the ideal America."[1] Ultimately, a visionary president can help change the terms of political discourse in the nation as arguably both FDR and Ronald Reagan managed to do.

In the words of presidential historian Robert Dallek, "There is something almost magical in the mass appeal of presidents who are devoted to high-minded, based purpose."[2]

> Vision gives leaders, including presidents, a sense of purpose. As I have written elsewhere, "Vision helps provide focus to presidential staff members and allows them to concentrate their energy and prevent drift. In the absence of a

DOI: 10.4324/9781003285229-2

strong vision, a president will be pushed and pulled in a thousand directions; he will become the object of the political process, not its master."[3] Guided by a strong vision or purpose, a president can establish clear priorities for his (or her) administration, make clear choices about where to invest human and financial resources, and make tough decisions when crises inevitably occur.

When we review the eight most recent presidential administrations, we see vastly different approaches to vision. Some of these differences emerge from the personalities or temperaments of the eight presidents, some from their paths to power, and some from their philosophical orientation to politics and leadership.

Jimmy Carter

When Carter announced his candidacy for president on December 12, 1974, at Washington's National Press Club, he declared himself "a farmer, an engineer, a businessman, a planner, a scientist, a Governor, and a Christian."[4]

As described by Carter's former White House domestic policy adviser, Stuart Eizenstat, the essence of the speech and the entire primary campaign was a clear anti-Watergate and anti-Washington message.[5] According to Eizenstat, "He hammered away at restoring trust in government through reforming the bureaucracy, tearing away secrecy in decision-making, and passing strict ethics laws to control lobbyists, and appoint … senior officials, diplomats and judges on merit and not on connections."[6] Indeed, the same themes had also been prominent in Mr. Carter's successful 1970 gubernatorial campaign in the state of Georgia. Carter's biographer, Betty Glad, characterized his appeal as follows:

> refusal to accept ideological labels; avoidance of controversy; emphasis on personality, morality, and integrity; preference for concrete proposals over broad political issues; ability to control a network of talented and energetic supporters, as well as disciplined, effective staff; and willingness to go for the jugular of his opponents when the situations seemed to demand it.[7]

Jimmy Carter's campaign for the presidency in 1975–1976 was premised on the belief that Americans were in search of a leader who was honest and ethical, and who would govern within the sometimes austere strictures of the checks and balances system of government established in the Constitution. These themes resonated strongly in a nation that had been traumatized by Watergate and Richard Nixon's "imperial presidency," which showed disdain for the checks and balances system. As stated by Eizenstat, "The Carter campaign was less about detailed issues than the broader themes of restoring the voters' trust in the presidency."[8]

In short, Jimmy Carter, while projecting desirable leadership qualities of humility and service, was not a visionary leader. He lacked a grand vision and never truly enunciated a purpose for his administration beyond the restoration of trust in the office. He possessed considerable skill in attacking the status quo and illuminating all its defects but was less eloquent in charting a course for the nation's future. According to Carter's speechwriter, James Fallows, Carter's speeches became more forceful when he talked about the subject that most inspired him—who he was instead of what he proposed to do. According to Fallows, "Where Lyndon Johnson boasted of schools built and children fed, where Edward Kennedy holds out the promise of the energies he might mobilize and the ideas he might enact, Carter tells us that he is a good man."[9]

The thrust of Carter's campaign for presidency was thematic, not programmatic. He presented himself as Nixon's opposite. According to Washington Post reporter Bob Woodward:

> But Carter ... was not Nixon. He was not a lawyer. He had never held office in Washington—the seat of a government few any longer trusted. He was an outsider and would tell the truth—always. He would divest himself of the trappings of the imperial presidency. He promised to remain close to the people. He would do what he deemed right, not what was politically expedient. Carter had fashioned a powerful message in the aftermath of Watergate .... The diagnosis was that government was corrupt to the core. The remedy was to make the government as good as he was by electing him.[10]

Jimmy Carter gained traction as a presidential candidate by portraying himself as a DC "outsider," who was not beholden to the political establishment and would be free to do the people's business unfettered by the claims of lobbyists or the Washington establishment. He would be guided by his deep religious convictions, moral probity, and prior state government experience in leading the nation forward. But the question is, lead them forward to what? What were the goals, the purposes of his administration? What beliefs, values, and policy preferences would animate his presidency? He was relatively silent on these kinds of questions during the campaign, which translated into confusion, lethargy, and leadership ineptitude in his presidency, as we will explore in the "politics" chapter (Chapter 3).

TAKEAWAYS FOR ALL LEADERS

- It's fine to campaign against the status quo or the past when seeking an office, but the real creativity of leadership is in the articulation of goals to be achieved going forward.
- Research has demonstrated that followers are inspired by leaders who are "forward-looking and inspirational."[11]

Ronald Reagan

There are many contrasts between Presidents Carter and Reagan, but perhaps none so pronounced as in their attachment, or lack thereof, to a "vision" or purpose. Reagan, a former Hollywood actor and two-term California Governor, was deeply motivated by purpose and ideas in seeking the presidency. He had developed strong conservative ideas over the course of his many years in the private sector, as head of the Screen Actors' Guild, and as governor of California. When he ran against Jimmy Carter in the 1980 presidential campaign, Reagan was assisted by speechwriter Peggy Noonan, who described his vision as having two parts: an aspiration for a freer and more peaceful world, and a nation that would be in "full and vibrant possession" of its economic freedoms.[12]

Noonan's statement revealed two dimensions of Reagan's vision: economic recovery for the United States, and the restoration of American global power and leadership to achieve a more peaceful world. In both aspects of his vision, Reagan was also willing to repudiate conventional thinking about the philosophical underpinnings of the welfare state and the doctrinal foundations of nuclear deterrence.[13]

Domestically, Reagan believed that the federal government had become too big, too bloated, too anti-business, and too invasive in American lives. Reagan opined that government does not solve problems, but merely subsidizes them. It stifles individual freedoms and restricts profits; overall, he believed, government is inimical to freedom.[14] Reagan believed that government was sapping the energy from America's productive enterprise. He was strongly influenced by the research of David Stockman (a Michigan Republican member of Congress who would become the Director of the Office of Management and Budget during Reagan's presidency) demonstrating the increasingly large outlays by the federal government for social welfare programs, known as "entitlements." Stockman's numbers indicated that 48 cents of every government dollar were going toward payments for social security, pension, and welfare programs.

Stockman's analysis, published in a 1975 issue the conservative journal *The Public Interest*, led him to the conclusion that the federal budget had become largely "uncontrollable," and that no matter who was president, the occupant of the White House would have little to say about budgetary allocations and priorities. In the Public *Interest* article, Stockman averred that "Special interest groups and advocates in the bureaucracy had made Congress a weak buffer group with revenues fully committed years in advance. The federal budget process ... has been reduced to a mere annual ritual of account juggling."[15]

As well, Reagan believed that Americans were paying excessive taxes. As a movie star, Reagan made $3,500 a week before WWII, and he paid

90 percent in income taxes. He claimed, bitterly, that the American tax system was created by Karl Marx![16] Underlying his zeal for tax cuts was Reagan's belief in "supply side economics," the idea that cutting taxes would benefit all Americans because citizens left with more disposable income would invest in productive enterprise and all Americans would benefit.

Shortly after Reagan's election, he delivered a speech in Pittsburgh (September 1980), drafted by his advisers Martin Anderson and Alan Greenspan. Reagan pledged a 30 percent cut in income taxes, a significant reduction in social welfare spending, a scaling back of government regulations, and a balanced budget.[17]

Reagan wanted to inspire an economic recovery concomitant with a reduction in the size and scope of government. He believed he could significantly reduce taxes, cut social welfare spending, increase defense spending, and balance the budget. In many ways the analysis was flawed and all its goals, when combined, were unachievable. According to political scientist Erwin Hargrove, Reagan had become "a true believer in the supply side theory and saw no contradiction in its claims."[18]

The second part of Reagan's vision, encapsulated in the Peggy Noonan quote, related to foreign policy. As I have written elsewhere, "Reagan strongly believed that the United States had let its guard down under Carter and previous presidents and Americans had dropped their focus on military preparedness and in consequence had failed to adequately back up their diplomatic interventions with military might, or perceived might."[19] Reagan advocated for a substantial increase in military spending.

He wanted to contain and turn back Soviet power because he believed its Communist regime was rotten to the core. Reagan's hatred of communism emanated from his personal recollections of the communist attempts to infiltrate Hollywood when he was president of the Screen Actors Guild. But he also strongly objected to the Communist Party's treatment of religious minorities in the USSR and elsewhere.[20]

These beliefs and others led him to believe that the United States would have to confront the Soviets from a position of strength, in order to achieve a freer and more peaceful world.[21] As I have written elsewhere, "Convinced that the Soviets represented an 'evil empire,' Reagan thought he could marshal the resources of the country to influence the Soviets to pursue negotiations and cooperate with the United States in finding a more stable world order."[22]

The vision bore fruit. Reagan's embrace of an assertive posture against the Soviets in his first term, and his baiting them into a costly arms race, laid the groundwork for a more conciliatory and peace-seeking approach in the second term.[23] "It is clear," as I said in *The President as Leader*, "that Reagan's success in negotiating with Gorbachev and encouraging the Russian leader's domestic reform initiative known as 'perestroika' helped accelerate the dissolution of the Soviet empire, which technically occurred during the administration of Reagan's successor, President George H.W. Bush"[24]

TAKEAWAYS FOR ALL LEADERS

- Having a strong vision or purpose helps define you as a leader and gives people a reason to follow you that goes beyond personal characteristics.
- The vision can shift over time as conditions change. A strong vision does not have to be a rigid one, and core ideology can remain stable as strategy shifts over time.

George H.W. Bush

George H.W. Bush ascended to the White House after a long, distinguished career in public service, culminating in his selection as Vice President by Ronald Reagan. Previously, Bush served as a member of Congress, chairman of the Republican National Committee, first liaison to China, Director of the CIA, and US ambassador to the United Nations.

In performing these multifarious roles of great responsibility, Bush was rarely guided by a grand strategy or a clearly enunciated vision. According to biographer John Meacham, "Bush came to the presidency as decent and caring man whose experience in life and government had taught him that there were few simple problems and even fewer perfect answers. He saw himself as a guardian, not as a revolutionary."[25]

Bush's political style was highly personal, pragmatic, and incremental. He expressed discomfort in grandiose and lofty pronouncements, and even about the "poetry" or dramatic language of some political campaigns. According to Dennis Ross, who served as director of the State Department's Policy Planning Staff and later as special envoy to the Middle East in the Bush administration, Bush was uncomfortable in a world of "philosophical absolutes."[26] As Bush said in *A World Transformed*, a book he coauthored with his national security adviser, Brent Scowcroft, "It was difficult for me to give dramatic speeches on my vision for the nation. I was certain that results would be far better than trying to convince people through rhetoric."[27] Nevertheless, he was guided by important principles and as he explained,

> Even if I could not express it as well as Reagan, I knew what I hoped for our country and for the world. I wanted to tackle the big problems facing us, such as lingering superpower confrontation. I was determined

to do what I could to make the world a better, safer place, where people would no longer fear imminent nuclear war.

I too had my own guiding principles and values. Everything I learned from history, from my father, Prescott Bush, everything I've learned from the US Navy reinforced the words "duty, honor, country. I believe one's duty is to serve the country."[28]

The foundation of Bush's political style, then, was not vision or lofty rhetoric; it was, instead, friendships and relationships. Over his many years in public service, Bush had developed close friendships with many political elites. According to Dick Cheney, who served as Bush 41's secretary of defense (and later as Vice President to Bush 43), "The personal relationships that the President had acquired was another ingredient that contributed to the administration's success. Basically, he knew everyone."[29]

In the realm of foreign policy, which was his strength, Bush clearly recognized the significant changes that were underway in the Soviet empire, accelerated by the rise to power of Mikhail Gorbachev in 1985 and the profound impact of his leadership would exert on US-Soviet relations. Several significant changes occurred during the Bush presidency, a "consequential time," which Henry Kissinger thought was the most tumultuous four-year period term since Harry Truman.[30]

The first three years of the Bush 41's presidency witnessed the collapse of communism in Europe, the demise of the Soviet Union, and the dramatic military triumph of a US-led military coalition over Saddam Hussein's Iraqi forces. Bush reacted to and in some cases accelerated these events; his comprehension of the complexities of international relations led him to emphasize the value of order and stability in world affairs, good personal relations among national leaders, and sensitivity to the interests and views of other nations.[31] The strategy that emerged from this amalgam of ideas amounted to what Barilleaux and Rozell call a "conservative internationalism": a desire to promote American ideas like liberty and democracy, but to do so through measures that ensured security and stability on the world stage.[32]

President Bush's "conservative internationalism" could also be observed in his clam, measured reaction to the fall of the Berlin Wall and to the ultimate reunification of Germany. According to the late Zbigniew Brzezinski, National Security adviser under President Carter:

It is impossible to overestimate the importance of the peaceful reunification of Germany in October 1990 …. The fall of the Berlin Wall a year earlier made reunification seem inevitable, but only if there was no regressive Soviet reaction to the Wall's removal. The Soviet army was still in East Germany ... Bush's performance deserves the highest praise. He cajoled, reassured, flattered, and subtly threatened his Soviet counterpart. ... At the same time, Bush had to reassure his British and French allies that a reunited Germany would not threaten their interests[33]

In foreign policy, then, President Bush was animated by the need to promote US interests through "steadiness, realism, and the search for further peace and stability."[34] He believed that it was important to maintain a semblance of order and stability within a rapidly changing international environment. He was careful in managing delicate relationships and a shifting power configuration.

In terms of his vision for domestic policy, Bush intended to continue the Reagan policies (tax cuts, social welfare cuts, etc.), but to reduce the most severe effects of those policies on the poor, reaching for a "kinder, gentler" approach.[35] He identified a domestic agenda that prioritized deficit reduction, education reform, and drug control policy; however, his approach, as described by Barilleaux and Rozell was one of moderation or "disjointed incrementalism."[36] As I have written elsewhere:

> His notion was to take one step at a time and guide the nation toward improvement. In his inaugural address, President Bush emphasized the policy limits imposed by a large budget deficit. He said that new programs and increased government spending were not the answers to the nation's problems. He opined that the United States had "more will than wallet" and needed to limit its aspirations for major changes in domestic policy. Instead, he called on the nation to renew its commitment to private acts of charity and "a thousand points of light" for the improvement of society.[37]

As mentioned earlier, Bush saw himself as a "guardian" president in domestic policy. According to political scientist David Mervin, guardians are largely satisfied with the status quo, even as they recognize the need for marginal change.[38] To a guardian, leadership is not about crusading, nor about working for a grand vision; it is about problem-solving on a case-by-case basis. Bush put it this way at the end of his 1989 inaugural address, "Some see leadership as high drama and the sound of trumpets calling, and sometimes it is that. But I see history as a book with many pages, and each day we fill a page with acts of hopefulness and meaning."[39]

Overall, George H.W. Bush was not a visionary but a skillful practitioner of power politics in the international arena. He saw himself as a problem-solver and relationship builder. And according to David Mervin, "Governance for a president like Bush was a low-key, low-profile affair with little room for ideology or flamboyant rhetoric. He preferred the term 'doer' to 'dreamer,' and expressed cynicism about the loftier and even public aspects of the presidency."[40]

TAKEAWAYS FOR ALL LEADERS

- Competence is a great leadership characteristic, but it is not a substitute for vision.
- A vision will be incomplete if it is developed in consultation with only "elite" communities.

William Jefferson Clinton

Vision was a key element in Bill Clinton's pursuit of the presidency during the 1992 presidential campaign. The two-term governor of Arkansas presented himself to the American people as a "New Democrat." Clinton had been a member of the Democratic Leadership Council, along with US Senators Sam Nunn (D, GA), Cuck Robb (D, VA), John Breaux (D, LA), and Paul Tsongas (D, MA) who, beginning in 1984, collectively argued that the Democratic Party had shifted too far to the left since 1972, and had been captured by organized labor and the urban poor and had lost touch with the middle-class.[41]

As a "New Democrat" Clinton's campaign was guided by the following philosophical principles:

- The Democratic Party must embrace change and be willing to chart a new direction, instead of being locked into the dictates of the New Deal and Great Society programs.
- The Democratic Party should not be perceived as antithetical to business, but seen as a party that could collaborate with business to develop innovative policy initiative and market-based solutions.
- Human capital is vital to human progress, and Democrats need to "put people first" in a progressive political party.
- The United States has entered a globalized environment and the distinctions between domestic and international progress may well be obliterated.
- Change may be the only constant on today's economy.
- Democrats share a responsibility to protect the environment.[42]

There was another aspect of Clinton's vision that he had exhibited as governor of Arkansas, and that would, again, help define him as a New Democrat: personal responsibility. As governor, Clinton had asked the Arkansas legislature to require welfare recipients with children three years or older to sign a contract, committing them to achieve independence through literacy, job training, and work.[43] Together with other governors, Clinton testified before the House Ways and Means Committee on welfare prevention and reform. He and his colleagues asked Congress to provide the states with tools to "promote work, not welfare, independence, not dependence." They advocated for programs that would keep people off welfare in the first place, including adult literacy, teen pregnancy prevention, and drug and alcohol prevention education.[44] In promulgating this picture of government reform, Clinton employed visionary terms "such as the 'New Covenant' to signal his expectation that government would not be in the business of giveaway, but in the business of investment."[45]

But if the era of "big government" was coming to an end, the era of better government was also part of Clinton's vision. President Clinton believed strongly in the power of technology to make government more efficient and accessible. In March 1993, he assigned Vice President Al Gore the responsibility of leading an effort to reinvent the federal government. The project became known as the National Performance Review (and later as the National Partnership to Reinvent Government). Its purpose was to create a government that "costs less and works better," especially in cutting red tape perfecting customer service in government, and empowering federal employees to innovate for results.[46] When he announced the idea of government reform at his inauguration, Clinton displayed the visionary basis of the effort:

> Our goal is to make the entire federal government both less expensive and more efficient and to change the climate of our national bureaucracy away from complacency and entitlement toward innovation and improvement. We intend to redesign, reinvent, to reinvigorate the entire national government.[47]

In foreign policy, Clinton's dominant vision was globalization. Former Carter National Security Adviser Zbigniew Brzezinski suggested that Clinton perceived that the disappearance of the Soviet Union and the "bipolar world" created three major opportunities for the United States:

- More opportunities for US and Russian initiative to limit the arms race.
- The possibility of a wider global security system.
- A larger, more robust Europe linked closely to the United States.[48]

Clinton's global vision led him to successfully advocate for the expansion of the number of countries associated with the North Atlantic Treaty Organization (NATO). In July 1997, Poland, the Czech Republic, and Hungary were officially invited to join NATO, followed soon thereafter by invitations to Bulgaria and Rumania.[49] Clinton also backed the establishment of the World Trade Organization (WTO), which was founded in January 1995 and marked a significant development in the emergence of a global economic order.[50]

On the other hand, Clinton's belief in the benefits of globalization, may have distracted him from recognizing the growing dangers in the North Korean refusal to allow inspections of its nuclear programs by the International Atomic Energy Agency (IAEA). Not only did the North Koreans refuse inspections, but they also openly announced their intent to withdraw from the Non-Proliferation Treaty (NPT), citing Article 10, which allows withdrawal on grounds of national security. Brzezinski, and others, faulted Clinton for not taking a more aggressive stand on several matters of North Korean defiance.[51] Clinton had a different interpretation in his autobiography. He reflected as follows, "In 1994, we reached an agreement with North Korea to end their threat of nuclear proliferation on the Korean peninsula."[52]

The agreed framework, signed by US negotiator Bob Gallucci and the North Koreans in 1994, committed North Korea to freeze all activity of existing nuclear reactors and allow inspectors to continue their work. In exchange, the United States offered improved trade conditions for North Korea.[53]

In sum, Clinton's visionary impulses were encapsulated in his redefinition of the Democratic party and in imagining a "third way" of governing America—one that tapped into new technologies, embraced progressive ideas from around the world as well as at home, and promoted a dynamic collaboration between business and government.[54]

TAKEAWAYS FOR ALL LEADERS

- Sometimes a leader must challenge established, even revered, institutions when they are not keeping pace with significant changes in the environment.
- The visionary leader must articulate an alternative to the status quo in a compelling and convincing manner and attract like-minded people to join him or her.

George Walker Bush

Although not truly an intellectual in orientation, nor drawn to "heavy" ideas and philosophical musings, President George W. Bush embraced the idea of visionary leadership. In his autobiography *Decision Points*, he explained the vision behind his bid for the presidency in 1999:

> I was concerned about the future of the country, and I had a clear vision of where I wanted to lead it. I wanted to cut taxes, raise standards in public schools, reform Social Security and Medicare, rally faith-based charities and lift the sights of the American people by encouraging a new era of personal responsibility.[55]

Bush had embraced similar ideas when he served as governor of Texas, and he embellished them when running for the presidency. As indicated in his quotation above Bush believed in "compassionate conservatism," that rested on the notion of faith-based solutions to social problems. Inspired by writer Marvin Olasky, who authored the book, *The Tragedy of American Compassion*, Bush believed that faith-based groups helped millions out of poverty with the detailed knowledge and flexibility needed to administer the combination of having compassion and rigorous discipline to improve peoples' lives.[56] The approach of government welfare programs, on the other hand, was, according to Olasky and his colleagues, to aid through bureaucratic structures and without compassion. It was not a great surprise that as governor of Texas, Bush issued an executive order making Texas the first state to introduce the option of using private and religious charities to distribute welfare services.[57] And in an early presidential initiative, Bush established a White House Office of faith-Based and Community Initiatives (OFBCI) to facilitate the use of federal funds for social purpose to be administered by faith-based organizations.[58]

Closely tied to his belief in compassionate conservatism was Bush's rejection of many of the tenets of the Great Society and welfare state. Like Ronald Reagan, he strongly embraced lower taxation and less government regulation.[59] Bush was strongly influenced by the negative views of the 1960s expressed in Professor David Horowitz's book, *Destructive Generation: Second Thoughts about the Sixties*, which his political adviser Karl Rove introduced him to.[60] Accordingly, it was not surprising that President Bush's first and largest legislative initiative was to propose an enormous tax cut—$1.6 trillion over ten years that included the reduction of top brackets, elimination of the estate tax, reductions in the marriage penalty, and increases in child credits. The House passed the bill, and the Senate, after considerable negotiations, went along and passed a slightly smaller $1.35 trillion cut.[61]

An additional aspect of W's domestic vision was his belief in the application of market solutions and business principles to government programs; he was, after all, the nation's first MBA president.[62] Perhaps the strongest expression of this aspect of his vision was in his unsuccessful attempt to privatize social security by advocating for the setting aside a portion of contributions to the fund for private investment in personal retirement accounts, allowing Americans to make their own investment decisions. The business perspective is also seen in the successful legislative effort to reform American education through the No Child Left Behind Act, which introduced mandatory standardized testing of students in grades 3 and 8 in reading and mathematics and made schools accountable for results—well performing schools would be rewarded financially while poor performers would be penalized.[63]

In terms of foreign policy, Bush, when he ran for the presidency on 1999, suggested that the United States should have a humble approach and was dismissive of the Democratic Party's alleged obsession with nation building. In a 1999 speech at the Reagan Presidential library, however, he used several phrases that telegraphed a more assertive US role: "The empire (Soviet Union) has passed but evil remains"; "America has determined enemies who hate our values"; "We must protect our homeland and our allies against missiles and terror"; and "In defense of our nation a president must be a clear-eyed realist."[64]

The inclinations implicit in the 1999 speech were transformed into strong policy directives and preferences after September 11, 2001, the day radical Islamist terrorists attacked the World Trade Center and the Pentagon and killed almost 3,000 innocent people. According to political scientist James Pfiffner, "thus were world history, international relation, American politics, and the Bush presidency transformed within minutes."[65]

Bush displayed clear, decisive leadership and planned the US response with confidence and effectiveness. He conducted a largely effective military campaign in Afghanistan, where the radical Taliban regime was harboring al Qaeda terrorists and leader, Osama bin Laden; provided swift and generous relief to New York City; introduced several legislative proposals to keep Americans safe; and presented himself eloquently and passionately to a nation that had been previously dubious about his leadership acumen.[66]

Beyond that, Bush conceptualized a broader security threat to the United States than the one represented by the al Qaeda terrorists. In his January 29, 2002 State of the Union address before a joint session of Congress, Bush outlined two specific goals: first to "shut down terrorist plans and bring terrorists to justice; second to prevent regions that sponsor terror from threatening America or our friends and allies with weapons of destruction."[67]

In his address to Congress, Bush proceeded to define three nations, North Korea, Iraq, and Iran, as part of an "axis of evil," and he was laying the groundwork to persuade the American people and the Congress that we would have to take action to prevent rogue nations from doing harm to the United States. He emphasized the need for preventive action, "We'll deliberate; yet time is not on our side. I will not wait on events while dangers gather. I will not stand by as peril draws closer and closer."[68]

It was not a long step from the rhetoric summarized above to action against the "axis of evil." Bush and his advisers were convinced that there was a strong case for military action against Iraqi leader Saddam Hussein. After all, they argued, Saddam fought a long and bloody war with Iran, invaded Kuwait, and threatened Saudi Arabia in 1991; brutally oppressed his people and used poison gas against the Kurds in Northern Iraq, launched Scud missiles into Israeli cities during the earlier Gulf War; and stockpiled and developed chemical and biological weapons and planned the development of nuclear weapons. As well, the Bush administration was convinced of a connection between the Iraqi government and the 9/11 terrorists.[69]

The notion of initiating an attack on a sovereign nation before that nation had attacked the United States, or even threatened an attack, represented a significant paradigm shift in US foreign policy. According to political scientists Raymond Tanter and Stephen Kerstig, writing on 2002, "George W. Bush had instigated the broadest reformulation of US grand strategy since the presidency of Franklin D. Roosevelt, based on the shock of a surprise attack."[70]

Bush and his national security team believed that the urgency spawned by the 9/11 attacks, augmented by the existence of rogue states that could harbor terrorists and share nuclear technology with them, called for a reformulation of US national security policy. In a July 2002 commencement speech at the US Military Academy at West Point, Bush explained the new approach:

> For much of the last century, America's defense relied on the cold war doctrines of deterrence and containment. In some cases, those strategies still apply, but new threats require new thinking. Deterrence—the promise of massive retaliation against nations—means nothing against shadowy terrorist networks with no nation or citizens to defend. Containment is not possible when unbalanced dictators with weapons of mass destruction can deliver those weapons or missiles or secretly provide them to terrorist allies. …[71]

Overall, President Bush developed a strong vision for America's role in the world. Alarmed by the incalculable tragedy of 9/11 and the perceived ongoing threat of radicalized terrorists and a dangerous "axis of evil," Bush envisioned his role as a wartime president with a strong mission. But he became nearly obsessed with this vision and it became overly grandiose and expansive, as is evident in his second inaugural address, delivered on January 20, 2005:

> And expose the pretensions of tyrants and reward the hopes of the decent and tolerant, and that is the force of human freedom …. So it is the policy of the United States to seek and support the growth of democratic movements and institutions in every nation and culture, with the ultimate goal of ending tyranny in the world.[72]

TAKEAWAYS FOR ALL LEADERS

1. A vision is a good thing, but an obsession can prove dangerous to a leader, as he or she holds on to strong beliefs in the face of contradictory evidence or shifting "facts on the ground."
2. A leader must always invite dissenting or challenging views as he sets out to implement his vision.

Barrack Hussein Obama

President Obama, the nation's first AA president, with relatively little national political experience, was determined.[73] Throughout his campaign, and in the early days of his administration, he described his purpose in transformational terms. When he announced his candidacy for president in Springfield, Illinois, on February 10, 2007, he told supporters that his purpose was "Not just to hold the office, but to gather with you to transform a nation"[74] And at an October 2006 Meet the press interview with Tim Russert, then US Senator Obama, who had not yet announced his presidential ambitions, described his view of a great president:

> When I think about great presidents, I think about those who transform how we think about ourselves as a country in fundamental ways so that, that, at the end of their tenure, we have looked and said to ours—that's who we are. And, and our, our—and for me at least, that means that we have a more expansive view of our democracy, that we've included more people into the bounty of this country. And, you know, there are circumstances in which, I would argue, Ronald Reagan was a very successful president, even though I did not agree with him on many issues, partly because at the end of his presidency, people, I think, said, "You know what? We can regain our greatness. Individual responsibility and personal responsibility are important." And they transformed the culture and not simply promoted one or two issues.[75]

Obama sought transformational change in both domestic and foreign policy. He assessed that the time was ripe for profound change due to what he perceived as pent-up demand and the egregious failures of the Bush 43 presidency. According to author Michael Grunwald:

> After eight exhausting years of George W. Bush—the partisan warfare, the nonexistent weapons of mass destruction, the surpluses alchemized into record deficits, the inept response to a drowned city, and finally the epic financial and economic collapse—millions of Americans were ready for a leap of faith.[76]

Obama's domestic vision focused on the role of government and on the value of fairness. He believed, for instance, that wealthy people should pay their fair share in taxes. As he said in his autobiography, "Getting the rich to pay more in taxes was not only a matter of fairness but also the only way to fund new initiatives."[77] He also expressed confidence in an expansive role of government in promoting social justice, reducing inequality, and countering the abuses of the private sector.[78] In short, although Obama acknowledged the importance of private responsibility and "rugged individualism," he clearly embraced the idea of a muscular role for the federal government in our democracy.[79] Certainly he did not attack "big government" the way that Reagan did, or even the way Clinton, at times, did.

In a March 2009 address to members of Congress involved in his health care fight, he revealed aspects of his vision by saying, "One of the unique and wonderful things about America has always been our self-reliance …. our healthy skepticism of government."[80] But then he went on to highlight the legacy of Senator Ted Kennedy (D, MA) and his passionate and long struggle to achieve universal health care for all Americans:

> That large-heartedness – that concern and regard for the plight of others – is not a partisan feeling. It's not a Republican or a Democratic feeling. It, too, is part of the American character – our ability to stand in other people's shoes; a recognition that we are all in this together, and when fortune turns against one of us, others are there to lend a helping hand; a belief that in this country, hard work and responsibility should be rewarded by some measure of security and fair play; and an acknowledgment that sometimes government has to step in to help deliver on that promise.[81]

It is equally clear that part of Obama's vision was a government that is reliable and competent. In his first inaugural address (January 20, 2009), he said that we should not be asking ourselves "whether our government is too big or too small, but whether it works—whether it helps families find jobs at a decent wage, care they can afford, a retirement that is dignified."[82] Government, according to Obama, also has a role to play in reducing the glaring disparities in wealth and opportunities that have existed for years in the United States. In *The Audacity of Hope*, he wrote: "I am very angry about policies that consistently favor the wealthy and powerful over average Americans, and insist that government has an important role in opening up opportunity to all."[83]

As discussed earlier, Obama's vision also included a strong embrace of fairness as a value. In part, this value was inherited from his mother and her life's work in eradicating poverty.[84] In part, he came to appreciate it through his own experiences. In his October 16, 2012, presidential debate with Republican presidential nominee, former Massachusetts Governor (and future US Senator, R, UT), Mitt Romney, Obama said:

> I believe that the free enterprise system is the greatest engine of prosperity that the world has ever known. I believe in self-reliance and individual initiative and risk takers being rewarded. But I also believe that everybody should have a fair shot, and everybody should do their fair

share, and everybody should play by the same rules ... And ... that is part of what is at stake in this election. There's a fundamentally different vision about how we move the country forward.[85]

In terms of his vision for foreign policy, Obama, as I have said elsewhere, was "equally determined to change the orientation and direction of American foreign policy, specifically to move it away from the bellicosity and military aggressiveness of the Bush administration toward a more realistic-oriented posture based on using persuasion and soft power."[86]

According to Derek Chollet, who served as Obama's director for strategic planning at the National Security Council, Obama sought to restore a sense of balance to American foreign policy: balance between American interests and values, balance between priorities at home and abroad; balance between US goals in different regions; and balance among the tools of strategy and influence.[87] In Obama's estimation, the United States had lost that sense of balance under President George W. Bush; the nation had become overly involved in the Middle East, ignored the Asia-Pacific region, and become obsessed with the military instruments of power. Obama, according to Derek Chollet, "wanted the US to be respected abroad not just for its military prowess," but also, for its growing economy, domestic vitality, and moral example."[88] Obama's foreign policy realism also underlined the value he placed on restraint. In an address to the US Military Academy at West Point in May 2014, President Obama declared:

Since World War II, some of our most costly mistakes came not from our restraint, but from our willingness to rush into military adventures without thinking through the consequences—without building international support and legitimacy for our action; without leveling with the American people about the sacrifices required.[89]

Another aspect of Obama's foreign policy vision was engagement, even with adversaries, so as to explore options for the peaceful resolution of conflict and "resetting" of relationships in a more positive direction. He attempted to apply the strategy of engagement with the Muslim community by making a major presidential address at Cairo University on June 4, 2009. He said, "I've come here to seek a new beginning between the United States and Muslim communities around the world, one built on mutual respect and one based upon the truth that America and Islam .... share common principles of justice and progress, tolerance and dignity of all human beings."[90]

The vision of engagement led President Obama to conduct negotiations with Iran about their nuclear weapons program. Following the application of harsh economic sanctions by the United States and its allies on Iran, and following the June 2013 election of a supposedly more moderate Iranian leader

(Hassan Rouhani), Obama and his second secretary of state, John Kerry, led a protracted series of negotiations with Iran that resulted in a deal to force the Iranians to limit their enrichment of uranium. The Joint Comprehensive Plan of Action (JPCOA) was signed in Vienna on July 14, 2015, by the E3/ EU+3 (China, France Germany, the Russian Federation, the United States, the United Kingdom, and the Islamic Republic of Iran).[91]

Overall, through his words and actions, Obama's domestic vision emphasized a strong role for the federal government, and specifically its chief executive, in helping to create a just and fair society where people play by the rules and inequalities lessen. While not driven by an ideology, he spoke consistently of the need for fair play in the US economy and on public life generally. He objected to excessive tax breaks for the wealthy, to prejudice against the LBGTQ community by the military, and eventually to discrimination against same-sex couples. While he did not draw attention to his identity as the nation's first African American president, he did have an appreciation for the significance of this fact and its potential to bring about transformational change in Washington. Nevertheless, to accomplish most of his larger goals—a huge economic stimulus program, a reformed US health care system, and profound financial reform—he relied on the more typical behaviors of transactional presidents to achieve the needed votes in Congress.[92]

In foreign policy, Obama aimed to move away from what he believed to be the dogmatic militarism of the Bush 43 years to a more sober, interest-based, pragmatic foreign policy that had more in common with the Bush 41 years. As I wrote previously:

> President Obama's foreign policy would be more calculating, cautious, precise, and engagement-oriented than was the previous administration's .... Obama sought to achieve a "long view" of US foreign policy and to protect his administration from reacting to events quickly and emotionally. If George W. Bush led with his heart, Obama wanted to lead with his head.[93]

TAKEAWAYS FOR ALL LEADERS

- There are ways for leaders to reach previously unmotivated or alienated voters or constituents in both symbolic and philosophical means.
- When the vision a leader enunciates seems consistent with the way he has lived his life, it is a powerful combination.
- Transformational leadership is a high benchmark, and transactional leadership is not to be taken lightly.
- A leader must consistently show strong conviction for his vision, even when it seems tedious or undignified.

Donald John Trump

It is challenging to decipher a coherent vision embraced by one of the most unconventional political leaders in US history; nevertheless, we can discover what Trump stood for and believed in from his words and actions. As indicated in my previous writing on the subject, Donald Trump campaigned for president on a promise to Make America Great Again, by restoring economic prosperity; repairing a rapidly deteriorating infrastructure; keeping US citizens safe from violent criminals, murderous terrorists, and unsavory immigrants; by negotiating more auspicious trade deals for the United States; and by putting "America First" in all foreign policy decisions.[94] In his January 20, 2017, inaugural address, he fiercely promoted that approach in what many described as a downcast speech:

> For many decades we enriched foreign industry at the expense of American industry .... We've made other countries rich while the wealth, strength, and confidence of our own country has disappeared over the horizon .... From this moment on it's going to be America First. Every decision on trade, taxes, on immigration, on foreign affairs, will be made to benefit American workers and American families.[95]

In terms of domestic policy, Trump's views, especially in the 2016 campaign, can be characterized as "heterodox." He expressed support for entitlement programs, like Medicare and social security, and promised he would sustain access to healthcare for all Americans, while reducing costs and enhancing quality.[96] He also promised to get tough on crime, while also appealing to minority voters to "give him a chance."

There was no coherence to the vision, nor did it emanate from any philosophical convictions or lead to anything like a grand strategy. It was primarily based on a list of grievances against the status quo and a rejection of the programs and policies of recent presidential administrations, especially Obama's. As well, Trump's vision was rhetorically aimed at rescuing the "forgotten men and women" and reducing the fear in society brought on by rapid social change.

Perhaps the closest Trump came to be articulating a "vision" for his presidency was in a speech he delivered in Gettysburg, PA on October 23, 2016. At that time, he said that his administration would pursue measures to "clean up the corruption and special interest collusion in Washington DC" (with measures for term limits on Members of Congress and a 5-year ban on White House and Congressional officials becoming lobbyists after leaving public service); "protect American workers" (with measure to renegotiate NAFTA and withdrawal from the Trans-Pacific Partnership); "restore American prosperity" (though a middle-class tax cut, a dramatic cutting of environmental and other regulations, and a repeal and replacement of Obamacare) "restore security and the constitutional rule of law" (with measures to cancel unconstitutional executive actions, memoranda and orders issued by President Obama, and cancelling all federal funding for Sanctuary Cities); and "protect our national security" (with measures to dramatically reduce the number of illegal immigrants entering the United States, and to build a wall on our southern border, which Mexico would pay for, as well as rebuilding our military and eliminating the defense sequester).[97] Some of the proposals above would require legislation and others could be accomplished through executive action. Trump summarized his views by saying, "On November 8, Americans will be voting for this 100-day plan to restore prosperity to our economy, security to our communities, and honesty to our government."[98]

There are additional elements of Trump's political vision, which relate to his views on leadership. Throughout his life, Trump vigorously embraced the values of winning and of strength and disdained the ideas of losing or weakness. Whether it's the United States in the global community, or Trump in the political one, the value of winning is the foundation of success. Many times, during the presidential campaign, as well as earlier in his life, Trump bemoaned the fact that "We don't win anymore!"

According to Washington Post columnist, Michael Gerson:

> More than an ideology or a governing philosophy, Trumpism is a certain view of strength. It is strong to crush those who challenge you … It is strong to strike back twice as hard and below the belt … Mercy is weakness. Empathy is weakness.[99]

During the coronavirus pandemic, which began in January 2020 and continues to the present day, scientists strongly advised US citizens to wear face coverings to protect the spread of the virus, and there was a great deal of scientific evidence to support this recommendation. President Trump, however, refused to wear a mask and, when asked about it responded, "We didn't want to give the press the pleasure of seeing it."

According to Gerson, "Trump clearly views any concession—even a concession to common sense and common decency—as a form of surrender."[100] Trump's failure to concede would be manifest again after the 2020 presidential election.

In his first year as president, Trump took additional actions to show his preference for strength over weakness. Over the weekend of August 11 and 12, 2017, hundreds of Neo-Nazis and white supremacists travelled to the college town of Charlottesville, Virginia, to protest the removal of the city's statue of Confederate General Robert E. Lee. When they arrived in Charlottesville, the protestors marched down the streets carrying torches and shouting slogans like "Jews will not replace us" and the Nazi slogan "Blood and Soil."[101] When the white supremacists and Nazi sympathizers were met by a group of counter-protestors; violence ensued, and one of the white nationalists drove his car into the crowd of counter-protestors, killing one woman and injuring 19 others.[102]

From his golf complex in Bedminster, NJ, Trump tweeted the following message, "We all must be united and to condemn all that hate stands for. There is no place for this kind of violence in America. Let's come together as one."[103] Later in the day, at an outline veterans bill signing, Trump read from a script saying, "We condemn in the in the strongest possible terms the egregious display of hatred, bigotry, and violence." And then he departed from the script and said, "On many sides, on many sides. It's been going on for a long time."[104]

Trump touched a nerve with his use of the phraseology "on many sides," suggesting an equivalency between the neo-Nazis and those opposed to white supremacy. Even Republican leaders questioned the wisdom of the phrase "on many sides." Senator Marco Rubio (R, FL), who had run against Trump in the primaries, tweeted, "Very important for the nation to hear @potus describe events in Charlottesville for what they are, a terror attack by #white supremacist." Senator Orrin Hatch (R, UT) tweeted, "My brother didn't give his life fighting Hitler for Nazi ideas to go unchallenged here at home."[105]

Rob Porter, the Staff Secretary to the President, drafted a statement for Trump to give the next day, August 19, at the White House. Trump reviewed the draft on the flight back to DC on Air Force One, and was unhappy with Porter's draft, sensing it was a capitulation to political correctness. Porter pushed back, arguing there was no advantage to refusing to condemn Nazis and racial animus unequivocally. And then Trump essentially delivered the speech Porter had drafted. He noted that the Department of Justice had opened a civil rights investigation, and then Trump told the television audience, "To anyone who acted criminally in this weekend's racist violence, you will be held fully accountable …. No matter the color of our skin, we all live under the same laws and salute the same flag. Racism is evil."

According to Washington Post reporter, Bob Woodward, "It was a five-minute speech that could have been given by President Reagan or Obama."[106]

Trump's staff complimented him on the speech; however, he regretted giving it, saying, "That was the biggest f.ing mistake I've made. You never apologize. I didn't do anything wrong in the first place. Why look weak?"[107]

The following day, President Trump held meetings in New York to discuss his infrastructure ideas for spending on roads, bridges, and schools. In the afternoon, he was scheduled to participate in a press briefing in the lobby of Trump Tower. Many of the questions posed by reporters related to the recent events in Charlottesville. He took out this Saturday statement and said, "As I said, we condemn in the strongest possible terms the egregious display of hatred, bigotry, and violence," and then added,

> The alt-left came charging at the rally. You had a group on the other side that was also, very violent. And nobody wants to say that, but I'll say it right now. Not all of those people were neo-Nazis, believe me. Not all of those people were white supremacists by any stretch. Many of those

people were there to protests the taking down of the statue of Robert E. Lee ... There is blame on both sides .... you also had people that were very fine people on both sides. You had a lot of bad people in the other group too .... there are two sides to a story.[108]

Trump was praised by David Duke, a former Ku Klux Klan leader; but each branch of the US military went on a social media offensive against their Commander in Chief, a stunning rebuke, according to Bob Woodward.[109]

Kenneth Frazier, the head of Merck, the giant pharmaceutical company, and one of the few African American CEO's of a Fortune 500 Company, announced he was resigning from Trump's American Manufacturing Council, a group of outside business advisers to the president. In addition, Trump's leading economic advisor, National Economic Council Director, Gary Cohen, threatened to resign in protest over Trump's statements, and all 16 members of the President's Committee on Arts and the Humanities resigned.[110]

But Trump had not bowed to what he perceived as political correctness. The president told his then chief-of-staff, John Kelly, that his wife liked the last version of the speech because it showed him being strong and defiant.[111]

The final and devastating expression of the Trumpian idea of "strength" came at the very end of his presidency, on January 6, 2021. Trump never accepted his defeat at the polls by former US Senator (D, DE) and Vice President (to Barrack Obama), Joe Biden. After losing over 50 attempts to declare the elections legally fraudulent through various levels of the judiciary, as well as attempting to pressure state election officials to find votes for him, Trump encouraged his supporters to come to Washington, DC on January 6, 2021 to protest the certification of Biden's victory by Congress. After describing, again, the "theft" of his presidential election victory by "leftist" elements and the media, Trump said:

> Now it is up to Congress to confront this egregious assault on our democracy. After this, we're going to walk down—and I'll be there with you—we're going to walk down to the Capitol, and we're going to cheer on our brave senators and congressmen and women. And we're probably not going to be cheering so much for some of them because you'll never take back our country with weakness. You must show strength, and you must be strong.[112]

Once again, we see the elevation of "strength" as a value in Trump's worldview. And although Trump encouraged the thousands of followers to protest "peacefully and patriotically," what ensued at the US Capitol was a paroxysm of violence and anger amounting to an attempted insurrection. Indeed, the activities of that day led to the passage a second round of impeachment resolutions against Trump by the House of Representatives (the first involved his attempt to bribe the government of Ukraine to open an investigation into Vice President Joe Biden). The Senate did not vote to convict, however, as it had not during the first one as well.

One additional element of Trump's domestic policy vision needs to be explored. A month after Trump's inauguration, his Chief Political Strategist, Steve Bannon, announced to a CPAC (Conservative Political Action Committee) conference the goal of "deconstruction of the administrative state."[113] He added, "If you look at the cabinet appointments, they were selected for a reason, and that is deconstruction. The way the progressive left runs is if they can't get it passed, they're just going to put in some sort of regulation in an agency."[114]

And closely aligned with Bannon's goal of "deconstructing the administrative state" was Trump's goal of "draining the swamp," a phrase that Trump invoked without clear definition. What Trump and Bannon were both referring to was the

> … ill-defined membrane that had grown between the public sector and the industries that haunted its borders: the lobbyists, contractors, the consultants, the media, the law, the defense-industrial complex, the non-profits and think tanks. And all these industries thrived because as the administrative state—that is the federal government in all its regulatory might—grew, it became more inefficient and unwieldy, the little prince propped up by his servile court.[115]

Not since Nixon had a president declared war on the federal bureaucracy the way Trump and Bannon did, and the consequences of this view were pervasive, as will be explored in the subsequent three chapters.

Trump's foreign policy vision was, as described earlier, based on the premise of "America First." Trump wanted to replace. The costly mantle of moral leadership, which he claimed characterized several previous administrations, with a focus on America's immediate economic interests. There was less interest expressed in his foreign policy decisions in preserving the "liberal world order" than there was on protecting US material interests and investments.[116]

Several of Trump's foreign policy decisions and actions reinforced the notion of "America First." For instance, in January 2017, he withdrew the United States from the Trans-Pacific Partnership (TPP), a 12-country Asia focused trade agreement that had been negotiated by the Obama Administration. Trump claimed the agreement did not sufficiently protect US interests. He made similar arguments when, in June 2017, he decided to withdraw the United States from the Paris Climate. This 195-country agreement would have directed the United States to voluntarily limit carbon emissions. Trump argued that the agreement constricted US sovereignty, harmed American workers, and disadvantaged the US economically.[117]

In January 2017, Trump signed an executive order banning nationals from six Muslim countries from traveling to the United States for 90 days. He later amended the measure to include two additional countries and impose a freeze on refugees from Syria. A few days after the first order was signed, a federal judge in the state of Washington ruled that part of the order was unconstitutional, setting the stage for a series of additional court challenges.[118] It took Trump's lawyers several tries to satisfy the constitutional objections to the ban by the federal judiciary. And in May 2018, Trump decided to withdraw the United States from the Joint Comprehensive Plan of Action, or the Iran Nuclear Deal, citing that it had not adequately curbed Iran's civilian nuclear program or its regional aggression. In withdrawing from the JCPOA, the Trump administration also announced the reinstatement of two sets of economic sanctions on Iran that had been waived with the deal's implementation.[119]

Overall, Trump was not a visionary president. His campaign was largely driven by grievance and appeal to a base of supporters who had many grievances of their own. His domestic policy was a pastiche of incoherent proposals and ideas that only partially followed through on his campaign to protect the "forgotten" people, and instead delivered a multitude of benefits to the wealthy. His view of the presidency was one of "strength" and assertiveness, but frequently without adequate recognition of or deference to the constitutional framework of Article II. His foreign policy was predicated on the idea that an avid pursuit of "America First" left little room for multilateralism, international agreements, human rights concerns, or other nuances of previous administrations.[120]

TAKEAWAYS FOR ALL LEADERS

- A vision based primarily on grievances aimed at the status quo or the establishment is not a sufficient guide for a leader's vision.
- A leader must be clear about what he stands FOR in addition to what he stands AGAINST.

Joseph Robinette Biden

Joe Biden's 36 year-long career as a US Senator (D) representing the state of Delaware, as well as his eight years as President Obama's Vice President, reflected the proclivities of a moderate, practical politician, not an ideologue. According to journalist Evan Osnos,

> In the Senate, Biden accrued a record, to today's progressives, resembles the counts in an indictment. He voted for the deregulation of Wall Street, the Defense of Marriage Act, the North American Free Trade

Agreement, the War in Iraq. During the 2020 primaries, Massachusetts Senator Elizabeth Warren faulted him for having legislated on the side of the credit card companies.[121]

Nevertheless, when he ran for president against Donald Trump, Biden sounded a more visionary message, openly favoring a competent, active federal government that cares for its most vulnerable populations, including those needing protection against the deadly pandemic known as COVID-19. As well, Biden promised a massive focus on improving and upgrading the US infrastructure and a "Build Back Better" agenda that would ultimately translate into proposing trillions of dollars of expenditures on fixing deteriorating roads and bridges, extending unemployment benefits, providing education assistance and getting COVID-19 relief to millions of Americans.

According to journalist Jonathan Alter, Biden found his "inner Roosevelt" (meaning FDR). In Alter's words, "His 'Build Back Better' agenda could be a less transparent but still historic vision of Roosevelt's New Deal."[122] As well, says Alter, Biden also uses a medical metaphor. He speaks of healing the nation from the divisions created by Trump and the stress of coping with COVID-19, "and like FDR, he fuses his personal suffering and resilience with the character of the American people."[123]

Jonathan Alter expands on the visionary similarities between FDR and Joe Biden:

- FDR put 250,000 young men to work clearing trails and planting trees in the Civilian Conservation Corps (CCC); Biden wants a US Public Health Corps to enlist 100,000 young people to handle COVID-19 tests and other health challenges.
- FDR's Work Progress Administration (WPA) and Public Works Administration (PWA) were among the agencies that built schools, hospitals, highways and bridges, dams, and post offices. Biden's "sustainable infrastructure" would make similar public initiatives and pump federal dollars into US-based jobs in clean technology.[124]

During the summer of 2021, Biden proposed a $3.5 trillion package to Congress that free community college, expansion of dental and vision benefits through Medicare, an increase in health care subsidies for people enrolled in the Obamacare programs, universal pre-kindergarten education, and lowering of the age for collecting social security. While passage of the massive spending bill is not assured as of this writing, the ambition of the agenda, and the vision underlying it, are apparent.[125]

As well, Biden emphasized the idea of UNITY in his campaign and in his early presidency. He urged a united response to COVID-19, a pulling together on improving infrastructure, and a call to unity around American values, especially as reflected in our foreign policy. In a speech at Shanksville, PA, Biden urged a return to national unity.

> We saw national unity bend. We learned that the unity is the one thing that must never break. Unity is what makes us who we are. America at its best. To me, that's the central lesson of September 11. It's that at our most vulnerable, in the push and pull of all that makes us human, in the battle of the soul of America, Unity is our greatest strength.[126]

In foreign policy, Biden sought to reaffirm America's commitment to human rights and to international institutions after the degradations of the Trump era. "He strengthened US commitments to institutions like NATO and emphasized US relations with allies and other friendly nations."

Application to Other Sectors

Visionary leadership is just as important in other sectors as it is in the White House.

Questions a leader in any sector should ask might include:

- Why do I want to lead this organization?
- What is my purpose?
- What do I want to accomplish during my tenure as a leader?
- How will my leadership make a difference in the lives of people in the organization and to stakeholders?
- What do I want my legacy to be?

Researchers and authors Jim Kouzes and Barry Posner have been studying leadership in many different sectors for almost four decades; in 1982 they began asking the hundreds of thousands of leaders in their longitudinal survey the following question: *What did you do when you were at your personal best as a leader?* Their findings indicate that while each leadership experience was unique, there were five described practices that united exemplary leaders in all sectors: model the way, **inspire a shared vision,** challenge the process, enable others to act, and encourage the heart.[127]

In terms of "inspire a shared vision," Kouzes and Posner explain that "Leaders envision the future by imagining exciting and ennobling possibilities."[128]And they continue with comments that clearly have ramifications in the White House, courthouse, C-suite, or and any leadership "house":

> The future holds little certainty. There are no guarantees, and circumstances can change in a moment. Pioneering leaders rely on their own internal compass and dream. …. Leaders look forward to the future. They hold

in their minds ideas and visions of what can be. They have a sense of what is uniquely possible if everyone works together for a common purpose.[129]

Research conducted by Mark Clark and Meredith Persily Lamel explored six paths to leadership in the public and private sectors. The authors focused on the PATH leaders took to achieve their position and considered the "insider" (promoted from within), the "outsider" (external hire), the "representative" (elected to the position), the "proxy" (appointed by a prescribed authority), the "creator" (founder of the organization), or the legacy holder (inherited from a family, etc.). In all six paths to leadership, the authors found that a common characteristic of successful leaders is "having a strong vision that sets the direction designed to attract stakeholders."[130]

In addition, James C. Collins and Jerry I. Porras concluded their research into successful companies by saying that "visionary" companies outlasted their competitors who lacked a visionary approach: 3M outlasted Norton, Boeing outlasted McDonnell Douglas, General Electric outlasted Westinghouse, IBM outlasted Burroughs, and Sony outlasted Kenwood. The endurance of the companies, in addition to several others, can be directly correlated to their enunciation of a vision and sense of purpose, according to Collins and Porras.[131] Consider the following quotation from Thomas Watson, former CEO of IBM, on the role of vision, core values, and beliefs:

> I believe the real difference between success and failure in a corporation can very often be traced to the question of how well the organization brings out the great energies and talents of its people. What does it do to help these people find common cause with each other? I think the answer lies in the power of what we call beliefs and the appeal these beliefs have for its people. ….. I firmly believe that any organization, in order to survive and achieve success, must have a sound set of beliefs on which it premises all its policies and actions. Next, I believe that the most important single factor on corporate success is faithful adherence to those beliefs.[132]

An essential component to the development of a meaningful vision is what author Joseph Nye calls "contextual intelligence"—the ability to focus on the current conditions or environment and the potential need to change to adapt to the environment.[133] (We saw this exemplified in the Reagan years, as discussed earlier.) Let us consider Amtrak, America's, passenger railroad which recently celebrated its 50-year anniversary.

As explained by Amtrak President Stephen Gardner, the nation's population has grown by 120 million people during the last 50 years (1971–2021), and it is time for reflection, to include a celebration of accomplishments and a look forward to see how Amtrak can fulfill its role and mission in support of the development and mobility of the nation.[134]

In articulating a vision for Amtrak's future, Gardner is asking people to imagine what an expanded rail network could look like by 2035. Imagine, he says, 39 new routes and increased frequencies on the existing 25 routes? That kind of expansion could mean 20 million more passengers annually using Amtrak, which had a record 32.5 million passenger trips prior to the pandemic. Among the new lines being contemplated is a train connecting Cincinnati, Columbus, and Cleveland in Ohio, and a new train in Atlanta with service to Nashville, as well as increased frequencies from Washington to Richmond and other parts of Virginia.[135]

A powerful vision statement embraces the beliefs of an organization, is focused on results, not process, and speaks directly to the needs of stakeholders. According to Kouzes and Posner:

> Call it what you will—vision, purpose, mission, legacy, dream, aspiration, calling of personal agenda—the result is the same. If you are going to be an exemplary leader, you must be able to imagine a positive future. When you envision the future, you want for yourself and others, and when you feel passionate about the legacy you want to leave, you are much more likely to take that first step forward.[136]

Vision is a critical element of leadership because it helps to answer the question Why should anyone be led by you?[137] The answer is because of who you are, in part; but the more important answer is because they believe in your vision, your purpose, and where you want to lead them. It is the leader's responsibility to help all people in an agency or organization comprehend the PURPOSE they are trying to accomplish and how their accomplishments will improve the lives of others.

Notes

1 Arthur M. Schlesinger, Jr., *The Imperial Presidency*. Boston, MA: Mariner Books, 2004, 438.
2 Robert Dallek, *Hail to the Chief: The Making and Unmaking of American Presidents*. New York, NY: Hyperion, 1996, Introduction.
3 Michael Eric Siegel, *The President as Leader*, 2nd ed. New York, NY: Routledge, 2018, 13.
4 Stuart E. Eizenstat, *President Carter: The White House Years*. New York, NY: St Martin's Press, 2018, 49.
5 Ibid.
6 Ibid, 48–49.
7 Betty Glad, *Jimmy Carter: In Search of the Great White House*. New York, NY: Norton and Company, 1980, 107.
8 Eizenstat, *President Carter: The White House Years*, 48.
9 James Fallows, "The Passionless Presidency: The Trouble with Jimmy Carter's Administration." *The Atlantic Weekly*, May 1979, www.theatlantic.com/unbound/flashbks/pres/fallpass.htm

10 Bob Woodward, *Shadow: Five Presidents and the Legacy of Watergate*. New York, NY: Simon and Schuster, 2000, 42.

11 James Kouzes and Barry Posner, *The Leadership Challenge: How to Make Extraordinary Things Happen in Organizations*, 6th ed. San Francisco, CA: Jose-Bass Publishers, 2017.

12 Peggy Noonan, "Ronald Reagan," in Robert A. Wilson ed., *Character Above All: Ten Presidents from FDR to George Bush*. New York, NY: Simon and Schuster, 1985.

13 Siegel, *The President as Leader*, 2nd ed., 74.

14 Lou Cannon, *President Reagan: The Role of a Lifetime*. New York, NY: Simon and Schuster, 1991, 90.

15 Ibid, 237.

16 Richard Reeves, *President Reagan: The Triumph of Imagination*. New York, NY: Simon and Schuster, 2005, 11.

17 Ibid, 164.

18 Erwin Hargrove, *The President as Leader: Appealing to the Better Angels of Our Nature*. Lawrence, KS: University of Kansa Press, 1988, 192.

19 Siegel, *The President as Leader*, 2nd ed., 76.

20 Paul Kengor, *God and Ronald Reagan: A Spiritual Life*. New York, NY: Harper Perennial, 2005.

21 Noonan, "Ronald Reagan," 204.

22 Siegel, *The President as Leader*, 2nd ed., 77.

23 James Mann, *The Rebellion of Ronald Reagan: A History of the End of the Cold War*. New York, NY: Viking Adult, 2009, 278.

24 Siegel, *The President as Leader*, 2nd ed., 77.

25 Jon Meacham, *Destiny and Power: The American Odyssey of George Herbert Walker Bush*. New York, NY: Random House, 2015, 255.27.

26 Dennis Ross, Interview with author, December 1, 2008, Washington, DC.

27 George H.W. Bush and Brent Scowcroft, *A World Transformed*. New York, NY: Vintage Books, 1999, 17.

28 Ibid.

29 Dick Cheney, "The Bush Presidency," in Kenneth W. Thompson, ed. *The Bush Presidency, Part Two: Ten Intimate Perspectives of George Bush*. New York, NY: University Press of America and the Miller Center, University of Virginia, 1998, 10.

30 Meacham, *Destiny and Power*, 356.

31 Ryan J. Barilleaux and Mark J. Rozell, *Power and Prudence: The Presidency of George H.W. Bush*. College Station, TX: Texas A&M University Press, 2004, 117.

32 Ibid, 118.

33 Zbigniew Brzezinski, *Second Chance: Three Presidents and the Crisis of American Superpower*. New York, NY: Basic Books, 2007, 57.

34 Meacham, *Destiny and Power*, 375.

35 Meacham, *Destiny and Power*, 375.

36 Barilleaux and Rozell, *Power and Prudence*, 12.

37 Siegel, *The President as Leader*, 2nd ed., 114.

38 David Mervin, *George Bush and the Guardianship Presidency*. New York, NY: St. Martin's Press, 1996, 32.

39 Siegel, *The President as Leader*, 2nd ed., 115.

40 Mervin, *George Bush and the Guardianship Presidency*. 27.

41 Siegel, *The President as Leader*, 2nd ed., 147.

42 Bill Clinton, *My Life*. New York, NY: Alfred A. Knopf, 2004, 326–332.

43 Bill Clinton, *My Life*. New York, NY: Alfred A. Knopf, 2004, 326–327.

44 Siegel, *The President as Leader*, 2nd ed., 154, and William Jefferson Clinton. "Inaugural Address, January 20, 1997," in Public Papers of the Presidents of the United States, Book I, January 1 to June 30, 1997. Washington, DC: Government Printing Office, 1997, 44.

45 William Jefferson Clinton, "State of the Union Address, 1995."
46 Al Gore, *Creating a Government that Works Better and Costs Less*. New York, NY: Plume, 1993, 5.
47 Clinton, Inaugural Address, 1997.
48 Brzezinski, *Second Chance*, 93–94.
49 Ibid, 106.
50 Ibid, 109.
51 Ibid, 97.
52 Clinton, *My Life*, 624–625.
53 Ibid, 97.
54 Siegel, *The President as Leader*, 157–158.
55 George W. Bush, *Decision Points*. New York, NY: Random House, 2010, 36.
56 Marvin Olasky, *The Tragedy of American Compassion*. New York, NY: Regnery Publishing Reprint, 1994.
57 Ibid, 8.
58 James P. Pfiffner, "Introduction; Assessing the Bush Presidency," in Gary L. Gregg II, and Mark J. Rozell, eds., *Considering the Bush Presidency*. New York, NY: Oxford University Press, 2004, 4.
59 Siegel, *The President as Leader*, 2nd ed., 205.
60 Bill Minutaglio, *First Son: George Bush and the Bush Family Dynasty*. New York, NY: Crown, 1999, 108.
61 Siegel, *The President as Leader*, 2nd ed., 205.
62 James P. Pfiffner, "The First MBA President: George Bush as Public Administrator." *Public Administration Review*, January/February, 2007, 67.
63 Siegel, *The President as Leader*, 2nd ed., 205.
64 Stanley A. Renshon, "The Bush Doctrine Considered," in Stanley A. Renshon and Peter Suedfelds, eds. *Understanding the Bush Doctrine: Psychology and Strategy on an Age of Terrorism*. New York, NY: Routledge, 2007, 12–13.
65 Pfiffner, "The First MBA President," 5.
66 Gary L. Gregg II, "Dignified Authenticity: George Bush and the Symbolic Presidency," in Gary L. Gregg II and Mark J. Rozell, eds. *Considering the Bush Presidency*, 88–92.
67 Siegel, *The President as Leader*, 2nd ed., 206.
68 George W. Bush, "Address before a Joint Session of Congress in the State of the Union," in Public Papers of the Presidents of the United States, January 29, 2002. George Bush. Book I, June 30, 2002. Washington, DC: Government Printing Office, 2004, 130–131.
69 Siegel, *The President as Leader*, 2nd ed., 207.
70 Raymond Tanter and Stephen Kerstig, "Grand Strategy and National Security Policy: Politics, Rhetoric, and the Bush Legacy," in Colin Campbell, Bert Rockman, and Andrew Rudalevige, eds., *The George W. Bush Legacy*. Washington, DC: Congressional Quarterly Press, 2002.
71 George W. Bush, "Commencement Address at the United States Naval Academy in West Point, NY," in Public Papers of the Presidents of the United States, 2002. George Bush, Book 1, January 1–July 31, 2002. Washington DC: Government Printing Office, 2002, 140.
72 George W. Bush, "Inaugural Address, January 20, 2005," in Public Papers of the President's of the United States, 2005. Book I. January 1 to July 30, 2005. Washington, DC: Government Printing Office, 2005, 66..
73 Siegel, *The President as Leader*, 2nd ed., 270.
74 Barrack Obama, "Remarks Announcing Candidacy for President," www.nytimes.Com/2007/02/11/us/politics/11obama.html?mcubz=1
75 Meet the Press, October 22, 2006, www.nbcnews.com/id/15304689/ns/meet_the_press/t/mtp-transcript-oct/#.VsPwmPkwiUK

76 Michael Grunwald, *The New New Deal: The Hidden Story of Change in the Obama Era*. New York, NY: Simon and Schuster, 2012, 2–3.

77 Barack Obama, *A Promised Land*. New York, NY: Crown, 2020, 605.

78 Colin Dueck, *The Obama Doctrine: Grand Strategy Today*. New York, NY: Oxford University Press, 2015, 3.

79 Siegel, *The President as Leader*, 2nd ed., 271.

80 Jonathan Alter, *The Promise: President Obama: Year One*. New York, NY: Simon and Schuster, 2010, 401.

81 Ibid.

82 "Inaugural Address, January 20, 2009," Public Papers of the Presidents of the United States, Barack Obama 2009 (in two books). Book 1, January 20–June 30, 2009. Washington, DC: US Government Printing Office, 2009.

83 Barack Obama, *The Audacity of Hope: Thoughts on Reclaiming the American Dream*. New York, NY: Crown, 2006, 10.

84 Barack Obama, *Dreams from My Father: A Story of Race and Inheritance*. New York, NY: The Free Press, 2004, 49.

85 October 16, 2012 Debate Transcript, President Barack Obama and Former Governor Mitt Romney Participate in a Candidate's Debate, Hofstra University, Hempstead, NY, www.debate.org/index.php?page=october-16-2012-the-second-obama-romney-preseitial-debate

86 Siegel, *The President as Leader*, 2nd ed., 276.

87 Derek Chollet, *The Long Game: How Obama Defied Washington and Redefined America's Role in the World*. New York, NY: Public Affairs, 2016, 216.

88 Ibid, Introduction, v.

89 Barack Obama, "Remarks by the President at the United States Military Academy Commencement Ceremony," White House, May 28, 2014, https://obamawhitehouse.archives.Gov/the-press-office/2014/05/28/remarks-president-united-states-military-academy-commencement-ceremony

90 Siegel, *The President as Leader*, 2nd ed., 276.

91 https://medium.com/@ObamaWhiteHouse/joint-comprehensive-plan-of-action-5cdd9b320fd/

92 Siegel, *The President as Leader*, 2nd ed., 304–305.

93 Ibid, 305.

94 Siegel, *The President as Leader*, 2nd ed., 342.

95 Donald Trump, "January 20, 2017 Inaugural Address,"

96 Michael Nelson, *Trump; The First Two Years*. Charlottesville, VA: University of Virginia Press, 2018, 33.

97 Anita Kelly and Barbara Sprunt, "Here is What Donald Trump Wants to do in His First 100 Days." https://www.npr.org/2016/11/09/501451368/here-is-what-donald-trump-wants-to-do-in-his-first-100-days

98 Ibid.

99 Michael Gerson, "Trump's Infantile Conception of Strength." *The Washington Post*, July 3, 2020, A21.

100 Ibid.

101 Complaint, Sims v. Files. Integrity First for America. Time.com/charlotessville-white-national-rally-clashes/

102 Ibid.

103 Bob Woodward, *Fear: Trump in the White House*. New York, NY: Simon and Schuster, 2018, 238.

104 Ibid.

105 Ibid.

106 Ibid.

107 Ibid, 243.

108 Ibid, 244.
109 Ibid.
110 Ibid.
111 Ibid.
112 CNN Transcript. Donald Trump, January 6, The Ellipse.
113 Alexander Nazaryan, *The Best People: Trump's Cabinet and the Siege on Washington.* New York, NY: Hachette Books, 2019, 6.
114 Ibid.
115 Ibid.
116 G. John Ikenberry, "The Plot Against Foreign Policy: Can the Liberal Order Survive?" *Foreign Affairs.* May/June 2017, 2.
117 Council on Foreign Relations, "Trump's Foreign Policy Moments, 2017–2021." https://www.cfr.org/timeline/trumps-foreign-policy-moments
118 Ibid.
119 Ibid.
120 Richard Haas, "Present at the Destruction: How Trump Unmade US Foreign Policy," *Foreign Affairs.* September/October 2020: 24–32.
121 Evan Osnos, Joe Biden: *The Life, the Run, and What Matters Now.* New York, NY: Scribner, 2020, 49.
122 Jonathan Alter, "The Biden-FDR Connection Runs Deeper Than You Think." *Foreign Policy,* September 14, 2020. https://foreignpolicy.com/2020/09/14/the-biden-fdr-connection-runs-deeper-than-you-think/
123 Ibid.
124 Ibid.
125 Sean Sullivan, Marianna Sotomayor, Tyler Pager, and Jeff Stein. "Divides Cloud Budges Package." *The Washington Post,* September 13, 2021, A1.
126 Katie Rogers, "Bush and Biden Join in Seeking Unity Amid Grief." *The New York Times,* September 12, 2021, A3.
127 Kouzes and Posner, The Leadership Challenge, 6th ed., 15. Also see the authors' more recent book, James M. Kouzes and Barry Z. Posner, *Everyday People, Extraordinary Leadership.* New York, NY: Wiley, 2021.
128 Ibid.
129 Ibid, 18.
130 Mark A. Clark and Meredith Persily Lamel, *Six Paths to Leadership: Lessons from Successful Executives, Politicians, Entrepreneurs, and More.* New York, NY: Palgrave Macmillan, 2021, 10.
131 James C. Collins and Jerry I. Porras, *Built To Last: Successful Habits of Visionary Companies.* New York, NY: Harper Business, 1997.
132 Ibid, 74.
133 Joseph S. Nye, *The Powers to Lead.* New York, NY: Oxford University Press, 2008, 85–86.
134 Luz Lazo, "Amtrak President Discusses New Routes—And the Challenges to Get There." *Washington Post,* June 20, 2021. C2.
135 Ibid.
136 Kouzes and Posner, *The Leadership Challenge,* 103.
137 Robert Geoffe and Gareth Jones, "Why Should Anyone Be Led by You?" *Harvard Business Review.* September/October 2000.

3

POLITICS (STRATEGY, EXECUTION)

Importance to Presidents and All Other Leaders

"Politics" captures the leader's ability to transform vision into reality, to get things done. As Mario Cuomo (former Democratic Governor of New York) often said, "You can campaign in poetry, but you must govern in prose."[1]

There are several relevant questions a president must ask here:

- How will I implement or execute my vision, my program?
- Upon whom will I rely to communicate my message?
- Who will manage congressional relations?
- What strategy will I use to influence the opposition party, or even members of my own party who may have their own political agendas?
- How will I lead or manage the executive branch of government of some 3 million people? How will I work with the press?
- How will I stay true to my agenda, fulfill my campaign promises, and still have time to reflect and assess what I am doing?
- How many issues will I tackle at one time?

There are two critical aspects of "politics" for a president to master: the details of implementation and the "retail politics", or persuasion skills of the job. First, the president must understand the requirements of policy implementation. A president cannot get things done alone. As Dwight Eisenhower observed at the end of his two-term presidency,

> the government of the United States has become too big, too complex, and too pervasive in its influence for one individual to pretend to direct all the details of its important and critical programming. Competent assistants are mandatory; without them the Executive Branch would

DOI: 10.4324/9781003285229-3

bog down. To command the loyalties and dedication and best efforts of capable and outstanding individuals requires patience, understanding, a readiness to delegate, and an acceptance of responsibility for any honest errors—real or apparent—those subordinates might make.[2]

In a more recent example of the importance of policy implementation, once again demonstrating the president's inability to act alone, President George W. Bush experienced frustration in implementing his human rights vision. In a June 2007 speech in Prague (Czech Republic), Bush vowed to order US ambassadors in unfree nations to meet with dissidents and lauded the fact that he had created a fund to help embattled human rights defendants. Nevertheless, the State Department never sent out a cable instructing ambassadors to sit down with dissidents until two months later. As of August 2007, not a penny had been spent on the program.[3] We can glean an insight into the idea of bureaucratic defiance to the president through the following discussion between a Bush Administration staff member and a State Department official shortly after Bush's Prague speech: Bush Administration Staffer: "It's our policy" (support of dissidents). State Department Official: "What do you mean?" Bush Administration Staffer: "Read the President's speech." State Department Official: "Policy is not what the president says in speeches. Policy is what emerges from interagency meetings."[4]

The second aspect of "politics" relates to a president's facility with persuasion and with "retail politics." For example, President Ronald Reagan displayed great dexterity in the art of persuasion, as he worked tirelessly in 1981–1982 to secure passage of his conservative political agenda in a Democratic controlled House of Representatives. Reagan relied heavily on the Washington insiders, including his chief-of-staff James Baker and congressional liaison Max Friedersdorf.[5]

The Reagan team met in chief-of-staff Jim Baker's office, hammering out details of how to get key legislation tied up and passed on Capitol Hill.[6] They addressed important persuasion questions, such as Who needed to be stroked in Congress? How? With what arguments? What interest groups needed to be mobilized? To pressure whom? How should the issue be framed for the press? What columnist needed special attention? What must the president do? Can members of the cabinet take some of the load?

Reagan's lobbying team prepared him effectively for the telephone calls he would make on behalf of his economic reform program. Congressional liaison Max Friedersdorf prepared "call lists" for Reagan accompanied by a short biographical and political summary of each congressional member he intended to persuade.[7] Reagan took the advice and guidance provided by his staff, and it proved very useful in his negotiations.

In short, negotiating, bargaining, influencing, building coalitions, enlisting the support of competent people—all of these are requisite skills of a successful strategic president. According to political scientists Robert Dahl and Charles Lindblom, in their classic text, *Politics, Economics, and Welfare*:

> Because he is a bargainer, a negotiator, the politician does not often give orders. He can rarely employ unilateral controls. Even as a chief executive or a cabinet official he soon discovers that his control depends on his skill in bargaining.[8]

James Earl Carter

Carter won the 1976 presidential election by 1.7 million votes. He received 50.1 percent of the popular vote compared to Republican candidate (and incumbent president) Gerald Ford's 48 percent. He won 11 of the 13 states in the South and the few Northern states that he needed to win: New York, Ohio, Pennsylvania, Massachusetts, Wisconsin, and Minnesota. The electoral college vote was 297-240; the smallest winning total since Woodrow Wilson's victory over Charles Evans Hughes in 1916.[9]

Upon entering the White House in January 1977, Jimmy Carter confronted two contextual factors that would influence his political fate. First, the excesses of the Nixon presidency, most egregiously exemplified in the Watergate crisis, had caused Congress to reinstate itself more aggressively into the overall scheme of government and public policy, and to begin to scrutinize or "oversee" the president more intensely than it had done before.

Three months after Nixon's resignation from the presidency, 75 new Democrats were elected to the House of Representatives. Called the "Watergate Babies," these men and women presented a different profile than did their counterparts of earlier years: they were younger, less indoctrinated into the "norms" of Congress, more willing to innovate with legislative initiatives, and more likely to challenge presidential leadership. They were less likely to play the traditional role of a new member, apprentice, and demanded full participation in congressional activities and in the oversight of the executive.[10]

The changes in Congress were compounded by Carter's inability to develop a viable strategy of working with Congress, as will be detailed later in this chapter. According to Gregory Paul Domin, "Ironically it was genuineness of Carter's anti-Washington position, so formidable to the public, that hindered his effectiveness once in the nation's capital."[11]

A second set of political obstacles Jimmy Carter faced when he assumed the presidency: the nation's economy was experiencing a period of hyperinflation, serious energy problems were looming, and the traditional ideas of the Democratic Party were inadequate to address these kinds of issues.[12] Indeed, Carter emphasized that he would stake out different ground and failed to be constrained by the practices and policies of previous Democratic presidents. According to James Sterling Young:

After Roosevelt's New Deal, Truman's Fair Deal, Kennedy's New Frontier, and Johnson's Great Society, here was a Democrat who not only spurned labels but presented a large legislative agenda with a drastically conservative cast. Carter moved to retrench and reform—not to extend—the welfare state that other Democrats had built; to reduce intervention in the private sector as a way of solving public problems in the long run; to deregulate and start relying on market forces in order to achieve desired revenue ends.[13]

As I have written previously, "Carter moved quickly, but not strategically, to achieve his policy objectives."[14] The day following his swearing in, President Carter issued an executive order pardoning Vietnam draft dodgers a decision that Senator Barry Goldwater (R, AZ) described as the "most disgusting thing a president has ever done."[15] In February, the second month of his presidency, he announced that by March he would send Congress plans for a new Department of Energy as well as a comprehensive energy program to be delivered to a joint session of Congress on April 20.[16]

At a March 9 press conference, President Carter offered a large number of domestic programs and foreign policy initiatives including a Youth Conservation Corps program, a Middle East settlement idea, gradual withdrawal of US troops from South Korea, and arms negotiations with Russia. He also revealed his tax rebate program, his plan to reorganize the federal government, and his opposition to "wasteful" water projects in the West.[17] Because the president had not established a prioritization for these issues, the chances of legislative action were problematic. According to Heineman and Hessler:

> The President sent a flotilla of major proposals to Congress in the first eighteen months of his administration—cuts in water projects, social security finance, a tax rebate scheme, hospital cost containment legislation …. Many of these proposals went to the tax-writing committees of Congress: Senate Finance and House Ways and Means. And because the President had overloaded the Congress and those committees with reforms that would not command ready assent, because he was not able to marshal the Administration's resources and develop political support for the major battles that were required, and because many of his top political lieutenants were untutored in the ways of Congress, most of these proposals were either sunk or badly damaged.[18]

In February 1977, Carter announced a series of budget revisions that he preferred, including the elimination of 19 water projects. Members in the affected congressional districts were not consulted in advance, but were informed by letters and phone calls from Carter's staff later in the same week the announcement was made. Members had already returned to their districts for the weekend and learned about the cuts from their local newspapers. Carter's Press Secretary said that the members were "basically informed."[19] Nevertheless, members were incensed, including Democrats like Colorado Senator Gary Hart who told the media he had been "blindsided" by Carter.[20] One of Carter's greatest admirers, Stuart Eizenstat, who served as his Domestic Policy Adviser, said of the water projects, "The President's head-on attack on an extraordinarily contentious issue exposed every weakness of the new administration."[21]

In general, President Carter failed to appreciate the importance of "retail politics"—the selling of one's ideas to key constituents—to presidential leadership. A telling example of this oversight comes from a book by Tip O'Neill, the Speaker of the House during the Carter years.

On February 2, 1977, Jimmy Carter delivered an energy speech on national television wearing a cardigan sweater. (In some respects, Carter was trying to emulate President Franklin Roosevelt and his "fireside chats.") Carter eloquently explained to the nation how the energy crisis demanded sacrifices of all Americans and that the White House was no exception. He told Americans that he had ordered all the thermostats at the White House to be set at lower temperatures, which was why he was wearing a sweater.[22] Carter explained that importing large quantities of foreign oil was a concern and that America "must face the fact that the energy shortage is permanent."[23] The president also explained a series of cutbacks on expenditures for the White House such as eliminating luxuries like door-to-door limo service for all staff, cutting staff size for the members of his cabinet, and asking the public not to mail gifts to the White House, implying that although he knew the intentions behind them, it was a financial expenditure people should not face. He also asked for support for an energy bill he had presented to Congress.[24]

The energy bill had been developed largely behind closed doors under the direction of Secretary of Energy James Schlesinger.[25] Key provisions of the bill included a tax on gasoline pegged to rise with consumption, a tax on gas-guzzling automobiles, numerous conservation measures including tax credits for investments in greater fuel efficiency of buildings, taxes on domestic crude at the wellheads to increase domestic process to world levels with a revenue rebate to the public, federal control of intrastate natural gas sales, tax incentives for industries to shift to coal, and an end to gasoline price controls.[26] The president wanted Congress to consider 113 interlocking provisions in one package. Yet no attempt had been made to build a coalition in Congress while these proposals were being developed.[27]

Five minutes after the speech, Speaker O'Neill called to compliment Carter on his speech and then asked that the president call all the chairpersons of the committees who would be dealing with the energy bill. Carter responded that he did not feel that was necessary, as all the committee chairs had heard the speech.[28]

President Carter's reaction to Speaker O'Neill's request reveals several dimensions of persuasion (and leadership) ineptitude. First, it is more than likely that each member of Congress who heard the energy speech may have actually heard a unique version of the speech, a version tailored to fit his or her own perceptions and needs. For example, the senator from Texas probably heard a different speech than did the senator from Vermont, given the different levels of oil production in the two states. Furthermore, people are rarely mobilized to action based on speeches alone. Presidents, like other leaders, must engage in "retail" politics and follow their oral presentations with persuasion activities to the unique needs of individual members of Congress. Finally, follow-up calls and meetings conducted by the president and his team signify to members of Congress, and to the public, the president's personal commitment to his program or proposal. President Lyndon Baines Johnson, for instance, called resistant Southern senators at all hours of the night (and into the early morning hours) to lobby them on his civil rights bills.[29]

Carter faced multiple challenges regarding congressional relations. He seemed to disdain the need for persuasion and retail politics, wanting to rely instead on his analytical and logical arguments alone. One of his aides expressed the problem this way:

> We used to always joke that the worst way to convince the President to go along with your position was to say this would help you politically, because ... he wanted to be a different kind of President. He was elected somehow to be a different kind of President. He was running against the sort of system of inside deals and so forth. He saw himself above that system. He did not enjoy politics per se in the same way that a Humphrey or a Johnson did ... It's not something that came naturally to him.[30]

Another dimension of the problem stemmed from the fact that Jimmy Carter surrounded himself with mostly Washington outsiders, men and women who were not well schooled in the norms of Capitol Hill. For the key White House positions, he chose Georgian political intimates. Carter named his old friend and political ally, Bert Lance, as director of the Office of Management and Budget. He named the director of the Georgia Office of Planning and Budget, James McIntyre Jr., as deputy director.[31] Carter appointed his Georgia friend, Frank Moore, to the post of director of congressional liaison; however, Moore was particularly unfamiliar with the inside workings of Congress.[32] Jody Powell was named Press Secretary, and Hamilton Jordan as special assistant to the president. Robert Lipshutz, the financial campaign manager in 1976, was named legal counselor to the president. All of these appointments were men whom Carter had worked with in Georgia; none had substantial Washington experience.[33]

According to Stuart Eizenstat:

> He also filled the ranks of his senior White House staff with Georgians and campaign aides who had been with him during the long political campaign, myself included. All had one thing in common: Except for me, not one senior executive aide had ever before set foot in the White House, lived in Washington, or knew anything about the operations of the U.S. Congress, or the massive federal government. Our home-grown, inexperienced team did not know its way around Washington and the city's multiple power centers – Congress, interest groups, the press.[34]

There was one additional aspect of President Carter's disdain for "retail" politics and presidential persuasion—he underestimated the importance of one-on-one, face-to-face time spent with key stakeholders, especially members of Congress. *Washington Post* journalist Bob Woodward presented a poignant example of this problem in his book, *Shadow: Five Presidents and the Legacy of Watergate*.[35] Jimmy Carter preferred to schedule the White House tennis courts by himself, and one Sunday he scheduled a tennis doubles match at the White House and invited Texas Senator (D) Lloyd Bentsen and three other senators to join him. The four men played a few sets of tennis, and immediately after the game, Carter walked off the court and the senators went home. Bentsen was surprised, even shocked! How many times do I get to spend private time with the president, he wondered to himself? He called the White House to complain, saying, "He did not offer us a drink, lemonade … there was no conversation, no lobbying, no relaxing."[36] Carter was asked about what transpired, and responded, "They don't want to sit up in the White House on the balcony and have a drink with me; they want to see their families."[37] As Woodward says:

> Carter the outsider didn't understand his own power and appeal, the centrality of the president to Washington, its own peculiar games and rituals. He was not only removed from the capital city but alienated from it. Watergate had helped produce the most unlikely president: a loner.[38]

Despite Carter's troubles, he had a moderately successful first year legislatively speaking. President Carter's proposals for the creation of a Department of Energy, for authority to reorganize the government, and for building a natural gas pipeline from Alaska were approved as was his economic stimulus package and a major public works program.[39] Carter's legislative success rate was 75.4 percent, however, compared to other Democratic presidents that score was not overly impressive, especially because Carter was working with a Democratic Congress. During President Kennedy's first year, he had achieved a legislative success rate of 81 percent, and Lyndon Johnson had scored 88 percent![40] And he certainly achieved a great success in mediating the Camp David Peace Treaty between Israel and Egypt.

But with a Democratic Congress he could have done much more. Looking back on the Carter administration, where he served as secretary of state, Cyrus Vance ruminated about the absence of "political" savvy in Jimmy Carter, saying, "I think [Carter] should have involved himself much more with the Congress than he did, and he should have used his White House staff more effectively in dealing with the Congress. The master at this … was Lyndon Johnson; he was superb."[41]

TAKEAWAYS FOR ALL LEADERS

- While part of leadership is conceptual, a large part is all about the leader's ability to build and sustain relationships and align people around a common goal.
- A leader needs to be very clear about his or her policy goals and objectives and pursue a limited number of them with doggedness and determination.

Ronald Wilson Reagan

Reagan was elected with 50.75 percent of the popular vote in a three-way race for the presidency in 1980 (Carter was the Democratic candidate and John Anderson was the third-party independent candidate). Former Governor Reagan swept the mega states on both coasts, the Midwest, and nearly all the Sunbelt. Carter won in Georgia, Maryland, West Virginia, Rhode Island, Minnesota, Hawaii, and the District of Columbia.[42] Reagan was reelected as president in 1984 by one of the largest landslides in the US political history, winning 49 of the 50 states. In the electoral college, the split was 525-13.[43]

Reagan was 69 years old when he entered the White House. Most of his friends and political associates were from California and were not Washington insiders. Nevertheless, Reagan understood, unlike Jimmy Carter, that his political success would be closely linked to his acceptance in Washington.[44]

President Reagan wasted no time in pursuing his focused agenda of cutting taxes and social welfare spending and increasing defense spending. He named James Baker, recently described as "the Man who ran Washington,"[45] as his chief-of staff.[46] It was apparent that Baker understood Reagan's policy objectives and clearly prepared administration recruits for what they would be doing. Ed Meese, counselor to the president, told newcomers, "We all know what the President wants, and our job is simply to go out and do it."[47]

Reagan's team, led by White House staff member David Gergen and pollster Richard Wirthlin, drafted an "Early Action Plan" for the first hundred days of his presidency. The plan was informed by research that Gergen and his team had conducted on the first hundred days of five previous nonincumbent presidents: Roosevelt in 1933, Eisenhower in 1953, Kennedy in 1961, Nixon in 1969, and Carter in 1977.[48] They studied how presidents managed their leadership activities during the first hundred days, including the legislative proposals, executive orders, symbolic gestures, meetings with Congress, introduction to the Supreme Court, speeches, press conferences, and even troop deployments. They drew the following conclusions:

- The public makes a fresh evaluation of the president the day he takes office. Now that he holds the reins of power, people want to know if he is up to the job? Do people trust him? Does he know what he wants to do? Does he have a central focus? The recent Carter experience revealed the dangers posed by a lack of focus.
- The early months provide a good chance for the president to put a firm thematic stamp on his administration. FDR called himself "Dr. New Deal" and Nixon focused on "Bring Us Together."
- The early months of an administration also could be a time peril for a new president as Kennedy learned from the Bay of Pigs, Ford by pardoning Nixon, and Carter by unilaterally cutting water projects as described earlier in the chapter.[49]

The Early Action Plan was developed by Gergen and Wirthlin at the helm, but benefitted from previous disciplined work on Reagan's agenda by a wide circle of advisers that the president had assembled at the White House. Reagan's wider team consisted of ideologues he brought with him from California, including Ed Meese (counselor to the president), Casper Weinberger (secretary of defense), Martin Anderson (chief domestic policy adviser), and William Clark (national security adviser, secretary of interior); but the team also included a sizable band of Washington insiders who were more identified with the Ford-Bush wing of the Republican Party, including James Baker (chief-of-staff), Richard Darman (deputy COS), Max Friedersdorf, and Ken

Duberstein (congressional relations). According to David Gergen, who was also part of the wider team, Reagan understood the need to combine ideologues with political pragmatists and this "coalition government that Reagan created in the White House in his early years was one of the strongest teams of the past fifty years."[50]

The Reagan persuasion process was spearheaded by his Chief-of-Staff, Jim Baker, who immediately identified a powerful ally in Senate Majority Leader Howard Baker (R, TN), who became Majority Leader with the GOP capture of the Senate in 1981 on Reagan's coattails. The team was also assisted by Reagan's congressional liaison, Max Friedersdorf, and later by Kenneth Duberstein.[51] During the first hundred days of his presidency, Reagan personally conducted 69 meetings with 467 members of Congress, prompting one of them to say that members saw more of Reagan during the first four months of his term than he had seen Carter during his entire four years.[52] On February 18, 1981, in a speech to a joint session of Congress, Reagan laid out his plan for economic recovery, framing his message in the parlance of "restoring the promise that is offered to every citizen by this, last best hope of man on Earth."[53] President Reagan called for cutting $41 billion from the Carter budget and making cuts in 83 federal programs. He attacked waste and fraud in the federal government and asked for a 30 percent tax cut over three years, as well as an increase in military spending. It was, according to journalist Richard Reeves, a "stunning speech, and two-thirds of viewers and listeners across the nation said that they agreed with Reagan's message."[54] The Reagan team limited the agenda to three major objectives: tax cuts, domestic spending cuts, and defense budget increases. As mentioned earlier, the team, called Legislative Strategy Group, met around Jim Baker's conference table to map out their approach. The political landscape was not totally hospitable to Reagan's proposals, because the Democrats still held a 53-seat advantage in the House of Representatives.[55] Nevertheless, a sizeable number of Democrats, called "Boll Weevils" leaned conservative and were open to Reagan's entreaties to find common ground. Reagan approaches them with inclusive language, such as, "I'm here tonight to ask you to join me in making our plan work."[56]

As well, Reagan's persuasion/lobbying team effectively prepared him for his one-on-one meetings with members of Congress on behalf of economic reform. Regan's congressional liaison, Max Friedersdorf, prepared call lists for the president, accompanied by short biographical and political summaries of each congressional member. For example, for his meeting with Massachusetts Representative Margaret Heckler, a Republican, the notes said,

> North suburbs of Boston and Vietnam Affairs Committee. Peggy wants to support the President but her district is likely to be reapportioned and she will be pitted against Barney Frank, a liberal Democrat.

Following the meeting with Heckler, Reagan wrote the following note:

> Has a very real problem …. Many of our cuts are extremely sensitive in her area. There is no doubt of her personal support and desire to be of help. We need to give her good rational explanations re: the cuts, such as student loans, etc.[57]

Several things stand out here. President Reagan displayed humility in knowing what he did not know and leaning on the experts on his team who had the knowledge. An arrogant leader might say, "I don't need your notes; I know what I'm doing!" Indeed, President Clinton probably would not need the notes, because he would have already known Heckler's situation. But Reagan knew that he was not a detail person and that he had to rely on the expertise of those around him. In addition, the anecdote demonstrates Reagan's appreciation of the fact that persuasion is a two-way process, and we can learn a great deal from the person we are trying to persuade.[58]

On the tax front, Jim Baker and his deputy chief-of-staff, Richard Darman, reached across the aisle to Representative Dan Rostenkowski (D, IL), the powerful Democratic Chairman of the House Ways and Means Committee. To mollify Rostenkowski's concerns, Baker and Darman agreed to delay the first year of the tax cuts and reduce the amount to 25 percent, resulting in a scheme to cut taxes across the board by 5 percent in 1981, 10 percent on 1982, and 10 percent in 1983. In addition, Baker told Boll Weevil Democrats that Reagan would not campaign against them in 1982 if they supported the tax cuts.[59]

Reagan and his team achieved remarkable results through their negotiations and focused attention to their agenda: Congress passed an 8.5 percent cut in domestic spending programs. And on July 31, 1981, the House approved the administration's military build-up by a vote of 354-63, joining the Senate in approving a $136 billion defense appropriations bill. Finally, Reagan achieved his tax cuts with the passage of the Economic Recovery Act of 1981. Sponsored by Congressman Jack Kemp (R, NY) and Senator William Roth (R, DE), the ERTA phased in a 25 percent cut in individual taxes, accelerated business depreciation, reduced windfall profit taxes, and allowed all working individuals to establish individual retirement accounts (IRA's).[60]

But Reagan's substantial legislative victories did not immediately translate into economic success. The short-term impact of his program for economic recovery included a decline in social services for the neediest Americans, an increase to 9 percent in unemployment and 17,000 business failures.[61] In the 1982 mid-term elections, the Republicans lost 22 seats in the House and 7 governorships, while still holding onto control of the Senate.[61] Nevertheless, Reagan stuck to his guns, refusing to raise taxes at the time. By early 1983, an unprecedented economic recovery began and continued through Reagan's second term and into the early years of the Bush administration. Eighteen million new jobs were created, inflation was brought down to 4.4 percent, and unemployment came down to 5 percent.[62]

Reagan would subsequently face serious challenges, including those created by his mercurial Secretary of State, Alexander Haig, the attempt on his life on March 31, 1981, global financial instability, and revelations of the Iran-Contra scandal revealing the administration had traded arms for hostages. Reagan's leadership throughout these crises was not always stellar, but he never abandoned the pursuit of his agenda nor his optimism. As I have written elsewhere:

> The Reagan political effort was very strong in the first administration. Reagan clearly communicated his beliefs and objectives, recruited talented staff and allowed them the freedom to maneuver, and they negotiated with confidence and determination on a limited agenda. The president maintained clear control of his agenda and found ways to exert damage control when events or personalities threatened to derail him.[63]

TAKEAWAYS FOR ALL LEADERS

- Strong, purposeful leaders recognize their own strengths and weaknesses and surround themselves with associates who have the strengths that they lack.
- Having a focused agenda will lead to leadership success, and being willing to compromise, even on strongly held beliefs, will help.
- Ideologues or purists will provide the intellectual and emotional passion for the leader, but the leadership team will also need practitioners and negotiators.

George Herbert Walker Bush

Following a bitter and, at times, nasty 1988 presidential election campaign, Republican candidate George H.W. Bush (Bush 41) defeated former Massachusetts Democratic Governor Michael Dukakis by winning 53 percent of the popular vote, 40 states of the union, and 426 of the 38 electoral votes.[64] Bush was the first president elected to succeed a predecessor of his own party since 1928 and the first sitting vice president elected since 1836.[65] Despite his impressive victory, however, Bush's triumph did not really give him much of a "mandate" to do anything, because, as *New York Times* journalist Tom Wicker put it, "He had not, after all, campaigned to do much of anything—only on the proposition that he was a tried and experienced leader, a man of conventional virtue, while his opponent was not to be trusted."[66]

Almost on script, Bush chose moderate insiders to staff his administration, experienced, competent professionals whose profile in a sense mirrored his own. Indeed, he avoided purists or ideologues and selected, instead associates from previous phases of his political career: Jim Baker (Secretary of State) and Nicolas Brady (Treasury Secretary) from his Texas days, Brent Scowcroft (National Security Adviser) and Dick Cheney (Defense Secretary) from the Ford and Reagan Administrations, and Richard Darman (Director of the Office of Management and Budget) from the Reagan years.[67]

In March 1989, President Bush's chief-of-staff, John Sununu, summarized what he would consider a successful presidency: "a checklist of bills passed that major constituencies would applaud, of bills vetoed that the other constituencies (especially conservatives) had despised; and a tally of presidential actions taken, crises handled, and opportunities seized."[68]

Having served in the House and presided over the Senate, Bush had many friends in both chambers and sought to work with Democrats to make progress on issues of mutual concern, such as curbing illegal drug use, stabilizing the bank and credit industry, and reducing the federal budget deficit, which had grown, in part, because of Reagan's economic policies.[69]

In his inaugural address, president gave strong voice to a bipartisan orientation:

> To my friends, and yes, I do mean friends—in the loyal opposition, and yes, I mean loyal—I put out my hand. I am putting out my hand to you, Mr. Speaker, our differences ended at the water's edge. ... Let us negotiate soon and hard. But in the end, let us produce. The American people await action.[70]

During the first half of 1989, Bush's first year in office, virtually all 100 Senators and at least half of the 435 House members had been to the White House for a function or ceremony.[71] In addition, 20 days after his inauguration, Bush gathered hundreds of the government's senior career civil servants at Constitution Hall to praise their dedication and to ask for their help in governing. He said, "I'm asking you to join me as full members of our team. I promise to lead and to listen, and I promise to serve beside you as we work together to carry out the will of the American people."[72]

While the Democrats controlled both chambers, the party had experienced some disarray, until finally, in June 1989, Thomas Foley (D, WA) was chosen as the Speaker of the House and Richard Gephardt as Majority Leader of the Senate. Bush was able to work successfully with the Democrats to resolve the savings and loan crisis. In the absence of government regulations and guidelines, savings and loan institutions had made exuberant and sometimes careless investments and were losing a great deal of money, necessitating a monthly infusion of $1 billion from the federal government to keep them operating. In August 1989, Bush and the Democratic Congress agreed to $157 billion bailout for the industry under the Financial Institution Reform, Recovery and Enforcement Act.[73]

But then Bush confronted a political problem that his unique political style, predicated on friendships and relationships, could not overcome. The Senate rejected his nominee for Secretary of Defense, former Senator John Tower (R, TX). Tower, who had been chairman of the Senate Armed Services Committee, and had actively campaigned for Bush in Texas, had earned a reputation of arrogance toward his staff, heavy drinking, and womanizing. Bush realized the nomination was in trouble when the sitting chairman of the Senate Armed Services Committee, Senator Sam Nunn (D, GA) said that he could not in good conscience support Tower's nomination. But Bush could not abandon his friend, who had also chaired the Iran-Contra Commission which treated then Vice President Bush with "kid gloves." The Senate went on to rebuke the president, defeating Tower by 11-9 in the Armed Services Committee and by 53-47 in the full Senate.[74]

Another political challenge occurred when Bush was forced by circumstance to reverse his pledge of refusing to raise taxes, reprised in his famous line, "Read My Lips, No New Taxes," at the Republican National Convention. The Omnibus Budget and Reconciliation Act of 1990 was the result of several months of closed-door negotiations, and the bill stipulated the following terms: $137 billion in revenue increases, including a rise in the marginal income tax for individuals from 28 to 31 percent, and limitations on tax deductions for the wealthy, an increase in gasoline prices by 5 cents a gallon, and a cut of $42.5 billion in Medicare funding.[75] When he signed the bill into law, President Bush called it "the centerpiece of the largest deficit reduction package in history."[76] But in March 1992—after losing his bid for reelection to White House to Bill Clinton—Bush stated that his turnaround on the tax pledge was his worst mistake as president.[77]

In terms of leadership, President Bush failed to adequately educate the public on the NEED to reverse course on taxes. Although the move was, in the words of Bush's budget Director, Richard Darman, an "inescapable strategic necessity" (because of the size of the deficit), the president relied on a closed-door process with other elites to resolve the matter. James Cicconi, who served in the Bush Administration, described the problem well:

> I think we also ignored the importance of popular political backing. If taxes are to be raised—again in defiance of a pledge not to do so—I think we never made ... a compelling case for this sort of dramatic shift ... I think we chose what I would call an "insider process" in place of a public process. We opted for private, behind closed-doors negotiations rather

than a more public process of debate over these very important issues that were going to affect all Americans: whether taxes were increased, whether we passed the burden of debt on to our children, whether and how much we cut spending, and how to deal with entitlements. These were all questions that the public itself had not really been willing to confront, and rather than choose a course of public debate in a democratic process, we chose a behind closed-door process. And again, I think a public process would have made much better use of the president's high approval ratings with the public, his popularity, his ability to lead ....[78]

On the other hand, in foreign policy, President Bush showed great dexterity and leadership acumen. Rapid change unfolding in Europe, as mentioned previously, culminated in the fall of the Berlin Wall in November 1989. Bush reacted happily, but quietly to this development, understanding that a more exuberant expression of celebration by POTUS would create problems for Soviet General Secretary Mikhail Gorbachev, who was allowing events to occur without interference.[79] Four days after the Wall crumbled, Bush convened a meeting at the White House with his Secretary of State, Jim Baker, National Security Adviser, Brent Scowcroft, and former Secretary of State Henry Kissinger, who believed the time was ripe for the Bush administration to begin discussions of German reunification.[80]

While German reunification seemed like a desirable and plausible goal to the United States, and even to many inside Germany, the idea was perceived as potentially treacherous to other countries in Europe, including Great Britain, France, and the USSR. One of the vexing issues was whether a reunited Germany would become a member of NATO, to which the Soviets initially strongly objected.[81] Through sustained and competent negotiations, the Bush team, led by President Bush and Secretary of State, Jim Baker, convinced the Soviets to allow Germany to make their own choice about NATO membership. President Bush posed the question to Gorbachev as to whether under the protection of the 1975 Helsinki Final Act of 1975—which was ratified by 35 nations, including the USSR—the Germans would be allowed to choose for themselves on the matter of NATO membership. Gorbachev said yes, and the deal was concluded. On October 12, 1990, the four powers (United States, France, Great Britain, and the USSR) relinquished the occupying rights of their defeated WWII enemy; Germany regained its complete sovereignty 45 years after the conflict. And according to journalists Peter Baker and Susan Glasser, "The Soviet Union had not only agreed to allow Germany to reunify, but to do so on Western terms."[82]

And then Bush confronted another huge challenge: the invasion of Kuwait by Iraq in August 1990. President Bush's success in what became known as Operation Desert Storm—the US-led coalition to oust Saddam Hussein's forces from Kuwait—led him to achieve one of the highest approval ratings ever achieved by a US President until that time, 89 percent in March 1991.[83] President Bush's effective management of Operation Desert Storm emanated, in part, from the strong personal relationships he had developed with foreign and domestic leaders during his many years of public service. According to his Secretary of Defense, Dick Cheney, "All of Bush's experiences came into play during the course of Operation Desert Storm."[84]

For example, Bush understood that launching military operations in Kuwait would require the cooperation of Saudi Arabia. He feared that Saddam's designs were not limited to Kuwait, which controlled 20 percent of the world's oil reserves, but extended to Saudi Arabia, which controlled over 30 percent.[85] President Bush also understood that he would have to obtain Saudi approval for the stationing of United States and coalition forces on Saudi soil in order to conduct an effective military campaign in Kuwait. He leveraged the relationship he had developed over several years with Saudi officials to achieve his goals in the Persian Gulf War. As vice president, Bush visited Saudi Arabia and established a friendship with King Fahd. The two men often dined together and enjoyed after dinner talks late into the night.[86]

Bush had maintained that link, regularly talking with King Fahd on the phone and sharing tidbits and gossip about political life in the kingdom and the states.[87] In the run-up to the Persian Gulf War, Bush sent Defense Secretary Dick Cheney to Saudi Arabia to discuss allowing United States and allied forces to be stationed there. Cheney met with King Fahd, along with General Norman Schwarzkopf (the US commander in Desert Storm) and Paul Wolfowitz (Undersecretary of State for defense policy). During the two-hour meeting, the US delegation explained why it was important for Saudis to join in the effort to defend the kingdom and defeat Saddam Hussein. After a five-minute discussion with his colleagues, King Fahd granted permission for the United States to undertake the mission. It would be the first time the Saudis would allow foreign troops on the holy soil of Mecca and Medina. Fahd said he would trust the United States (including trusting that they would leave) because he "trusted George Bush."[88]

President Bush was tireless in building an international coalition against Saddam Hussein. He also deployed his Secretary of State, Jim Baker, who raced 100,000 miles around the world in two weeks and met with more than 200 heads of state and foreign ministers.[89] Bush himself made 62 calls to heads of state and government during the first 30 days of the conflict.[90]

The results of the prodigious diplomatic efforts were impressive: 35 countries Joined the Bush-led coalition by contributing militarily, countries ranging from Afghanistan and Australia, to Norway, Canada, and Turkey.[91] The 700,000 thousand troops (including 23,000 non-US ones), vanquished the Iraqi forces quickly and decisively. The Iraqis lost 90 percent of their tanks and 20,000 army dead. The US lost only 148 troops.[92] According to political scientists Barilleaux and Rozell:

The conclusion of the Persian Gulf War was both remarkable and controversial. It was remarkable for the speed with which it occurred and the relatively small loss of life by coalition forces that accompanied it. Barely a hundred hours after it had begun, the ground offensive was halted and President Bush declared victory. The abrupt closure made the war's conclusion controversial, for Bush was criticized then and later for not going all the way to Baghdad and completing the destruction of Saddam Hussein.[93]

In fact, Bush argued that the UN mandate did not authorize going all the way to Baghdad, but merely throwing the Iraqis out of the sovereign nation they had attacked. Years later, Bush's son George W., would take up the job of destroying Saddam Hussein and liberating Iraq: however, his actions would lead to a long, protracted, and ultimately unpopular war.[94]

TAKEAWAYS FOR ALL LEADERS

- A leader who is an "insider" gains great leverage from friendships and relationships, which can provide a foundation for reaching deals or introducing change.
- An "insider" leader must also be aware of the potential dangers posed by and over-reliance on closed-door negotiations.
- All leaders must be willing to explain their actions and decisions to all stakeholders and followers, not just to fellow insiders.

William Jefferson Clinton

Although Bill Clinton's political aspirations began when he was just 16 years old,[95] his ascent to the White House in 1992 was a remarkable achievement requiring him to overcome several inauspicious conditions, including a difficult childhood spent in a small, poor southern state. On his path to the White House, he served one term as the Arkansas Attorney General and 14 years (two terms) as governor of that state.

Following a bruising campaign, that included three candidates—Clinton, George Bush (the incumbent president), and Ross Perot (a Texas billionaire)—Clinton was elected with 43 percent of the popular vote. He accumulated 370 electoral votes and won 32 states and the District of Columbia. Bush won 37.4 percent of the popular vote, 18 states, and 168 electoral votes. Perot won an astounding 19 percent of the popular votes and no votes in the electoral college.[96]

There were great hopes and expectations for the Clinton presidency among Democrats, as the party had been out of power in the White House for 12 years and had been playing defense, according to Clinton campaign leader (and future White House staffer) George Stephanopoulos.[97] Nevertheless, Clinton's early days in the White House were problematic. He won office, as mentioned, with only 43 percent of the popular vote. Only two other presidents had entered the office with such a slim plurality, Woodrow Wilson in 1912 with 42 percent and Richard Nixon in 1968 with 43 percent. But on both of those cases, the president's party had gained seats on Congress. In Clinton's case, on the other hand, the Democrats lost ten seats in the House in 1992 and one in the Senate a short time later.[98] According to David Gergen (who joined the White House staff in early 1993), "Clinton had neither a mandate nor coattails. He had won office but not power."[99]

Given these challenges, Gergen suggests, one would have expected Clinton to buckle down and map out a serious, sustaining strategy for governing, as Reagan had done with a much larger margin of victory. But Clinton, naturally inclined to procrastination, let the time slip away from him. As Gergen opines, Clinton was still in campaign, and not yet in governing mode.[100] We can confirm Gergen's point by noting that Clinton's selections for White House staff were almost exclusively men and women from his campaign: George Stephanopoulos, Communications Director, Dee Dee Myers, Press Secretary, Rahm Emanuel, Assistant to the President for Political Affairs, and Gene Sperling, National Economic Council. These four individuals provided the backbone for the first successful Democratic presidential campaign for the White House in 16 years, but as Gergen notes, "they were also young and inexperienced in governing."[101]

In addition, Clinton's designation of Mack McLarty as chief-of-staff demonstrated his over-reliance on friendships and under-appreciation of DC insiders. McLarty was CEO of a Fortune 500 company and a lifelong friend of Bill Clinton. He had offered himself as a potential liaison to the business community, but Clinton insisted he take the COS position. McLarty proved to be a weak chief-of-staff, and Clinton replaced him with a former member of Congress, Leon Panetta in 1994.[102]

On the other hand, Clinton effectively assembled a first-rate economic team, established a personal bond with Federal Reserve Chairman Alan Greenspan, and moved decisively to bring down the deficit. Clinton had focused on the economy more than he had on any other issue during the campaign, and organized the economic team in the White House to favor deficit hawks who believed that if the deficits of the Reagan/Bush era—estimated to be over $300 billion in Clinton's first year in office—could be controlled, interest rates would be reduced, and the economy would grow.[103] Deficit hawks would lead his economic team: Texas Senator (D) Lloyd Bentsen, chairman of the Senate Finance Committee, as Treasury Secretary; Congressman Leon Panetta (D, CA), chair of the House Budget Committee, as head of the Office of Management and Budget; and Robert Rubin, former co-chairman of Goldman-Sachs as head of the National Economic Council.[104]

Nevertheless, the early days of the Clinton administration continued to be problematic. Clinton's first two choices for attorney general were forced to withdraw due to a "nanny problem" (nominees Zoë Baird and Kimba Wood had not been paying social security taxes for domestic workers they had employed at their homes). The president tried but failed to redeem a campaign promise to allow gay people to freely enlist in the military, and had to settle on a strange compromise policy of "Don't Ask, Don't Tell."[105]

Clinton was so frustrated after his first few months in the White House, that he called David Gergen in early 1993 and exclaimed, "I'm in trouble; I need your help!"[106] Gergen, who had previously worked primarily for Republican Presidents, joined the Clinton White House staff as a counselor and to assist with the administration's communications efforts.[107] Over the next several months, President Clinton began to turn things around and to breathe life onto his presidential aspirations. The first big victory was achieved on the budget situation. Clinton had promised a middle-class tax cut; however, his team conducted an early analysis of the deficit and discovered that it was larger than they had previously believed and could be closed only through fiscal discipline.[108] Leon Panetta calculated that the deficit would reach $360 billion by the end of fiscal year 1997.[109] Accordingly, Clinton, in consultation with Bentsen, Rubin, and Panetta, proposed a budget plan that would increase the top income tax rate from 31 to 36 percent on incomes over $180,000, with a 10 percent surcharge on incomes over $250,000; in addition, he proposed an increase in the corporate income tax from 34 to 36 percent on incomes over $10 million.[110] Through his plan, Clinton aspired to reduce the deficit by raising taxes on the wealthiest Americans (top 5 percent income bracket), while cutting taxes for the poor and middle class.[111]

President Clinton introduced the budget plan on national television and then mounted a vigorous campaign of "retail politics" to get it passed. The president became the lobbyist-in-chief, and he "called, cajoled, begged, pressured, and promised—whatever it took.[112] He explained to wavering Democrats that he was the first Democrat in the White House in twelve years, and they could not allow him to fail. Howard Paster, Clinton's congressional liaison, assisted in the lobbying effort, as did George Stephanopoulos. The Clinton team developed printouts for each member, showing how many people in their congressional district would get a tax cut under EITC (Earned Income Tax Credit), compared to those who would get an increase.[113] The Republicans mounted an aggressive campaign against Clinton's economic plan, characterizing it as "the biggest tax increase in the history of the universe."[114] President Clinton achieved the slimmest of victories, gaining passage of his budget bill by a vote of 218-216 in the House of Representatives (with no GOP support) and a 50-50 tie in the Senate, with Vice President Gore casting the deciding vote.[115] Nevertheless, the budget victory proved to be a substantial one for Bill Clinton's presidency. He had pleasantly surprised Wall

Street by moving in a fiscally conservative direction. With the budget deficit seriously diminished, Alan Greenspan's Federal Reserve Board felt it was safe to lower interest rates. The economy grew rapidly, inflation fell, and the stock market gained strength.[116]

Subsequently, Clinton managed to win a legislative victory with the passage of the North American Free Trade Agreement (NAFTA), which was intended to ease trade barriers from the north of Canada to the southern tip of Mexico. Allowing some 400 million people to share the economic and social benefits of free trade.[117] The negotiations for this trade agreement had begun in the Bush years, and during the 1992 presidential campaign Clinton had only given it tepid support, as organized labor and some environmentalists opposed it. And now the Clinton administration was split over NAFTA, with Treasury Secretary Lloyd Bentsen strongly supporting it for its economic benefits and Secretary of State Warren Christopher lauding positive diplomatic effects. The political advisers, however, opposed NAFTA. Stephanopoulos, Begala, and Hillary all lined up against it because of the affront it presented to labor.[118] Clinton held his ground and solicited lobbying assistance for NAFTA from Bill Daly, a Chicago business executive who would also serve briefly as President Obama's chief-of-staff, from Mickey Kantor, Clinton's trade representative; and from Bill Frenzel, a former Minnesota Congressman (D). Clinton spoke forcefully for passage and worked the Hill tirelessly, making a side agreement on citrus for the Florida delegation and one on sugar for Louisiana, to secure victory. Al Gore went on national television to debate billionaire Ross Perot, who vociferously opposed NAFTA. With the support of 132 Republicans in the House, including Speaker Newt Gingrich (R, GA), the House adopted NAFTA. The Senate did as well, with a 61–38 vote.[119]

Clinton's positive momentum extended to the realm of foreign policy. Capitalizing on an informal peace process that had taken place between Israelis and Palestinians in Oslo, Norway during the early 1990s, President Clinton had the rare opportunity of presiding over a historic event at the White House in September 1993: the signing of a Declaration of Principles by Israeli Prime Minister Yitzhak Rabin and Palestinian Liberation Organization (PLO) Chairman Yasser Arafat.[120] The Declaration committed the PLO to recognize the state of Israel, and Israel to recognize the PLO (and later the Palestinian Authority) as the legitimate representative of the Palestinian people. It also created a process by which Israel would gradually relinquish its control over some aspects of Palestinian lives, including a timetable for the creation of a Palestinian Authority, starting Gaza and Jericho.[121] The mood of the day was perhaps most elegantly expressed by Rabin, who said, "Enough of blood and tears."[122]

Clinton's achievements resulted in an upswing in his approval ratings from 38 percent in May 1993 to 58 percent by December.[123] But the positive political momentum was interrupted by President Clinton's attempt to reform health care. Clinton had identified healthcare reform as a priority for his administration; he wanted to address the anxieties of many about the rising costs of health care and the fact that 37 million Americans had no healthcare coverage.[124]

On January 5, 1994, Clinton went to the podium of the US House of Representatives to deliver the State of the Union address and presented a proposal that the first lady, a strong advocate for healthcare reform, had developed as head of the president's healthcare task force. In the address to Congress, President Clinton announced that his proposal was intended to overhaul the nation's healthcare insurance and delivery system, and that he was willing to compromise on the details, but one element of the plan was nonnegotiable: universal coverage.[125]

The healthcare reform plan concocted by Hillary Clinton and her deputy, Ira Magaziner, preserved some aspects of the status quo. For example, it stipulated that private insurance, not government, would continue to finance health care for most Americans, albeit with close federal supervision. As well, the plan provided that employers, from whom most people already received insurance, would remain the primary place where they would obtain service.[126] But they also added two novel concepts. The first known as "Managed competition," envisioned a process where insurance companies would compete for customers under rules strictly enforced by the government. The government would guarantee customers a minimum level of benefits, and the insurance companies would be guaranteed a fixed amount of money for each participant in the plan. Insurance companies competing for customers would also motivate hospitals and physicians to find efficiencies, thereby holding costs down while increasing their profits.

The ideas were certainly creative, but once translated into programmatic details they became enormously complex. Clinton's healthcare bill was 1,342 pages long when it was presented to Congress.[127] To implement managed competition, the president proposed a series of regional cooperatives that would raise money from employers, negotiate benefits packages with insurers and regulate the quality of care.[128] Lobbyists sprang into action, mostly in opposition to the plan. For instance, the insurance industry prepared a series of advertisements featuring "Harry and Louise," a young couple trying to comprehend the Clinton healthcare plan but growing increasingly alarmed as they examined the details at their kitchen table.[129]

According to Clinton adviser and author David Gergen, the proposal could have been saved had the Clinton administration been willing to compromise and support a more modest, bipartisan plan. Early in 1994, Senate Majority Leader Bob Dole (R, KS) was genuinely interested in reaching a deal, as was the Democratic member of the Senate Finance Committee, Daniel Patrick Moynihan (D, NY).[130]

But Hillary Clinton was not amenable to compromise, and, instead launched attacks on the lobbyists and on doctors and insurers. In a speech before the American Academy of Pediatrics, the first lady became so angry about the "Harry and Louise" ads that she discarded her prepared remarks and offered a vitriolic outburst to the audience, saying, "Insurance companies like being able to exclude people from coverage, because the more they can exclude the more money they can make."[131]

In June, Senator Moynihan, in an appearance on "Meet the Press," suggested that there was no chance of achieving Clinton's goal of universal coverage in a year; it would, in fact, take a decade. He suggested that Clinton try to pass a more modest reform, achieving perhaps 91 percent coverage, which would mean substantial progress over the current rate of 85 percent. He said that 91 percent could be presented as a victory, not a failure.[132]

Moynihan's compromising language was consistent with President Clinton's governing style, but Hillary warned publicly about accepting anything short of universal coverage. When the president himself alluded to a willingness to accept 95 percent coverage in a speech to the National Governors Association in Boston, and indicated flexibility on the question of employee mandates, Hilary demanded that he back off, which he did. The following day, the president issued a humiliating retraction of his remarks to the Governors Association.[133]

David Gergen, who participated in several White House discussions of health care, opined that if the president had paid more attention to the initiatives and ideas of Moynihan, as well of those of the Secretary of Health and Human Services, Donna Shalala, and Treasury Secretary Lloyd Bentsen, a compromise could have been reached with Dole and the Republicans.[134] Instead, according to Gergen, "the biggest initiative of Clinton's presidency died in committee."[135]

Gergen outlined several leadership errors that Clinton made during the healthcare reform effort:

- Clinton and his team misjudged the values of the country and proposed a healthcare program that sounded like a government takeover.
- They misjudged the president's political strength. The Democrats had a rather slender margin in Congress to pass one of the most sweeping reforms of the century.
- There was an unrealistic belief in the White House that Clinton could "sell anything"!
- They misjudged Congress. Clinton attempted to bypass traditional committee hearings (and a potential Senate filibuster) by including healthcare reform in a budget reconciliation bill in 1993. But Senator Robert Byrd invoked the Byrd Rule to prevent that maneuver.
- They misjudged the interest groups. The AFL-CIO and AARP were not as effective as expected, and the Health Associates of America and National Federation of Independent Business aggressively opposed the Clinton plan.

- They allowed the excellent to become the enemy of the good. Treasury Secretary had crafted a compromise plan that would have attracted bipartisan support.[136]

Finally, Gergen added that the president was not fully himself during the fight for healthcare reform. "He was not as engaged political and intellectually as I saw him in the Budget and NAFTA struggles," said Gergen.[137]

The political consequences of the healthcare debacle were fast and furious. In the 1994 congressional elections, the Democrats suffered a significant defeat, losing 8 seats in the Senate and 54 in the House. As well, the center of gravity for the Republican Party shifted notably rightward. The Republicans elected Representative Newt Gingrich of Georgia as Speaker of the House. Gingrich and his colleagues pledged themselves to a "Contract with America," promising to achieve a balanced budget, a limitation on the "unfunded mandates" that the federal government could require of the states, a congressional accountability act (which would provide congressional staffers workplace rights enjoyed by all other workers), and the return of prayer to the public schools.[138] Gingrich also introduced a more confrontational, combative style of political leadership, based on a ruthless form of partisanship that eschewed compromise with the Democrats and focused on maintaining partisan power.[139]

For his part, Clinton clearly comprehended the importance of the 1994 congressional elections and moved toward a strategy of "triangulation," which had been suggested by his long time political adviser, Dick Morris. Triangulation amounted to moving back toward the center of the political universe or finding a mid-point between left and right.[140] As part of the triangulation strategy, Clinton supported and then signed a landmark welfare reform bill, which had passed with a bipartisan majority in both chambers of Congress. The legislation retained the federal guarantee of medical care and food aid and increased child care assistance by 40 percent; however, it also ended the federal guarantee of a fixed monthly benefit to welfare recipients, placed a five-year limit on welfare benefits, and cut overall spending on the food stamp program.[141]

By the spring of 1995, Clinton was poised to recapture the political momentum from Speaker Gingrich. During the fall of 1995, the president fought a fierce battle with Speaker Gingrich over the federal budget. The Republican budget called for significant cuts in Medicare, Medicaid, education, and environmental protection, all of which Clinton opposed. Unable to find a viable compromise by midnight, November 13, the two sides faced the prospect of a government shutdown. Clinton took a firm stance, telling Gingrich and Senate Majority Leader Bob Dole, "I do not care what happens. I don't care if I go to 5 percent in the polls, I am not going to sign your budget. It is very bad for the country."[142] The following morning the government shutdown, and afterwards most citizens blamed Gingrich, while Clinton's standing improved.[143]

It is, nonetheless, ironic that on the first night of the government shut-down, November 14, 1995, President Clinton encountered Monica Lewinsky, a young White House Intern, roaming the halls of the White House, while most employees were on furlough. The two began an affair in the Oval Office that would endanger Clinton's marriage as well as lead to impeachment hearings against him in the second term. Despite these and other obstacles, Clinton won a second term in the 1996 presidential election, winning 49.2 percent of the popular vote, compared to Bob Dole's 40.8 percent and Ross Perot's 8.5 percent. Clinton became the first Democratic president since FDR to be reelected, and also to win alongside a Republican legislature.[144]

TAKEAWAYS FOR ALL LEADERS

- When a leader is strongly engaged in the fight for a cause and is willing to use a full array of persuasion and negotiation tools, he or she can substantially increase the chances for success.
- A leader needs to surround himself/herself with strong, capable professionals, not with friends.
- A leader needs to preserve his physical energy and exert the necessary personal and organizational discipline for the most important matters at hand.
- A leader who asks for help when he or she needs it is a wise leader!

George Walker Bush

The tight 2000 presidential race between Texas Republican Governor George W. Bush and Democratic Vice President Al Gore was not resolved on the day of the election. The race was too close to call when most Americans went to bed on Tuesday night, November 7, 1999. The challenge to a clear electoral outcome was in the state of Florida and its 25 electoral college votes. Although the television networks had declared Bush the winner in Florida, and the presidency, and although Gore had actually called Bush to concede, Bush's lead in the popular vote in Florida began to narrow, as more votes were counted. The final tally was so close that an existing Florida law forced an automatic (electronic) recount. Gore retracted his concession, and when the second recount did not go in his favor, he initiated a 36-day legal battle to determine the true winner of the state's electoral votes.[145]

For more than a month the identity of the 43rd president was unresolved, as neither candidate had attained the 270 electoral votes needed to secure the office; Bush had 246, and Gore had 266. Gore called attention to a series of voting irregularities in several Florida counties and on November 9 requested a manual recount of all ballots in four Florida counties. The situation became more complex, as Florida's Secretary of State, Katherine Harris, moved to certify a Bush victory (based on a new machine recount result), the Florida Supreme Court decided to allow the hand recount to continue, and the Bush team, led by James A. Baker, decided to appeal the case to the US Supreme Court.[146] In Bush v. Palm Beach County Canvassing Board, et al., the majority of the court ruled that the Florida Supreme Court had not adequately justified its decision to extend the vote certification deadline and allow time for hand recounts in the first place, essentially the court was asking the Floridians to explain their ruling.[147] As manual recount proceeded, vote counters were held to varying standards of what constituted a vote. Meanwhile, the Florida Supreme Court ruled in Gore's favor, ordering a statewide recount of 14,000 "under vote" ballots that had not been acknowledged in the machine recount.[148]

Bush again appealed to the US Supreme Court. In their 5-4 ruling in Bush v. Gore, the Justices (per curium) argued that the manual recount process was too complicated to complete before the December 12 deadline for states to appoint their slate of electors. The majority also noted that voters' rights under the Equal Protection clause of the 14th Amendment were being violated, because not all counties or precincts statewide received the same strict scrutiny as the ballots in Miami-Dade and Palm Beach counties would under the planned recount.[149]

In a bitter dissent, Justice John Paul Stevens opined:

> One thing .... is certain. Although we may never know with complete certainty the identity of the winner of this year's Presidential election, the identity of the loser is clear. It is the Nation's confidence in the judge as an impartial Guardian of the rule of law.[150]

Justice Stevens' dissent notwithstanding, the Supreme Court effectively gave George Bush Florida's 25 electoral votes, and the presidency. Bush received 271 electoral votes, compared to Gore's 266. On the other hand, Gore won 50.26 percent of the popular vote, compared to Bush's 49.73. A president had been elected while losing the popular vote![151]

Fortunately, Bush and his team had begun planning for the transition in the spring of 1999, when Bush asked his friend from Yale days, Clay Johnson, to start the process. Johnson reacted swiftly and reached out to James A. Baker and George Schultz for advice.[152] And Bush's running mate, Dick Cheney, with his deep knowledge of American Government, was also heavily involved in the transition process, including "crafting his future role as the most powerful vice president in history."[153]

In June 2000, Johnson described the components of a successful transition effort, reflecting lessons learned from the Clinton experience:

- Pick a chief-of-staff early.
- Identify cabinet secretaries by mid-December, and senior staff earlier.
- Hire based on Bush 43's policy priorities.
- Develop a clear set of policy goals.
- Recognize that Congress and career executives will pay attention to how a new administration reaches out and communicates with them.[154]

Bush took Jonson's advice and, unlike Clinton, hit the ground running. By January 4, he had chosen almost his entire team.[155] He chose Andrew Card as his chief-of-staff, before election day: Card had served as deputy chief-of-staff for Bush 41. Card, with strong input from Cheney, announced the first set of appointments on December 17: Condoleezza Rice as National Security Adviser, Alberto Gonzalez as White House Legal Counsel, Karen Hughes as Counselor to the President, Mitch Daniels as Director of the Office of Management and Budget, Joshua Bolton and Joe Hagin as deputy chiefs-of-staff, Nick Calio as legislative affairs director, and Margaret LaMontagne Spellings as assistant to the president for domestic policy.[156] According to the *National Journal*, a prestigious Washington political journal, the Bush Team was "one of the most experienced senior staff in modern history."[157]

Bush also quickly announced a surprisingly diverse slate of cabinet picks:

- Four women (Elaine Chou for Labor, Ann Veneman for Agriculture, Gale Norton for Interior, and Christine Todd Whitman for the Environmental Protection Agency (EPA)).
- Two African-Americans (Colin Powell for State and Roderick Page for Education).
- One Arab American (Spencer Abraham for Energy).
- Two Asian Americans (Elaine Chou and Norman Mineta, who was also a Democrat, for Transportation).[158]

One distinguishing feature of the Bush 43 administration was the notably large portfolio assigned to Cheney, which was reflected in his central role in staffing the Bush presidency and in the integration of his personal staff with the president's. For example, Cheney had domestic and national security policy staffs, a press secretary, and chief-of-staff, in essence an organization that paralleled the president's.[159] He also had more and earlier access to the president and his decisions. According to Washington Post reporter, Barton Gellman,

Vice presidents traditionally joined the president at "policy time," if the President so desired. Cheney intended to get involved sooner, long before the moment of decision. Cheney would exert a quiet dominance over meetings in which advisers framed their goals, narrowed options, and decided when or whether to bring them to the president. Cheney's presence unavoidably changed this tone, and often the outcome.[160]

Bush was aware of the political realities of his administration. His Republican Party held a slim majority of seats in the House of Representatives (222-211), with two independents, while in the Senate there as an even 50-50 seat split, meaning that the vice president would need to cast a tie-breaking vote on legislation that was close.[161] The realities of the power distribution in Congress, perhaps reinforced Bush's claim to govern in a bipartisan manner, as he had done as Governor of Texas. The bipartisan focus would be demonstrated in his quest for educational reform. His first legislative accomplishment occurred on June 7, 2001, when Bush signed a major tax cut. Bush effectively worked with Congress to achieve his goal, including reaching a compromise on the size of the cut; he proposed a cut of $1.6 trillion over ten years and accepted the figure of $1.35 trillion after negotiations.[162]

His second initiative, education reform, demonstrated his interest in a bipartisan approach, as after securing the support of Republican leadership for his ideas, he reached out to Democratic Senator (Massachusetts), Edward Kennedy. Kennedy told him, "I want to help you do this," and Bush replied, "I'll pledge that we will work together ... and resolve our differences."[163] With Kennedy's support, Bush achieved passage of the No Child Lefty Behind Act, which he signed into law on January 8, 2002.[164] The bill mandated standardized testing in all public schools and connected federal funding to the results of the tests.

But it was the terrorist attacks of September 11, 2001, that would come to dominate the political and emotional life of the nation, and the president for several months of the young Bush presidency. And Bush rose to the challenge. According to political scientist Gary L. Gregg, "In the days, weeks, and moths following the terrorist attacks, George Bush seemed to have met his place in history, and the public was rallying to his side."[165]

President George Bush demonstrated strong leadership during this time.

He projected reassurance. On the morning of the attacks, Bush pledged the full resources of the federal government to help the victims and first responders and promised to "hunt down and find the perpetrators." Later that day, from Barksdale Air Force Base (where the Secret Service persuaded him to land) he explained his intent to his staff as follows: "I think it's important for people to see the government is functioning. The government is not chaotic; it is functioning smoothly."[166] And in his remarks to the nation that evening, he reassured the public of the continuity of government operations, of the high alert status of the military, and that the nation would pass the test.[167]

He reflected the public mind. President Bush demonstrated an impressive ability to project the extent to which he shared the pain of American citizens as well as their demand for justice. The public was also seeking retribution. From the Oval Office on the evening of September 11, he expressed "disbelief, sadness, and a quiet unyielding anger" that he also sensed among the public. And a few days later he visited the site of the collapsed World Trade Center in New York City; and with his arm draped around a firefighter, speaking through a bullhorn to the assembled iron workers and firefighters who were having trouble hearing him, said, "I can hear you. The rest of the world will hear you, and the people who knocked down these buildings will hear all of us soon."[168]

He instructed the public mind. Bush wisely clarified who the real "enemy" was and was not. He stated emphatically that the US was not at war with Islam. He was wary of repeating the kind of racism that led to seclusion of Japanese Americans in internment camps during WWII.[169] Bush included an Islamic cleric as part of the National Prayer Service and visited Washington's largest Islamic Center where, with shoes off, he declared that "the face of terror is not the face of Islam."[170] And in his nationally televised address to a joint session of Congress in September 20, which journalist Robert Draper described as the best speech of his presidency,[171] Bush separated the terrorists from Islam, explaining that the terrorists practiced a fringe form of the religion that had been rejected by most Muslim scholars and clerics.[172]

Then he appealed directly to the Muslim community:

> We respect your faith. It's practiced freely by millions of Americans and by millions more in countries that America counts as friends. Its teachings are good and peaceful, and those who commit evil in the name of Allah blasphemies the name of Allah. The enemy of America is not our many Muslim friends; it is not our many Arab friends. Our enemy is a radical network of terrorists and every government that supports them.[173]

In another educational effort, President Bush advised patience. He took great care to remind Americans that this new kind of war would be unconventional, frequently unpublicized, and would require a great deal of persistence. He repudiated the idea of a quick military stroke that would be immediately popular, but not effective.[174]

He balanced the realities of war with a hope for peace. In addition to President Bush's vows to achieve justice and "smoke out the terrorists," was his call for humanitarianism. For instance, the president noted that the

US "respects the people of Afghanistan" and would use airplanes to deliver humanitarian assistance, even while other planes carried out military operations.[175] Furthermore, on November 17, 2001, Laura Bush delivered the president's weekly radio address, the first time a First Lady had ever done so; and she spoke directly to the women of Afghanistan, saying the "fight against terrorism is also a fight for the rights and dignity of women."[176]

President Bush had found a new identity as a wartime president, and was "perfectly at ease with the role," according to journalist Robert Draper.[177] And Congress was at his side; whatever he asked for Congress gave him, and with decisive majorities. He won quick approval for a $40 billion aid package for New York City, a massive bailout for the nation's airlines, and a huge tax cut. He won overwhelming support for the Authorization for the Use of Military Force (AUMF), to authorize his intent to intervene militarily on Afghanistan. In the Senate, the AUMF was approved by 99-1, and the bill was introduced by a Democrat, Senator Tom Daschle of South Dakota. In the House, the AUMF was adopted with 420 members voting "yes."[178]

Nevertheless, the bipartisanship that Bush championed, and that was evident in the early days of his administration and immediately after 9/11, began to erode. In the 2001 budget cycle, Bush slashed funding for No Child Left Behind by $90 million, prompting Senator Kennedy and Representative George Miller (D, CA) to call him a liar.[179] Furthermore, as the administration proceeded to lay the groundwork for the 2002 invasion of Iraq, Bush and his deputies moved away from a bipartisan and conciliatory approach toward an aggressive and "frenzied" one, in the words of congressional scholar Louis Fisher.[180]

The Bush administration was already convinced of the need to attack Saddam Hussein's Iraq, and the leadership went onto an aggressive marketing campaign for the war.[181] In an August 22, 2002, address, Vice President Cheney said that Saddam Hussein would possess nuclear weapons "fairly soon," and we needed to launch a preemptive strike. Moreover, the administration wanted Congress to quickly authorize military action. Bush asked that Congress act prior to leaving for the 2002 congressional elections.[182]

According to Louis Fisher, there was political calculation behind the push for quick congressional action. Republican candidates in the 2002 elections compared their "strong stand" on Iraq to the "weak position" of their Democratic opponents. Several key congressional races were decided based on candidates' positions on the war issue. At that point, Democrats were unable to focus on their political agenda, which included issues such as corporate crimes, a falling stock market, and a struggling economy. In a September 23 speech in Trenton, NJ, Bush accused the Democrats of being "more interested in special interests in Washington than with the security of the American people."[183]

But prominent military officials expressed serious reservations about a military strike on Iraq, and about the policy of preemption in general.[184] Several generals expressed specific concerns, including the possibility that an invasion would prompt Saddam to use weapons of mass destruction (assuming he had them), the dangers of being mired in urban warfare, and the tremendous costs we would face on a post occupation Iraq.[185]

For their part, the Democrats, including those who anticipated entering the 2004 presidential race folded their tents and joined the chorus in favor of war. House Minority Leader Dick Gephardt (D, MO) and Senator John Edwards (D, NC) came out in support of an authorizing resolution. Massachusetts Senator John Kerry (D, MA), who would be the Democratic Party's nominee in 2004, expressed concern, but ultimately voted for the resolution. On the eve of the vote, which occurred a month before the 2002 congressional elections, Kerry stated, "We are affirming a president's right and responsibility to keep the American people safe."[186] But, as Fisher argues, trust in the president and a call for bipartisanship do not adequately substitute for an analysis by Congress of the justification for using military force against another nation.[187]

Bush received a strong, but nowhere near unanimous, endorsement for going to war in Iraq: 296-123 in the House, and 77-23 in the Senate.[188] Then, in the 2002 mid-term elections, the Republicans gained two Senate seats, giving them a narrow (51-49) majority, and, defying historical trends, picked up 6 House seats to expand their majority slightly (229-205).[189] In December 2002, several national security experts and Mideast scholars met for two days at the National Defense University, a premier military education institution in DC, and concluded that "occupying Iraq will be the most daunting and complex task the US and the international community will have undertaken since the end of WWII."[190]

Although the US scored a quick military victory, taking control of Baghdad within a month of the beginning of hostilities, the military was unable to establish control or unify the country in a common purpose. By the fall of 2003, the tragedy of Iraq was beginning to become clear. The Iraq Study Group, co-chaired by former Secretary of State, James A. Baker, and former Indiana Representative and former chair of the House Foreign Affairs Committee, Lee Hamilton (D), described the situation in Iraq as "grave and deteriorating."[191]

Overall, we can conclude that Bush 43 achieved a high level of success politically during his first two years: he overcame the challenges posed by a hotly contested election outcome; achieved two major legislative victories in the massive tax cut and No Child Left Behind; unified and led the country with great acumen after 9/11; and showed growth in his demeanor and gravitas with respect to the presidency. But his vision about fighting the terrorists, expanded to a fight against "tyranny" in his Second Inaugural

Address, became more like an obsession. He abandoned his interest in bipartisanship, failed to lead effectively during Katrina, one of the worst hurricanes to hit the United States in decades, and continued to claim "victory" in Iraq, despite the increasing evidence to the contrary. And by 2007, he had to confront a serious national economic crisis, caused by the subprime mortgage issue. Although he won a second term in 2004, in 2006 his party was trounced at the polls by the Democrats, partly due to the unpopularity of the Iraq War.[192]

TAKEAWAYS FOR ALL LEADERS

1. Leaders must confront a crisis with confidence, composure, competence, and compassion. Followers are particularly attuned to leader behaviors during crises.
2. Leaders can grow in office; they can mature and develop new skills.
3. A leader's influence will decline if he or she becomes obsessed with a single idea or policy and stops paying attention to a changing environment or a full range of stakeholders.

Barack Hussein Obama

Many of his supporters viewed Obama's 2008 presidential election victory as a truly transformational political event. After all, Obama, the first African-American elected to the White House, won 28 states and a higher percentage of the two-party vote than any other candidate in two decades. He won 52.9 percent of the popular vote compared to Arizona Republican Senator John McCain's 45.6 percent.[193] Obama won "red" states like Indiana and made significant inroads in Republican strongholds, including North Carolina and Virginia. On his coattails, Democrats gained 21 seats in the House of Representatives and 8 in the Senate.[194]

Nevertheless, a fundamental question, posed by journalist Jonathan Alter, remained: Could Obama convert widespread disappointment with the Bush Administration into faith in a new political order?[195] In many ways, the stage was set for Obama's transformational leadership in 2008: there was a financial crisis begging for a talented problem-solver; he had a substantial majority in Congress to help advance his agenda, a rare gift for oratorical inspiration, a supple mind, and a supreme level of confidence. Yet, as Alter says, "None of this could assure successful navigation of the treacherous currents of the American presidency. The expectations were immense, as people around the world held up the promise that leadership mattered."[196]

Obama presented an ambitious agenda in his "Blueprint for Change,"[197] and in his Campaign manifesto, "Change We Can Believe In: Barack Obama's Plan to Renew America's Promise."[198] Some of the action items included:

- Making government more effective and cutting wasteful spending.
- Restoring fiscal discipline to the federal government.
- Making sure Americans have an affordable healthcare system that improved (but maintained) the private insurance, preserving Medicare, and providing coverage to those who cannot afford it.
- Adding new jobs through investment in infrastructure.
- Protecting social security.
- Promoting energy independence.
- Ending the war in Iraq through a "responsible phased withdrawal."
- Supporting Israel.
- Finishing the fight against al Qaeda and the Taliban in Afghanistan.

To help advance these goals and deal with the challenges expressed by Alter, Obama chose experienced insiders for his team: 50 percent of his appointees had served in the Clinton administration.[199] He chose a former member of Congress and of the Clinton White House, Rahm Emanuel as his chief-of-staff, signaling the new president's appreciation to Rahm's deep knowledge of Congress and the White House.[200] Interestingly, Obama chose Robert Gates as his Secretary of Defense. Gates had served several Republican presidents in high level positions dealing with national security, but Obama respected his competence and was determined to display the bipartisanship that he had favored in his famous 2006 speech at the Democratic National Convention in Boston and in his subsequent campaign speeches. He chose Timothy Geithner, president of the Federal Reserve Bank in New York, to be his Secretary of Treasury. Geithner shared Obama's nonideological problem-solving sensibilities, and could help Obama address the deepening economic crisis. The president also decided that he would receive a daily economic briefing, like the daily national security briefing, and that the briefer would be Larry Summers, former president of Harvard University, who would also be the Chair of the National Economic Council.[201]

The most celebrated—and somewhat surprising—appointment of the first Obama administration was Hillary Clinton as Secretary of State. Obama believed that Hillary's stature abroad meant that she could carry his message faster and farther than anyone else could.[202] Also, Obama was inspired by the "team of rivals" concept developed by presidential historian Doris Kearns Goodwin, where she examined how President Abraham Lincoln gained valuable advice and support during the civil war from his former political opponents whom he included in his cabinet.[203]

No matter what he had intended to accomplish during his term, Obama had to confront the growing economic crisis in the United States and abroad. As I have written elsewhere,

> When Obama swore the oath of office, the US economy was experiencing the deepest recession since the Great Depression, the automobile and housing industries were in crisis mode, and the financial system was in a serious economic contraction. The economy was losing 740,000 jobs a month, and most investment indices had fallen by 40 percent in 2008 alone.[204]

Obama and his team began working on a large stimulus program to save the economy. In fact, according to author Michael Grunwald, Obama's transition became a "frantic policymaking exercise."[205] With input from Jason Furman, a 37-year-old political activist (who had overseen economic policy for Senator John Kerry's 2004 presidential campaign), Larry Summers, Rahm Emanuel, and Timothy Geithner, among others, Obama developed a $787 billion stimulus plan, which was translated in the American Recovery and Reinvestment Act of 2009. It had three major components:[206]

- One-third of the funds were for middle-class tax cuts, mostly in the form of tax credits and rebates.
- One-third was designated for "state stabilization," to ensure that States, including those with large deficits, would not have to lay off public servants, like teachers and police.
- One-third was designated for infrastructure (roads, bridges, etc.).

Obama assembled a lobbying team to promote the stimulus package to Congress. In addition to Jason Furman, he included Rob Nabors, who had been chief-of-staff to Representative David Obey (D, WI), the former chair of the House Appropriations Committee, and Rahm Emanuel. Vice President Joe Biden, with 36 years of experience in the US Senate, also joined the lobbying effort. Obama had a good relationship with Speaker of the House, Nancy Pelosi (D, CA), and with the Senate Majority Leader, Harry Reid (D, NV). The Democrats had a majority of 257-178 in the House and 58-41 in the Senate.[207] The lobbying team presented the stimulus plan as a starting point, as not definitive, and Rahm Emanuel set an ambitious deadline of February 16, 2009 (Presidents' Day), so the Administration could heal the economy and start creating jobs.[208]

The Republicans, however, were not ready to play ball. Senate Minority Leader Mitch McConnell (R, KY) declared that he was encouraging opposition to the stimulus program "en masse."[209] Leader McConnell and his colleagues portrayed the stimulus program as yet another example of the

Democratic tendency to throw money at problems. They identified the most egregious cases of questionable spending within the proposal, such as the "Mob Museum," or the expenditure to repair the lawn on the national mall.[210]

Obama was surprised by the intensity of the Republican opposition, but he benefitted from Joe Biden's great counsel and assistance. Biden focused on a few key senators whose support could help the bill succeed. For example, Biden worked assiduously on Senator Arlen Specter, a moderate Pennsylvania Republican, who, as a cancer survivor, was appalled that there was not enough money on the proposal for cancer research. Biden called Specter at least 14 times and obtained his support for the stimulus bill on the condition that it would include $10 billion for cancer research. The Obama team also negotiated heavily with moderate Republican Senators, Susan Collins and Olympia Snowe, who wanted to support the president, but became concerned when the price tag for the proposal went over $800 billion.[211]

The bill passed in February 2009, meeting Emanuel's deadline, with 61 "yes" votes in the Senate (including the three Republicans) and without a single Republican vote in the House. President Obama predicted the stimulus program would create 3 or 4 million jobs by the end of 2010 and would make the most significant investment in America's bridges, roads, and mass transit since the creation of the interstate highway system. He added that middle-class families would get tax cuts and the most vulnerable would get the largest assistance in decades.[212]

While he achieved passage of a major bill in a short period of time, Obama also lost his first "message battle."[213] Although the president had wisely augmented the lobbying resources to achieve the bill's passage, he had not publicly explained or celebrated his achievement. For instance, he could have barnstormed across states like Pennsylvania and Maine, whose senators voted for the bill, to raise public sympathy for his projects.[214] David Axlerod, a key presidential adviser, remarked, "We were so focused on the process that we failed to use the greatest tool we have, the Bully Pulpit."[215]

The benefits of the stimulus package were not immediately apparent for ordinary Americans. The Congressional Budget Office (CBO) estimated that, ultimately, the stimulus may have saved as many as 3.3 million jobs: nevertheless, the unemployment rate was higher in December 2010 (9.8 percent) than it had been when the bill was passed (8.2 percent).[216] In addition, a CBS/New York Times survey found that one-third of the public believed that taxes had increased, while only 8 percent accurately recognized that they had decreased, with the remainder of people saying they had stayed the same.[217]

Obama was determined, nonetheless, to continue pursuing his agenda by accomplishing healthcare reform, even though this had not been a major plank in his campaign and despite the expressed skepticism of Vice President and Chief-of-Staff Rahm Emanuel. Obama was motivated to try to refashion one-sixth of the nation's economy because of a promise he had made to

Senator Edward Kennedy (D, MA) when Kennedy endorsed him for president in 2008.[218] Kennedy had asked that, in return for his support, Obama make health care his top domestic project and strive to achieve universal coverage. As well, Obama believed that providing coverage to millions of Americans who currently lived without it, was a fundamental matter of fairness, and fairness was core to his vision, as developed on the previous chapter. In his travels around the country in 2007–2008, Obama also heard gut-wrenching stories of medical bankruptcies or callous treatment of clients by insurance companies. Finally, Obama believed that his chances for a legislative success were relatively good with a Democratic majority in both houses of Congress, which might not (ad did not) exist after the 2010 mid-term elections.[219]

While the odds were clearly against him, President Obama worked hard to build an effective healthcare reform team, including Jim Messina, the White House deputy chief-of-staff, Nancy-Ann De Pearle, director of the White House Office of Health Reform (and a former Rhodes scholar who had also run Tennessee's healthcare system). Rahm Emanuel was also part of Obama's healthcare team, and to help avoid the problems the Clinton administration had experienced with healthcare reform (which Emanuel had been part of), he suggested the following guidelines:[220]

- Allow Congress to write the bill, instead of presenting them with a finished product, as Hillary had done.
- Focus intensely on rising costs, a big concern of the middle-class and corporate America.
- Find ways to accommodate special interests and industries.

Obama announced the following goals in proposing the legislation:[221]

- Provide coverage to 31 million Americans out of the 47 million uninsured.
- Create mandates compelling employees and employers to buy insurance or face financial penalties (the "individual mandate" would be challenged and ultimately upheld by the US Supreme Court).
- Extend "subsidies" to help the uninsured purchase policies on new "healthcare exchanges."
- Provide help to small business owners to enable them to insure employees.
- Institute Medicare cuts and industry givebacks to cut costs.
- Impose new regulations on the insurance industry, preventing discrimination against those with preexisting conditions, and new incentives for preventive care.

When fleshed out, the proposals had several complexities. A big question at the outset was how to pay for the implementation of the envisioned massive overhaul, estimated to cost $1 trillion over ten years.[222] Obama took a step toward addressing the cost issue by assembling a large group of potential supporters in the White House in March 2009 to initiate a dialogue about implementation and funding. The 150 people included Democratic and Republican lawmakers, leaders of organized labor and the American Medical Association, corporate executives, consumer advocates, and members of the Chamber of Commerce.[223] Several members of the Clinton healthcare reform effort also attended, including W.J. "Billy" Tauzin, a former member of Congress now representing the Pharmaceutical Research and Manufacturers of America, along with Karen Ignagni, representing health insurers.[224] A dramatic highlight of the day was the appearance of Senator Edward Kennedy, who was recovering from cancer surgery. In what would be his last public appearance, Kennedy exclaimed, "I am looking forward to being a foot soldier in this undertaking. And this time, we will not fail."[225]

The bill was shepherded through the Senate by US Senator Max Baucus (D, MT), who was chair of the Senate Finance Committee. To help Obama obtain the money he needed to launch the reform program, Baucus negotiated with drug manufacturers. He told them they were poised to gain tens of millions of new customers in an expanded healthcare system; and to Baucus the logical tradeoff was for the industry to help offset the cost by accepting smaller federal reimbursements or paying a new fee to the government. He wanted to squeeze $100 billion in savings from the drug sector over 10 years.[226] Tauzin believed that drug companies would cooperate and were also willing to offer discounts on prescription medicines purchased through Medicare. Continued negotiations reduced the figure to $80 billion over a decade, which Obama described as a "historic agreement to lower drug costs for seniors."[227] Separate negotiations produced an agreement by the hospitals to forgo $155 billion in government reimbursements over ten years.[228]

As the reform process progressed through the Senate, the anti-healthcare activists gained momentum. Senator Joseph Lieberman (I, CT) raised strong objections to a "public option" that was included on the original bill. Lieberman saw the public option resembling a "single payer" idea and as a back-door path to a government takeover of the healthcare system.[229] Senate Majority Leader Harry Reid (D, NV) offered an alternative idea to mollify Lieberman: in place of the public option, a provision allowing people between the ages of 55 and 65 the chance to "buy-in" to the Medicare Program, opening Medicare to millions of pre-retirees.[230] Lieberman rejected Reid's idea, and Reid pulled the public option out of the bill. On December 24, 2009, the Senate convened the first Christmas Eve session since 1895, and Obama's healthcare plan passed by a vote of 60-39.[231]

In the House, meanwhile, Speaker Nancy Pelosi (D, CA) confronted her own obstacles in getting the Obamacare bill over the finish line. As an accomplished vote-counter, Pelosi calculated that she already had 200 solid commitments for passage of the bill, but she needed at least a dozen more.

One challenge to gaining the additional votes was Representative Bart Stupak (D, MI), a former police officer, who wanted to place strict abortion limits in the bill. He pushed an amendment prohibiting coverage for the procedure in any health plan subsidized by the federal government. Although Stupak's amendment was defeated, his cause was taken up by the Catholic bishops. In August 2009, at Senator Kennedy's funeral in a church in Roxbury, MA, Cardinal Sean O'Malley privately approached President Obama and said, "The bishops are anxious to support health care. It's very important. But we are very concerned that this not be public funding for abortion."[232] Then the bishops sent a notice marked "urgent" to every US parish advocating defeat of the healthcare bill unless it included the Stupak amendment.[233] Speaker Pelosi, to her chagrin, was forced to include the Stupak amendment, and the bill passed the House by a vote of 220-215.[234]

Instead of experiencing the thrill of victory, however, Obama faced a loud chorus of opposition. Between December 2009 and March 2010, public opinion polls registered great opposition to the bill.[235] In addition, the late Senator Kennedy's Massachusetts senate seat was won by Scott Brown, a conservative Republican, thereby ending the filibuster-free senate for the Democrats.[236] Several of Obama's closest advisers and some Democratic congressional leaders reacted to Brown's unlikely victory in MA by urging him to adopt a scaled-down version of the healthcare bill to attract wider support. But Obama rejected the idea and reiterated his commitment to a far-reaching bill that now awaited conference committee action to iron out differences between House and Senate versions. Obama and Pelosi convinced the House to accept the Senate bill so that "reconciliation, a special Senate procedure designed for Budget bills and requiring a simple majority, could be used."[237] Obama signed the Affordable Care Act, calling it "the most expansive piece of social legislation enacted in the United States in over four decades."[238]

The healthcare reform experience revealed Obama's strengths and weaknesses as a political leader. It certainly showed his courage in undertaking a massive reform project that no other president had succeeded in accomplishing, and several, like Bill Clinton, had failed miserably. It also showed his pragmatism and his willingness to make deals where they could be made. In this regard he was more of a transactional, than transformational, leader.

On the other hand, it revealed some of Obama's weaknesses especially in the area of persuasion and "retail politics." During the summer of 2009, opposition to Obamacare crystallized in the ferocious politicking of the Tea Part at congressional town hall meetings.[239] Obama was not sufficiently vocal or visible to calm the waters and educate the public on the importance of what he had accomplished. According to his adviser, Valerie Jarrett, for months the president had trouble "finding the right vocabulary on health care … It was like trying to find the combination of a lock … how to say this in a way people would understand."[240]

In an October 2010 interview with the *New York Times*, Obama reflected on the lessons he had learned on the early years of his presidency; we can see the themes discussed in this chapter on his comments:

> Given how much stuff was coming at us, we probably spent too much time trying to get the policy right rather than the politics right. There is probably a perverse pride in my administration—and I take responsibility for this; this was blowing from the top—that we are going to do the right thing even if short term it was unpopular. And I think that anybody who's occupied this office has to remember success is obtained by an intersection of policy and politics and that you can't be neglecting of marketing and P.R. and public opinion.[241]

Subsequent events would reveal the accuracy of Obama's insights. During his first term, his leadership resulted in an ironic combination of "legislative success and political failure."[242] In the 2010 mid-term elections Obama's Democratic Party suffered a crushing defeat at the polls, with Republicans gaining 64 seats in the House (giving them a 242-193 advantage), and 6 Senate seats (reducing the Democratic majority to 53-47).[243]

Nevertheless, Obama, with the help of former MA Senator John Kerry, was able to successfully negotiate an agreement with Iran, slowing down the development of their nuclear weapons program under a strict regime of inspections and monitoring. And the deal was achieved with the cooperation of Russia and China.[244]

Obama won a second term in 2011, defeating Republican presidential candidate (and former MA Governor), Mitt Romney with 51.06 percent of the popular vote to Romney's 47.2 percent. Obama secured 322 electoral college votes compared to Romney's 206.[245]

In summary, as I have written elsewhere:

> Obama assumed office in a highly challenging environment, inheriting from his predecessor an economy on the brink of disaster and a nation involved in two wars. His agenda was, in short, not really of his making, as he had to manage extant crises in an environment where he lacked a faithful partner. In spite of his party having control of both houses of Congress during his first two years as president, Obama had to use every ounce of his energy to achieve passage of his major legislation, such as the stimulus bill; Congressional Republicans had united visibly around the goal of defeating Obama in the moment and in the next election.[246]

TAKEAWAYS FOR ALL LEADERS

1. Leaders who pursue fundamental changes in their countries or organizations will succeed if they mobilize a coalition for change, listen to dissenters, and show a willingness to compromise.
2. Leaders who achieve a significant change to the status quo need to EXPLAIN the changes in terms that will be meaningful to a wide variety of constituents.
3. Leaders can aim for "transformational" leadership but will still have to rely on "transactional" deals to reach their goals.[247]

Donald John Trump

When real-estate mogul and reality-TV star Donald J. Trump descended the escalator from his luxurious New York Fifth Avenue penthouse, on June 16, 2015, to announce his candidacy for president, the world's premier betting firm, Paddy Power, predicted his chances of winning at 100 to 1. As late as October 2016, he was described as having a less than one in five chance of beating his Democratic opponent, former Secretary of State, US Senator (D, NY), and First Lady Hillary Rodham Clinton.[248]

And yet, with no political experience, a threadbare campaign, a paucity of endorsements from Republican Party elites, and at least 16 GOP rivals, most of whom had considerably more political experience than he did, Trump defied the odds to become the 45th President of the United States. After a tumultuous and often nasty 2016 presidential campaign, Trump achieved an electoral college victory, while losing the popular vote to Secretary Clinton by almost 3 million. Trump won the key eastern swing states, including Florida, North Carolina, and Ohio. He pushed Clinton to the limit in Virginia before finally losing the state to her. He won Wisconsin, Michigan, and Pennsylvania, breaching the vaunted "blue wall" of Midwestern states that Democrats had long counted on. Altogether, Trump won 30 states with 306 electoral votes, while Clinton won 20 states with 232 electoral votes. In the popular vote, Clinton won 48 percent compared to Trump's 46 percent. Her lead reached almost 3 million votes, partly explained by her 4.3 million vote advantage in California, where she won a higher percentage of votes than Obama had in 2012.[249]

Trump's victory was augmented by positive results for the Republican Party in the US Senate and House elections, as well as in state legislatures. The Democrats, with fewer Senate seats to defend, gained only two seats in the Senate, instead of the five they needed to secure a majority in the chamber. And with a near-record 98 percent of House incumbents reelected, the Democrats gained only six seats in the House, leaving Republicans in control of both chambers, as well as the White House, a condition last achieved in the Eisenhower years.

Trump's transition process was "haphazard and dysfunctional," according to two *Washington Post* reporters.[250] It is not surprising, then, that his approach to the political dynamic of leadership was equally chaotic. There was no compelling grand vision to animate his presidency, as there had been for Ronald Reagan, and certainly, no mastery of the details of governance and the legislative process, as there was in the Clinton administration, Trump was left to his own devices, his instincts, and the limited networks he could access to staff and lead his presidency. He filled most high-level White House positions with people he had become familiar with during the campaign. These included Republican National Committee chair Reince Priebus as his chief-of-staff; foreign policy adviser and former general Michael Flynn as national security advisor; campaign spokesman Sean Spicer as press secretary; senior campaign strategist Steve Bannon as senior political strategist; senior campaign advisor Stephen Miller as Senior White House policy advisor; and election lawyer Donald McGhan as White House Counsel. He also designated his daughter Ivanka and her husband, Jared Kushner as free-floating advisors. Trump gave Kushner an enormously wide policy portfolio, including lead responsibility for the Arab Israeli conflict, government efficiency reforms, criminal justice reform, and the opioid crisis.[251]

Given Trump's unfamiliarity with public administration, he placed his aides in unusual relations to each other. For example, Bannon was granted a seat on the National Security Council's Principals Committee, while the chairman of the Joint Chiefs of Staff and the CIA director were assigned a purely advisory role. As Bannon's equal partner, Priebus was denied real authority to direct and discipline the rest of the staff, a role usually played by the chief-of-staff.[252] According to presidential scholar Michael Nelson, "Lines of responsibility were notoriously unclear in the Trump White House. Factions formed on ideological differences and personal rivalries. Staff members leaked disparaging comments about each other to the press corps."[253]

And there was a considerable amount of turnover in the White House staff, a pattern that would continue for the entire four years.[254] By the end of Trump's second hundred days as president, the White House had seen the firing or resignation of the first national security advisor (Flynn), chief-of-staff (Priebus), chief strategist (Bannon), press secretary (Spicer), and other aides. By November 2017, most of Trump's original staff was gone, causing him to quip, "I'm doing a great job, but my staff sucks!"[255]

On July 31, 2017, Trump designated John Kelly, the administration's highly respected secretary of the Department of Homeland Security and previously four-star Marine Corps General, to become the chief-of-staff, replacing Reince Priebus. Kelly tried desperately to tighten the discipline and order in the White House, instituting, for example, "decision memos" that integrated the issues perspectives of relevant departments and agencies before they went to the president, as well as increasing the amount of vetting of executive orders before they were issued. But as Kelly and others learned, "the long-term reining in of a seventy-one-year-old man who rose high in the business and entertainment worlds, and was elected president by doing things in a loose, personal and spontaneous way, was not easy to accomplish."[256]

In filling his cabinet positions, Trump was drawn to people who had succeeded in domains he admired, business and the military. From the business world he selected Rex Tillerson (former CEO of Exxon-Mobil) as his secretary of state; Steven Mnuchin (former investment banker and executive at Goldman Sachs) as secretary of treasury; and Alex Azar (former president of Lilly USA) as his second secretary of health and human services (after the departure of Tom Price). From the military community, he chose Four-star Army General James Mattis as secretary of defense (admiring the general's moniker of "mad dog") and General John Kelly as secretary of homeland security (and as chief-of-staff as mentioned earlier). And finally, he turned to a small set of Republican politicians who supported his election bid, especially Alabama Republican Senator Jeff Sessions, whom he chose as attorney general, and former neurosurgeon and GOP presidential candidate Ben Carson, who he nominated to be secretary of housing and urban development.[257]

While Trump enjoyed a Republican majority in Congress, the margin of his party's edge was perilously thin in both chambers. In the House of Representatives, Republicans outnumbered Democrats by 241-194, and in the Senate by 52-48.[258] In the face of cohesive Democratic opposition, any legislation proposed opposed by just 10 percent of GOP House members was unlikely to be enacted. Republican leaders would have to keep the party's extremely conservative nearly three-dozen strong, and highly unified Freedom Caucus on board in order to prevail, without alienating Tuesday Group moderates, greater in number but less disciplined.

Moreover, Trump's victory has been narrow and carried no clear policy mandate.[259] By the anniversary of Trump's election, Congress had yet to pass a single piece of administration-sponsored legislation.[260] It was not from a lack of trying, however. From the beginning of the Trump presidency, Republican leaders joined hands with the president in trying to fulfill their shared campaign promise to repeal and replace Obamacare. For Republicans, this had been a consistent goal ever since they regained control of the House of Representatives in 2010, with no less than 50 attempts to overturn Obamacare. When the Senate joined the House in doing so in 2015, Obama vetoed the measure. During the presidential campaign Trump promised repeatedly to "end, terminate, repeal Obamacare and replace it with something really, really great that works."[261]

With little guidance from the administration, Republican House leaders began 2017 by writing a bill that the nonpartisan CBO estimated would leave 24 million more Americans uninsured within ten years than if Obamacare remained intact. Speaker of the House Paul Ryan (R, WI) cancelled a scheduled floor vote on March 24 when it became clear the bill would not pass. Freedom Caucus members objected to the measure's four-year extension of expanded Medicaid payments to the states, while Tuesday Group Republicans bristled at the proposed reduction in the size of those payments. Then Ryan and his Republican colleagues modified the bill, with Vice President Pence helping to broker a deal that mollified conservatives by allowing states to opt out of certain provisions of the new bill and moderates by supplementing coverage for people with preexisting conditions. Although the CBO still estimated that 23 million more Americans would still be uninsured, the House passed the revised bill on May 4 by a vote of 217-213, with the Democrats unanimous in opposition.[262]

The bill went to the Senate where it was modified further by Senate Majority Leader Mitch McConnell (R, KY), but did not come close to uniting enough Republicans to bring it to the floor. McConnell worked assiduously to revise the bill, finding that to mollify the moderates he would lose the support of the hard-liners. As for Trump, during this time, he took four positions in three days: first he supported the McConnell bill; then he proposed repealing the ACA without replacing it; then he suggested that Republicans should let Obamacare fail by doing nothing at all; and finally he pressured Republican senators to replace it after all.[263]

Desperate to pass something, McConnell brought the proposed bills to the Senate floor during the last week of August. Once again, Republican defections doomed all three. Nine Republican senators voted against the repeal-and-replace measure, seven against a repeal only measure, and three against a "skinny repeal," which would preserve Obamacare while abolishing the individual mandate. On September 30, the last day of the fiscal year, GOP Senators Bill Cassidy (LA) and Lindsey Graham (SC) proposed a bill that would have replaced Obamacare with block grants to the states. Senator John McCain frustrated that the Senate had not at any point considered a bill with "regular order"—with extensive hearings, debate, and amendment—led a group of moderate Republicans in defeating the Cassidy-Graham bill.[264] McCain famously signaled his opposition with a visible thumbs-down gesture for the cameras!

Trump's intervention in the healthcare debate had been so clumsy in the House, according to political scientist Michael Nelson, that McConnell politely declined the president's request to help in the Senate.[265] According to Nelson:

> Trump's public rhetoric was erratic, swerving from one petty complaint to another on Twitter instead of consistently rousing public opinion to support any of his policy proposals. Even when he did talk about health care, Trump veered from praising the House bill as a "great plan" that

was very, very, incredibly well-crafted" to condemning it as "mean" rather than "generous, kind, with heart." Legislators seldom forget casting a tough vote in support of a president only to have him criticize them for it later.[266]

Afterwards, Trump blamed Congressional Republicans, especially John McCain, for the failure to repeal and replace Obamacare. He also attacked Senators Dan Heller (R, NE), Lisa Murkowski (R, AL), and Susan Collins (R, ME). According to Professor Michael Nelson, "Underlying all these sources of Trump's ineffectiveness with Congress was his lack, in the absence of factual knowledge about his own proposals, of consistent guiding principles that could make up for it, as they did for Ronald Reagan."[267]

President Trump achieved greater success in the next set of issues he took on, specifically, taxes and the national debt. After failing to repeal Obamacare, the GOP was under enormous pressure not to fail on taxes. But the commitment to reducing that goal was more complicated than is apparent. One of the realities of economic policy at the national level is the connection between taxing and spending. Specifically, when spending outstrips taxation in a particular fiscal year, a budget deficit is created, which increases the national debt.

In spite of the federal government collecting nearly $3.5 trillion in taxes in the fiscal year that ended on September 30, 2017, deficit spending added $666 billion to the national debt, raising it above the $19.808 trillion ceiling allowed at that time by law. The deadline for Congress to raise the debt ceiling was September 29, the day after which the federal government would no longer be able to pay its bills unless Congress acted. House Freedom Caucus members vowed that they would not vote to raise the debt ceiling without exacting cuts in federal domestic spending. Trump sought assistance from Democratic congressional leaders Representative Nancy Pelosi (CA) and Senator Chuck Schumer (NY). On September 6, in an Oval Office meeting they indicated that they would encourage Democrats to vote to raise the debt ceiling for another three months, but they would not allow cuts in domestic spending.[268]

The Democratic leaders took advantage of another looming deadline to win additional concessions from Trump. On September 30, the federal government would run out of money to meet its ongoing expenses and have to shut down all but essential services without additional funds appropriated for the new fiscal year (beginning on October 1). Trump indicated that he would allow a shutdown to occur if the congressional appropriation did not include $1.6 billion for the construction of a wall along the southern border of the United States.[269] But Trump had little leverage, and Puerto Rico required an urgent federal response (for hurricane relief); and the president had already sent a $14.5 billion emergency relief bill to Congress with tens of billions in additional requests to follow. The country would not understand or accept shutting down the government in the immediate aftermath of a natural disaster. With Trump acquiescing to Pelosi and Schumer, Congress voted to raise the debt ceiling and fund the government until December as part of the hurricane relief bill. The Senate vote on September 7 was 80-17, and the House vote the next day was 316-90, with all the "no" votes coming from Republicans.[270]

But the budget resolution for the new fiscal year had not yet been passed. Passage of the bill was a necessary precondition for folding tax reform legislation into a reconciliation process.[271] On October 5, the House, overcoming united Democratic opposition and substantial challenge within the GOP, passed a budget resolution calling for a $4 trillion cut in taxes over the next ten years and an equal amount of spending reductions and loophole closings to offset them. Hours later, the Senate Budget Committee sent its own budget measure to the full Senate, which passed it on a straight party line vote. It allowed for $1.5 more in tax cuts than in reduced spending and increased revenue. The lateness of the Senate action left little room for a conference committee to smooth out the differences between the two versions: on October 26, House Republicans, encouraged by Speaker of the House Paul Ryan (R, WI) and President Trump had little choice but to pass the Senate version as written.[272]

On August 30, after being distracted by controversies like the border wall and the Charlottesville situation, Trump presented at least the "glimmerings" of a plan in a speech on Missouri. Offering few details, Trump promised a tax cut that was "the biggest ever, including a steep reduction in the corporate tax rate that would be partially offset by "eliminating loopholes and complexity that primarily benefit the wealthiest and special interests."[273]

By the end of September, working closely with Republican (but not Democratic) members of Congress, Treasury Secretary Stephen Mnuchin and National Economic Council director Gary Cohn developed a proposal to collapse the seven individual tax brackets into three (12 percent, 25 percent, and 35 percent); preserve the deductibility of mortgage interest and charitable donations for those who itemize, and for those who do not, nearly doubling of the standard deduction to $12,000 for individuals and $24,000 for couples, increase the child tax credit; and reduce the corporate tax rate from 35 percent to 20 percent.[274]

Neither the administration's plan nor the congressional budget resolution passed in October specified how to offset most or all of the cost of the tax cuts over the next ten years, except for directing the Senate Energy and Natural Resources Committee to come up with $1 billion in savings—amounting to a thinly veiled nod to committee chair Senator Lisa Murkowski of Alaska to proceed with oil drilling in the Arctic National Wildlife Refuge, fulfilling a long-standing goal of hers and other Republicans, to authorize oil drilling in the Arctic National Wildlife Refuge. Both chambers eased the challenge of deficit reduction by making optimistic assumptions about how fast the economy would grow.[275]

Trump would ultimately sign the Tax Cut and Jobs Act on December 17, 2017.[276] On the way to passage, the House and Senate proposed slightly different bills, but both generally embraced a greatly reduced corporate tax rate, a reduced individual rate, and a $10,000 limit on individual deductions for property taxes. This deduction was costing the federal government $100 billion in revenue each year. The high tax states were also, perhaps unsurprisingly, highly politically "blue" states, including California, New York, New Jersey, and Illinois.[277] Congressional Democrats generally opposed both versions, and adversely affected interest groups, including the National Association of Realtors, the National Association of Home Builders, and the American Association of Retired Persons (AARP) mobilized in opposition.

On November 13, three days before the scheduled vote on the House plan, Trump complicated the situation by abandoning his support for a higher tax on for the wealthy and tweeted that instead Congress should repeal the "individual mandate" in Obamacare, thereby saving enough money (more than $300 billion that the federal government would otherwise have spent) to cut the top tax rate to 35 percent, with all the rest going to middle-class tax cuts.[278] Republican Senators quickly endorsed the idea, and the Senate Finance Committee added the new provision to its modified version of the tax measure.

The major provisions of the Tax Cuts and Jobs Act of 2017 included:

- A reduction of the top marginal individual tax from 39.6 to 37 percent. The remaining rates would be 10, 12, 22, 24, 32, and 35 percent.
- Doubling of the standard deduction from $13,000 to $24,000 for married couples, and from $6,000 to $12,000 for single filers.
- A limit of $10,000 on deductions for state and local property taxes.
- An increase in taxpayer deductions for interest on mortgage payments to $1 million purchase price of a home, from the previous limit of $750,000.
- A reduction of the top corporate income tax from 35 percent to 21 percent.
- And a 100 percent bonus depreciation for qualified property purchases for 5 years.[279]

Trump claimed a great victory, saying "It's going to be a fabulous thing for the American people. It's going to be fantastic for the recovery."[280] In addition, Trump and his allies claimed that the tax bill would pay for itself; however, the Joint Committee on Taxation and the CBO estimated it would reduce federal revenues by about $1.5 trillion by the end of 2027.[281]

A good part of the remainder of Trump's presidency was consumed by his evading several legal and political challenges, facilitated in part by the success of the House Democrats in the 2018 mid-term election; the Democrats gained 40 seats and now held a 235-199 edge, while the Republicans gained 2 seats in the Senate, giving them a 53-47 advantage in that chamber.[282] The Democratic majority in the House would be quite important in the initiation of two impeachment proceedings against Trump.

But first came the Mueller Report, released in March 2019, which resulted from the "commander-in-chief's rage."[283] The rage was directed at FBI Director James Comey, who had been investigating the 2016 presidential election, but refused to tell the world that the president was not being scrutinized personally. On May 9, 2017, Trump, defying years of tradition and political norms, decided to fire Comey. He conveyed the news in a terse, hand-delivered letter to FBI headquarters by his former bodyguard.[284]

Lawmakers were livid. And Rodd Rosenstein, the second-in-command at the Department of Justice, was incensed that the White House was placing all the blame for Comey's removal on him, even though he had endorsed Comey's firing. Rosenstein considered resigning, but instead, turned to Robert S. Mueller III, a venerated DC lawyer who had himself previously served as FBI Director, notably during the September 11 terrorist attacks. On May 27, 2017, Rosenstein announced the appointment of Mueller to lead an independent investigation, under the auspices of the Department of Justice, into the 2016 presidential election and other matters that might stem from the inquiry.[285]

During the next 22 months, Mueller quietly and methodically investigated Trump and nearly everyone in his orbit, trying to determine whether anyone had conspired with the Russians to tilt the elections and whether the president had tried to obstruct justice.[286] Mueller and his team only "spoke" to the public through indictments and cryptic court filings. In federal court, the team of prosecutors charged 34 people, including 26 Russian nationals. They secured guilty pleas from 7 people, including a former national security adviser and the chairman of Trump's campaign.[287] The investigation culminated on March 22, 2019, when Mueller concluded his study and submitted a final report to Attorney General William P. Barr.[288]

The Mueller Report drew the following conclusions: The Russian government interfered in the 2016 presidential election in "sweeping and systematic" fashion. (a) A Russian entity carried out a social media campaign that favored candidate Donald Trump and disparaged Hillary Clinton, and (b) A Russian intelligence service conducted computer-intrusion operations against entities, employees, and volunteers working for Clinton's campaign, and then released the documents.[289]

Although the investigation identified numerous links between the Russian government and the Trump campaign, the investigation did not establish that members of the Trump campaign conspired or coordinated with the Russian government in its election interference activities.[290] And then the Report spoke to the specific question of Trump's role and whether he obstructed justice, and concluded that

> ... If we had confidence after a thorough investigation of the fact that the President did not commit obstruction of justice, we would so state. Based on the facts and the applicable legal standards, however, we are unable to reach that judgment. The evidence we obtained about the

President's actions and intent presents difficult issues that prevent us from conclusively determining that no criminal conduct occurred.

Accordingly, while the report does not conclude the President committed a crime, it also does not exonerate him.[291]

But Trump was eager to claim that he had been exonerated. He had an ally in Attorney General Barr, who held a news conference on April 18, less than two hours before the Mueller Report would be turned over to Congress. Barr noted repeatedly that the Report found no "collusion," a phrase Trump had uttered several times as he attacked the investigation.[292]

Trump's challenges continued in December 2019, when the House of Representatives voted to impeach him for "abuse of power" and "obstruction of Congress." The first article of impeachment (abuse of power) passed by a majority of 230-197, with only two Democrats and all the Republicans voting in opposition; the second one (obstruction of Congress) passed by 229-198, with one additional Democrat voting in opposition.[293] The impeachment was based on Trump's "corrupt" use of the levers of government to solicit election assistance from Ukraine in the form of investigations to discredit his Democratic political rivals.[294]

The impeachment proceedings were initiated following the disclosure of a half-hour telephone call between President Trump and Ukrainian President Volodymyr Zelensky. The Ukrainian leader thanked Trump for US military support and indicated that they were ready to purchase more Javelins from the United States, and to receive some $400 million in assistance. Trump answered Zelensky by asking for a favor: that Ukraine gets information about Joe Biden's son, which Trump said had been interrupted by Joe Biden. He asked Zelensky to "please look into it."[295]

Nevertheless, on February 6, 2020, the US Senate voted to acquit Trump on the charges drawn up by the House. The votes were as follows: First article, Abuse of Power, 52-48 (a strict party split) and Second article, Obstruction of Congress, 53-47 (with one Republican Senator, Mitt Romney (UT), voting with the Democrats).[296]

Before the end of his first term, Trump did achieve an additional political "win," facilitating the signing of the Abraham Accords between Israel and its Arab neighbors. The Abraham Accords are a series of treaties normalizing diplomatic relations between Israel, the United Arab Emirates (UAE), Bahrain, Sudan, and Morocco, facilitated by the Trump Administration between August and December 2000.[297] The Accords extended medical, scientific, and economic cooperation between Israel and the aforementioned countries as they all fought the ravages of COVID-19 and sought improved peace and prosperity for their citizens.

In November 2019, Trump lost his bid for reelection to former Vice President and US Senator (D, DE) Joe Biden, but refused to concede, claiming instead that there had been massive voter fraud in the 2020 presidential election. The refusal to concede started a process that led to a second impeachment of President Trump, in January 2021, after had already left office. Asserting that the election results were the product of widespread fraud—a charge repudiated by at least 60 federal and state court proceedings—Trump argued that they should not be accepted by the American people or by state and federal officials.

On January 6, 2021, pursuant to the 12th Amendment to the US Constitution, the Vice President of the United States, the House of Representatives and the Senate met at the US Capitol for a Joint Session of Congress to count the votes of the electoral college. Shortly before the Joint Session commenced, President Trump addressed a crowd at the Ellipse, only a short distance from the Capitol. There he reiterated his claim that he won the 2020 election "by a landslide." He also made a statement that, in context, encouraged—and fore-seeably resulted in—lawless action at the Capitol, such as "if you don't fight like hell, you're not going to have a country anymore." Inspired by Trump, members of the crowd he addressed in an attempt to interfere, among other objectives, with the Joint Session's constitutional duty to certify the results of the 2020 presidential election, "unlawfully breached and vandalized the Capitol, injured and killed law enforcement officers, menaced Members of Congress, the vice president, and congressional personnel, and engaged in other violent, deadly destructive and seditious acts."[298]

The House passed the article to impeach Trump, and then the process moved to the Senate, as prescribed by the constitution. And once again, the Senate voted to acquit him, with 43 Senators voting "not guilty" and 57 voting "guilty." This time 7 Republicans broke with Mr. Trump and voted "guilty;" however, 67 votes are needed to convict a president on an article of impeachment.[299]

TAKEAWAYS FOR ALL LEADERS

- A leader can influence a great number of people through charisma and showmanship; this is a leadership asset, as well as a potential danger.
- A leader will lose persuasive power when he or she lacks knowledge about critical issues, and instead enunciates confusing and contradictory messaging.
- The President of the United States must operate within the rather austere constitutional boundaries on the exercise of power or be able to articulate cogent reasons for exceeding those boundaries. Leaders in other sectors must also respect the boundaries they confront.
- Urging followers to resort to violence, or even extremism, is not a hallmark of strong leadership in a democratic society.

Joseph Robinette Biden, Jr.

After a long and nasty campaign, Joe Biden was elected president on November 3, 2020 capturing 51.3 percent of the popular vote to Donald Trump's 46.8 percent, and wining 306 electoral votes to Trump's 232 votes.[300] Kamala Harris, former US Senator (D, CA) was elected as Vice President; she was the first woman, first African-American, and first person of South Asian descent to be elected as Vice President.[301] The Democratic Party maintained a slim advantage, as a result of the 2020 congressional elections. In the House they had 222 seats (having lost 14 and gained 3), to 213 for the Republicans (who gained 15 and lost 3).[302] Andin the Senate, the Democrats and the Republicans each had 50 seats, with the Democrats gaining 4 and losing 1, and the Republicans gaining 1 and losing 4.[303]

Like presidents before him, Biden inherited a challenging situation, and he identified four major crises: the coronavirus, the economy, racial inequity, and climate change.[304] Perhaps the biggest immediate challenge was the persistence of the COVID-19 pandemic and the thousands of Americans dying from the virus as Biden assumed the office. The new president acted quickly and decisively to expand vaccinations, from 770,000 a day when he assumed office to 3 million a day by his 100th day in office.[305] According to two *Washington Post* reporters, "Now, nearly 100 days in to the Biden presidency, the pace of coronavirus vaccinations has far exceeded his initial promise."[306] Moreover, on his first day in office, through an Executive Order, President Biden brought the United States back into the Paris Climate Agreement, an international protocol to arrest climate change by reducing carbon emissions.[307]

Biden worked hard to unify the country and lobbied for the passage of a huge $1.9 trillion aid package, that he signed on March 12, 2021 as The American Rescue Plan Act.[308] In response to the economic hardships and damages caused by COVID-19, and to stimulate the economy, the bill provided $363 billion to state and local recovery funds, $656 billion in financial assistance (stimulus checks, tax credits, paycheck protection), $56.27 billion for assistance to individuals and families (SNAP nutrition assistance), and $211 billion to education and childcare.[309] It was, according to NY Times reporter Emily Cochrane, "the largest injection of federal aid since the Great Depression."[310]

While Biden aimed for a bipartisan effort on the bill, the vote on the bill largely broke down on party lines, and the Democrats were forced to use a process of reconciliation to secure passage. The bill passed by a 50-40 margin in the Senate, and by 220-211 in the House.[311]

Application to Other Sectors

In their path-breaking research on leadership effectiveness, authors Jim Kouzes and Barry Posner interviewed thousands of experienced leaders to determine when they felt they were at their "personal best" as a leader.[312] Without any prompting from the researchers, the vast majority of experienced leaders in both the private and public sectors talked about "times of challenge, turbulence, and adversity."[313] Kouzes and Posner suggest that the leaders' responses can be explained as follows: "…. because personal and business leadership have a way of making people come face to face with who they are and what they are capable of becoming."[314] In a similar vein, former First Lady Michele Obama, told the delegates at the 2012 Democratic National Convention, that, "being president doesn't change who you are, it reveals who you are."[315]

Kouzes and Posner emphasize that in conducting their research they did not ask people to talk about change, but an enormously high percentage of leaders they interviewed chose to frame the "personal best" leadership stories around changes they introduced in response to challenges they faced. "The study of leadership, according to Kouzes and Posner, is the study of how men and women guide others through adversity, uncertainty, and other significant challenges."[316] The skill of "adaptive leadership"[317] is certainly important for US presidents, corporate leaders, and educational and nonprofit executives.

Exemplary leaders are constantly looking for opportunities to improve the status quo, and they earn the respect of followers when they show a curiosity about how to do that. Kouzes and Posner report on a conversation they had with a new leader who joined Hewlett Packard and took on a very broad assignment with the company's global business services finance group. She described the reaction of direct reports and her boss, "They saw me as an advocate who was trying to simplify their lives and make their jobs a little easier, while my boss saw my desire to improve the current state of affairs even in the face of adversity."[318]

A fascinating example of a leader taking the initiative to introduce change to improve the status quo comes from the development of Starbucks's Frappuccino. A Starbucks district manager was frustrated that her customers were going to competitors' stores for blended drinks, which Starbucks did not offer. Indeed, corporate leadership declined numerous requests to introduce the drink. Undaunted, the district manager persuaded a colleague in retail operations in Seattle to be her ally, and he bought her a blender to experiment with in making the drink. They made the product in the district manager's store and tested it with customers. As more and more people requested the product, the company's leadership was persuaded to invest in the drink and, after several trials, to bring it to market. Frappuccino became the most successful new launch in their company's history.[319]

Leaders, like US presidents, must know why they want to bring about change, but as we have seen in previous sections of this chapter they also must be mindful of the dynamics of persuasion and of retail politics. The skills needed in change management are remarkably similar in different sectors. Harvard Business School Professor John Kotter advises leaders to consider eight factors in introducing and managing change:[320]

Establish a Sense of Urgency

Leaders must convince followers that there is an urgency to the change. Political leaders, for instance, are constantly struggling with creating a sense of urgency about climate change. People like former US Vice President Al Gore are passionately warning us about the dangers of complacency and attempting to create a sense of urgency. As discussed earlier in this chapter, US presidents have had to work hard to convince citizens and Congress of the need to reform health care or welfare policies. Similarly in the corporate world, people in a stagnant culture tend to argue that problems are so deep and entrenched that there is no point in trying to solve them.

Create a Guiding Coalition

As evidenced with US presidents, a leader cannot bring about change on his or her own, but needs a committed and capable coalition to develop momentum around the change. For a president, the chief-of-staff can be an invaluable asset in this regard. As well, interest groups or part leaders can increase support and enthusiasm for a change effort. In the business world, there are also people within the CEO's orbit who can assist.

Develop a Vision and Strategy and Communicate the Change Vision

We have discussed these concepts in the previous chapter of this book.

Empower Employees for Broad-Based Action

Leaders can engage employees in change efforts by encouraging them to take initiative. As Kouzes and Posner state, "Change requires leadership and every person, down to the most junior member of the organization, can drive innovation and improvement in a team's processes."[321] When they asked thousands of employees the question, "Would you work harder and for longer hours if the job demanded it?", they discovered that respondents' responses tied directly to the extent that they felt leaders provided them with opportunities to take initiative.[322] In addition, Kouzes and Posner learned that people are watching their leaders to see if THEY are people willing to take initiative, and state, "Our data shows that the more people observe their leaders as role models for taking initiative, testing skills and abilities, and learning from experience, the more favorably they feel about their workplace."[323]

Generate Small Wins

While leaders like to contemplate introducing transformational and profound change, most progress occurs in smaller increments, in "small wins." Many years ago, University of Michigan professor emeritus Karl Weick urged leaders to celebrate the achievement of small wins, "concrete, complete, implemented outcomes of moderate importance."[324] Kouzes and Posner agree, and indicate that the scientific community has always understood that major breakthroughs result from the work of hundreds of researchers, as countless contributions finally begin to add up to a solution.[325]

Consolidate Gains and Produce More Change

As discussed earlier in this chapter, one of the ways leaders can help to consolidate gains is through education and outreach. People at all levels of the organization, or in society, need to understand how the change will impact their lives in specific terms. As Doug Smith indicates leaders need to explain how organizational changes will influence the daily lives of staff, and how they will have to move from one set of activities and routines to a new one.[326]

Anchoring New Approaches in the Culture

It is essential that leaders seek out opportunities to embed organizational changes into the culture of the agency. And one of the best ways to accomplish this, according to a study published in the MIT *Sloan Management Review*, is to provide managers in the organization with concrete guidelines, while also allowing them enough flexibility to "seize novel opportunities, mitigate unexpected risks and adapt to local conditions." The authors develop several specific guidelines, which reinforces points made earlier in this chapter. For example, they suggest that leaders LIMIT the number of priorities to a handful. Readers will recall the problems encountered by the Carter administration when President Carter attempted 26 political/legislative changes at one time. In addition, the authors suggest a focus on mid-term objectives, providing concrete guidelines to staff, addressing organizational vulnerabilities and aligning to top team.[327]

Finally, the leader in business or the nonprofit sector must develop influence and persuasion skills, just like US presidents must. Effective persuasion, as argued earlier in the book, is a two-way process, a dialogue instead of a monologue. Persuasive leaders frequently approach people from a posture of curiosity and empathy.[328] According to author Jay Conger (quoting Professor Kathleen Reardon),

> The most persuasive people listen, empathize, negotiate, motivate, and reward skillfully. These people select strategies with the needs and desires of the persuade in mind. They know just as the perfect gift is not something the giver would like for himself but something the recipient would prize, so too the most effective persuasion strategies are the ones responsive to the needs of the persuade.[329]

Notes

1 Drum Major Institute for Public Policy, "Campaign in Poetry, Govern in Prose." www.dmiblog.com/archives/2007/09/campaign_in_poetry_govern_in_p.html

2 Ben W. Heineman and Curtis A. Hessler, *Memorandum for the President: A Strategic Approach to Domestic Affairs in the 1980's.* New York, NY: Random House, 1980, 4.

3 Peter Baker. "As Democracy Push Falters, Bush Feels Like a Dissident," *Washington Post*, August 20, 2007, A1.

4 Ibid.

5 Siegel, *The President as Leader*, 2nd ed., 16.

6 Lou Cannon. *President Reagan: The Role of a Lifetime.* New York, NY: Simon and Schuster, 1991, 182.

7 Siegel, *The President as Leader*, 2nd ed., 17.

8 Robert A. Dahl and Charles Lindblom. *Politics, Economics, and Welfare.* New York, NY: Harper and Row, 1953, 333.

9 Betty Glad. *Jimmy Carter in Search of the Great White House.* New York, NY: Norton and Company, 1980, 400.

10 Heineman and Hessler, *Memorandum for the President*, 92–95, and Roger Davidson and Walter J. Oleszek, *Congress and Its Members*, 11th ed. Washington, DC: Congressional Quarterly Press, 2007.

11 Gregory Paul Domin. *Jimmy Carter, Public Opinion, and the Search for Values.* Macon, GA: Mercer University Press, 2003, 65.

12 Erwin Hargrove. *Jimmy Carter as President: Leadership and the Politics of the Public Good.* Baton Rouge, LA: Louisiana State University Press, 1988, 21–22.

13 Ibid.

14 Siegel, *The President as Leader*, 2nd ed., 52.

15 Ibid.

16 Jimmy Carter, "Reorganization Plan Authority Remarks on Transmitting Proposed Legislation to the Congress," February 4, 1977; and John T. Woolley and Gerhard Peters, *The American Presidency Project.* Santa Barbara, CA: University of California, nytimes.com/1977/02/03/archives/the-text-of-jimmy-carter's-first-presidential-report-to-the-american.html

17 Jimmy Carter, "The President's News Conference of March 9, 1977," in *Public Papers of the President of the United States of America, 1977, Book I January 1 to June 30, 1977.* Washington, DC: Government Printing Office, 1977, 340, 348.

18 Heineman and Hessler, *Memorandum for the President*, Preface, xix.

19 Glad, *Jimmy Carter in Search of the Great White House*, 418–419.

20 Ibid.

21 Eizenstat, *President Carter: The White House Years*, 250.

22 Jimmy Carter, "Report to the American People—Remarks from the White House Library," in *Public Papers of the President of the United States*, 1977, 71.

23 Ibid.

24 Ibid.

25 Hargrove, *Jimmy Carter as President: Leadership and the Politics of the Public Good*, 50–51.

26 Bob Rankin, "Carter's Energy Plan: A Plan of Leadership," *Congressional Quarterly Weekly Report*, April 23, 1977, 727–728.

27 Hargrove, *Jimmy Carter as President: Leadership and the Politics of the Public Good*, 51.

28 O'Neill, Man of the House, 80.

29 Robert Dallek. *Flawed Giant: Lyndon Johnson and His Times 1960–1973.* New York, NY: Oxford University Press, 1998, 114–120.

30 Hargrove, *Jimmy Carter as President: Leadership and the Politics of the Public Good*, 17.

31 Glad, *Jimmy Carter: In Search of the Great White House*, 4.

32 Ibid., 414–415.

33 Ibid.

34 Eizenstat, *President Carter: The White House Years*, 69.

35 Bob Woodward. *Shadow: Five Presidents and the Legacy of Watergate*. New York, NY: Simon and Schuster, 1999.

36 Ibid., 55.

37 Ibid.

38 Ibid.

39 Glad, *Jimmy Carter: In Search of the Great White House*, 423.

40 Ibid.

41 Cyrus Vance, "Carter's Foreign Policy: The Source of the Problem," in Kenneth W. Thompson, ed., *The Carter Presidency: Fourteen Intimate Perspectives of Jimmy Carter*. Lanham, MD: University Press of America, 1990, 135–144.

42 David Gergen. *Eyewitness to Power: The Essence of Leadership from Nixon to Clinton*, 164.

43 Joseph A. Pika, John Anthony Maltese, and Andrew Rudalevige. *The Politics of the Presidency*, 10th ed. Washington, DC: Congressional Quarterly Press, 2021, 666.

44 Lou Cannon. *President Reagan: The Role of a Lifetime*. New York, NY: Simon and Schuster, 1991.

45 Peter Baker and Susan Glasser. *The Man Who Ran Washington: The Life and Times of James A. Baker III*. New York, NY: Doubleday, 2020.

46 Gergen, *Eyewitness to Power*, 165.

47 Richard Reeves. *President Reagan: The Triumph of Imagination*. New York, NY: Simon and Schuster, 2005, 27.

48 Gergen, *Eyewitness to Power*, 16.

49 Ibid.

50 Ibid.

51 Cannon, *President Reagan: The Role of a Lifetime*, 113.

52 Ibid., 114.

53 Ibid., 118.

54 Ibid.

55 Richard Reeves. *President Reagan: The Triumph of Imagination*. New York, NY: Simon and Schuster, 2005, 22.

56 Siegel, *The President as Leader*, 2nd ed., 81.

57 Laurence I. Barrett. *Gambling with History: Reagan in the White House*. New York, NY: Penguin Books, 146.

58 Jay Conger. "The Necessary Art of Persuasion." *Harvard Business Review*. May/June 1998, vol. 76, Issue 3, 86.

59 Baker and Glasser, *The Man Who Ran Washington*, 170.

60 Office of Tax Analysis, United States Department of the Treasury, *Revenue Effects of Major Tax Bills*, Working Paper 81, 12, http://www.ustreas.gov/offices/tax-policy/library/ota81.pdf, accessed November 10, 2009.

61 Siegel, *The President as Leader*, 2nd ed., 83.

62 Ibid.

63 Ibid., 85.

64 Michael Beschloss. *American Heritage Illustrated History of the Presidents*. New York, NY: Crown Publishers, 2000, 494.

65 James P. Pfiffner, "Establishing the Bush Presidency." *Public Administration Review*, January/February 1990, 6.

66 Tom Wicker. *George Herbert Walker Bush*. New York, NY: Penguin Books, 2004, 105.

67 Kerry Mullins and Aaron Wildavsky, "The Procedural Presidency of George Bush." *Political Science Quarterly*, 107, No. 1, Spring, 1992, 41.

68 Mervin, *George Bush and the Guardianship Presidency*, 15.
69 Barolleaux and Rozell, *Power and Prudence: The Presidency of George H.W. Bush*, 137.
70 Bush, "Inaugural Address."
71 Pfiffner, "Establishing the Bush Presidency," 70.
72 Max Stier. "A Lesson for Obama on Reaching Out to the Federal Workforce." *The Washington Post*, December 26, 2008.
73 Siegel, *The President as Leader*, 2nd ed., 119–120.
74 Ibid., 120.
75 Duane Windsor. "The 1990 Deficit Reduction Deal," in Richard Himelfarb and Rosana Peterson, eds. *Principle Over Politics? The Domestic Policy of the George H.W. Bush Presidency.* Westford, CT: Greenwood Publishers, 166.
76 George Bush. "Statement at Signing Ceremony for the 19909 Omnibus Budget and Reconciliation Act." *Congressional Almanac*, 1990. Washington, DC: Congressional Quarterly, 1991, 166.
77 Mervin, *George Bush and the Guardianship Presidency*, 156.
78 James Cicconi. "Discussant: James W. Cicconi." In Himelfarb and Perotti, *Principle Over Politics?*, 50.
79 Siegel, *The President as Leader*, 2nd ed., 112.
80 Baker and Glasser, *The Man Who Ran Washington*, 362.
81 Ibid., 366–390.
82 Ibid., 389.
83 Fred I. Greenstein. *The Presidential Difference: Leadership Style from FDR to George Bush.* Princeton, NJ: Princeton University Press, 2004, 160.
84 Cheney, "The Bush Presidency," 9.
85 Baker and Glasser, *The Man Who Ran Washington,* 395.
86 Michael Duffy and Dan Goodgame. *Marching in Place: The Status Quo Presidency of George Bush.* New York, NY: Simon and Schuster, 1992, 142.
87 Ibid.
88 Cheney, "President George Bush," 10.
89 Baker and Glasser, *The Man Who Ran Washington*, 412.
90 Duffy and Goodgame, *Marching in Place*, 153.
91 Mecham, *Destiny and Power*, 437.
92 Ibid., 461.
93 Barilleaux and Rozell, *Power and Prudence*, 130.
94 Siegel, *The President as Leader*, 2nd ed., 125.
95 Bill Clinton. *My Life.* New York, NY: Alfred A. Knopf, 2004, 63.
96 Ibid., 444.
97 Siegel, *The President as Leader*, 2nd ed., 125.
98 Gergen, *Eyewitness to Power*, 256.
99 Ibid.
100 Ibid., 257.
101 Ibid., 259.
102 Siegel, *The President as Leader*, 2nd ed., 160.
103 Gergen, *Eyewitness to Power*, 262.
104 Clinton, *My Life*, 451–452.
105 Siegel, *The President as Leader*, 2nd ed., 161.
106 Gergen, *Eyewitness to Power*, 265.
107 Siegel, *The President as Leader*, 2nd ed., 162.
108 Stephanopoulos, *All Too Human*, 176.
109 Martin Walker. *The President We Deserve.* New York, NY: Crown, 1996, 172.
110 Clinton, *My Life*, 496.
111 Ibid.

112 Gergen, *Eyewitness to Power*, 279.
113 Clinton, *My Life*, 535.
114 Stephanopoulos, *All Too Human*, 177.
115 Gergen, *Eyewitness to Power*, 279.
116 Ibid.
117 Ibid., 280.
118 Ibid.
119 Ibid., 224, and Senate.gov/legislative/LIS/roll-call_votes/vote_103_1_0083.htm. Congress=103 $sessoin&1vote.
120 Dennis Ross. *The Missing Peace: The Inside Story of the Fight for Middle East Peace.* New York, NY: Farrar, Strauss, and Giroux, 2004, 120–121.
121 Ibid., 122.
122 Ibid.
123 Gergen, *Eyewitness to Power*, 274.
124 Harris, *The Survivor*, 114.
125 Jacob S. Hacker. *The Road to Nowhere: The Genesis of President Clinton's Plan for Health Security.* Princeton, NJ: Princeton University Press, 1997, 10.
126 Ibid., 113.
127 Ibid.
128 Ibid.
129 Ibid.
130 Ibid., 118.
131 Harris, *The Survivor*, 242.
132 Ibid.
133 Ibid.
134 Gergen, *Eyewitness to Power*, 303.
135 Ibid.
136 Ibid., 304–306.
137 Ibid., 307.
138 Siegel, *The President as Leader*, 168.
139 Julian E. Zelizer. *Burning Drown the House: Newt Gingrich, the Fall of a Speaker, and the Rise of the New Republican Party.* New York, NY: Penguin Press, 2020, 4–5.
140 Harris, *The Survivor*, 164.
141 Clinton, *My Life*, 720.
142 Harris, *The Survivor*, 216.
143 Siegel, *The President as Leader*, 2nd ed., 170.
144 Ibid., 176.
145 Correspondents of the New York Times. *36 Days: The Complete Chronicle of the 2000 Presidential Election Crisis.* New York, NY: Henry Holt, 2001.
146 Baker and Glasser, *The Man Who Ran Washington*, 529–542.
147 Bush v. Palm Beach County Canvassing Board, et al., 531 US 70, 2000. Ordering a statewide recount of 14,000 "under vote" ballots that had not been acknowledged.
148 Correspondents of the NY Times, *36 Days*.
149 *Bush v. Gore,* 531 US 98 (2000).
150 John Paul Stevens, dissenting in *Bush v. Gore.*
151 James E. Campbell. "The 2000 Presidential Election of George W. Bus: The Difficult Birth of a Presidency," in John Kraus, Kevin J. McMahon, and David M. Rankin, eds., *Transformed by Crisis: The Presidency of George W. Bush and American Politics.* New York, NY: Palgrave MacMillan, 2004, 9.
152 John P. Burke, "The Bush Transition," in Gary L. Gregg and Mark J. Rozell, eds., *Considering the Bush Presidency.* New York, NY: Oxford University Press, 2003, 22.

153 Shirley Anne Warshaw. *The Co-Presidency of Bush and Cheney*. Stanford, CA: Stanford University Press, 2009, 1.
154 Kathryn Dunn Tenpas and Stephen Hess. "Organizing the Bush Presidency," in Gregg and Rozell, *Considering the Bush Presidency*, 39.
155 Ibid., 38.
156 Barton Gellman. *Angler: The Cheney Vice Presidency*. New York, NY: Penguin Press, 2008, 28.
157 Alexis S. Mendinger. "Stepping Into Power." *National Journal*, 4, 2001, 246.
158 Warshaw, *The Co-Presidency of Bush and Cheney*, 50.
159 Ibid., 5.
160 Gellman, Angler, 55.
161 James P. Pfiffner. "The First MBA President: George Bush as a Public Administrator." Public Administration Review, January/February 2007, 4.
162 Ibid.
163 Robert Draper, *Dead Certain: The Presidency of George W. Bush*. New York, NY: The Free Press, 2007, 116.
164 Dana Milbank. "With Fanfare Bush Signs Education Bill: President, Lawmakers Hit 3 States in 12 Hours to Tout Biggest School Change Since 65." *The Washington Post*, January 9, 2002.
165 Gary L. Gregg, "George W. Bush and the Symbolic Presidency," in Greg and Rozell, *Considering the Bush Presidency*, 88.
166 Bill Sammon. *Fighting Back: The War on Terrorism from Inside the Bush White House*. Washington, DC: Regency Publishing, 2002, 113.
167 Ibid.
168 Greg, "George W. Bush and the Symbolic Presidency," 97.
169 Siegel, *The President as Leader*, 2nd ed., 216.
170 Greg, "George W. Bush and the Symbolic Presidency," 98.
171 Draper, *Dead Certain*, 140.
172 Greg, "George W. Bush and the Symbolic Presidency," 98.
173 George W. Bush. "Address before a Joint Session of the Congress of the United States-Response to the Terrorist Attacks of September 11, 2001," in *Public Papers of the Presidents Of the United States*, George Bush, 2001, Book II, July 1–December 31, 2001. Washington, DC: US Government Printing Office, 2006, 1141.
174 Siegel, *The President as Leader*, 2nd ed., 216.
175 Greg, "George W. Bush and the Symbolic Presidency," 101.
176 George W. Bush, *Decision Points*, 200–201.
177 Draper, *Dead Certain*, 166.
178 THOMAS. Legislative Database. The Library of Congress. https://Thomas.loc.gov.egi-bin/bk
179 Draper, *Dead Certain*, 164.
180 Louis Fisher, "The Way We Go to War," in Gregg and Rozell, Considering the Bush Presidency, 109.
181 Scott McClellan. *What Happened? Inside the Bush White House and Washington's Culture of Deception*. New York, NY: Public Affairs, 2008, 112.
182 Fisher, "The Way We Go to War," 113.
183 Ibid., 114.
184 Thomas Ricks. *Fiasco: The American Military Adventure in Iraq*. New York, NY: Penguin, 2007, 40.
185 Ibid.
186 Fisher, "The Way We Go to War," 117.
187 Ibid.
188 Draper, *Dead Certain*, 184.
189 Siegel, *The President as Leader*, 2nd ed., 220.

190 Ricks, *Fiasco*, 72.
191 The Iraq Study Group. https://www.usip.org/programs/iraq-study-group
192 Siegel, *The President as Leader*, 2nd ed., 240.
193 Pika, Maltese and Rudalevige, *The Politics of the Presidency*, 10th ed., 667.
194 Andrew Rudalevige and Bert Rockman, "Introduction: A Counterfactual Presi-
     dent," in Andrew Rudalevige, Bert Rockman, and Colin Campbell, *The Obama
     Presidency: Appraisals and Prospects.* Washington, DC: Congressional Quarterly
     Press, 2013, 3.
195 Jonathan Alter, *The Promise: President Obama, Year One.* New York, NY: Simon
     and Schuster, 2010, 43.
196 Ibid., 44.
197 *Blueprint for Change.* www.barackobama.com
198 Barack Obama. "Change We Can Believe In: Barack Obama's Plan to Renew
     America's Promise." New York, NY: Three Rivers Press, 2008.
199 Joel D. Aberbach, "'Change We Can Believe In' Meets Reality," in Rockman,
     Rudalevige, and Campbell, eds. *The Obama Presidency*, 16.
200 Siegel, *The President as Leader*, 2nd ed., 280.
201 Andrew Rudalevige, "Rivals or a Team: Staffing and Issue Management in the
     Obama Administration," in Rickman, Rudalevige and Campbell, *The Obama
     Presidency*, 181–182.
202 Ibid., 183.
203 Doris Kearns Goodwin. *Team of Rivals: The Political Genius of Abraham Lincoln.*
     New York, NY: Simon and Schuster, 2005.
204 Siegel, *The President as Leader*, 2nd ed., 252.
205 Michael Grunwald, *The New New Deal: The Hidden Story of Change in the Obama
     Era.* New York, NY: Simon and Schuster, 2012, 93.
206 Ibid.
207 Ibid., 130.
208 Siegel, *The President as Leader*, 2nd ed., 282.
209 Grunwald, *The New New Deal*, 149.
210 Ibid.
211 Ibid., 210.
212 Statement on Signing the American Recovery and Reconstruction Act of 2009,
     February 17, 2009. *Public Papers of the Presidents of the United States* Barack Obama
     2009, Book I, January 20–June 30, 2009, 109.
213 Grunwald, *The New New Deal*, 244.
214 Ibid., 234.
215 Alter, *The Promise*, 160.
216 Gary Jacobsen. "Legislative Success and Political Failure: The Public's Reaction
     to the Early Obama Presidency." *Presidential Studies Quarterly*, 41, No. 2 (June
     2011), 226.
217 Ibid.
218 The Staff of The Washington Post. *Landmark: The Inside Story of America's Health
     Care Law—The Affordable Care Act—and What It Means for Us All.* New York, NY:
     Public Affairs, 2010, 7.
219 Siegel, *The President as Leader*, 2nd ed., 284.
220 Staff of the Washington Post, *Landmark*, 16.
221 Alter, *The Promise*, 258.
222 Ibid.
223 Staff of the Washington Post, *Landmark*, 16.
224 Ibid.
225 Ibid., 17.
226 Ibid., 19.

227 Ibid., 22.
228 Alter, *The Promise*, 254.
229 Staff of the Washington Post, *Landmark*, 40.
230 Ibid., 41.
231 Ibid., 47.
232 Ibid., 27.
233 Ibid., 32.
234 Ibid., 39.
235 Bert A. Rockman, Eric Wattenberg, and Colin Campbell, "Presidential Style in the Obama Presidency," in Rockman, Rudalevige and Campbell, eds. *The Obama Presidency*, 334.
236 Ibid.
237 Ibid.
238 Ibid.
239 According to journalist Jonathan Alter, the Tea Party emerged when a reporter named Rick Santelli, went on a tirade against Obama on the floor of the Chicago Board of Trade. He opposed healthcare reform and Obama's plan to help homeowners, and exclaimed, "How many of you want to pay for your neighbor's mortgage when he has an extra bathroom and can't pay his bills." He promised a "tea party" for the summer and then disappeared from the scene. A young conservative teacher in Washington State named Keli Calinder was credited as the first Tea Party organizer. Alter, *The Promise*, 262–262.
240 Alter, *The Promise*, 262.
241 Peter Baker, "Education of a President." *New York Times Magazine*, October 12, 2010.
242 Jacobsen, "Legislative Success and Political Failure," 220.
243 Ibid.
244 Chollet, *The Long Game*, 198–200.
245 nytimes.com/elections/2012/results/Presidents/exitpolls/pdf
246 Siegel, *The President as Leader*, 2nd ed., 305.
247 The distinction between "transformational" and "transactional" leadership was developed by Professor James MacGregor Burns in his classic book, *Leadership*. New York, NY: Harper and Row, 1978, 4.
248 Andrew W. Ceasar, Andrew E. Busch, and John J. Pitney, *Defying the Odds: The 2016 Election and American Politics*. New York, NY: Rowman and Littlefield, 2017, Preface, vii.
249 Ibid.
250 Philip Rucker and Carol Leonnig, *A Very Stable Genius: Donald J. Trump's Testing of America*. New York, NY: Penguin Press, 2020, 12.
251 Michael Nelson. *Trump: The First Two Years*. Charlottesville, VA: The University of Virginia Press, 2018, 34.
252 Ibid., 36.
253 Ibid.
254 Kathryn Dunn Tenpas. "Tracking Turnover in the Trump Administration." *Brookings Institution*, August 2019. URL: www.brookings.edu/research/tracking-turnover-in-the-trumpadministration
255 Nelson, *Trump: The First Two Years*, 37.
256 Ibid., 40.
257 Ibid., 42.
258 Ibid., 7.
259 Ibid., 79.
260 Ibid., 85.
261 Ibid., 85.

262 Ibid., 85.

263 Ibid., 86.

264 Ibid.

265 Ibid., 85.

266 Ibid., 86–87, and Thomas Kaplan, Jennifer Steinhauser, and Robert Pear. "Trump in Zigzag, Calls House Republican Bill 'Mean.'" *New York Times*, June 13, 2017.

267 Nelson, Trump, *The First Two Years*, 84.

268 Ibid., 91.

269 Ibid.

270 Ibid.

271 Ibid.

272 Reconciliation is a parliamentary process of the US Congress that expedites the passage of budgetary legislation. The Senate filibuster effectively requires a 60-vote super-majority for the passage of most legislation in the Senate, but reconciliation provides a process to prevent a filibuster and allows passage of a bill by a simple majority of the Senate. Reconciliation bills can be passed on spending, revenue and the federal debt, and the Senate is allowed to pass one bill per year that way affecting each of the enumerated topic area.

273 Nelson, *Trump: The First Two Years*, 91.

274 Ibid.

275 Ibid.

276 nbcnews.com/politics-news/trump-signs-tax-cut-bill-legislativewon-N832141

277 Ibid., 94.

278 Ibid., 95.

279 Brookings.edu/wp-content/uploads/2018/06/es-2018608-tcja-summary-paper-Final.pdf

280 Naomi Jacobs. "Trump Signs Tax Bill into Law," *The Hill*, January 22, 2017.

281 Brookings.edu/wp-content/uploads/2018/06/es-2018608-tcja-summary-paper-Final.pdf

282 politico.com/election-results/2018/house, and Financial Times, "US Midterm Elections 2018 Results," Ig.Ft.com/us-midterm-elections/

283 Rosalind S. Helderman and Matt Zapotosky of the *Washington Post*, "Introduction: A President, a Prosecutor, and the Protection of American Democracy," in The Washington Post, *The Mueller Report*. New York, NY: Simon and Schuster, 2019, 19.

284 Ibid.

285 Ibid., 9–10.

286 Ibid.

287 Ibid., 13.

288 Ibid.

289 The Washington Post, *The Mueller Report*, 59.

290 Ibid., 59.

291 Ibid., 264.

292 Helderman and Zapotosky, "Introduction." 10.

293 Nicholas Fandos and Michael D. Sher. "Trump Impeached for Abuse of Power and Obstruction of Congress." *New York Times*, December 18, 2019, updated February 10, 2021.

294 Ibid.

295 Trump's Ukraine Phone Call, annotated, cnn.com/interactive/2019/09/politics/trump-ukraine-transcript-annotated/

296 Lisa Mascaro, Mary Clare Jalonick, and Erick Teicher. "Not Guilty: Senate Acquits Trump of Impeachment Charges," APNews.com/articles/Donald-trupm-op-top-news-ut-state-uni-acquitalls-93c85dcFOe6b21839165e77.

297 US State Department. "The Abraham Accords," at https://state.gov/the-abraham-accords

298 From House Resolution 24. In the Senate of the United States, January 25, 2021. Resolution Impeaching Donald John Trump for High Crimes and Misdemeanors. Congress.gov/bill/117tth Congress/house-resolution/24/text.

299 Weiyi Cai, Annie Daniel, Jon Huang, Jasmine C. Lee, and Alicia Parlapiano. "Trump's Second Impeachment: How the Senate Voted." *The New York Times*, February 13, 2021.

300 NBC News. "US Presidential Election Results 2020: Biden Wins," nbcnews. com/politics/2020/-elections/president-results, and Jonathan Martion and Alexander Burns, "Biden Beats Trump," *The New York Times*, November 8, 2020, A1.

301 CNN News. "Joe Biden Wins Election to be 46th US President." cnn. com/2020/11/07/politics/joe-biden-wins-us-presdeint-election/hielix.html

302 "House Results." CNN News. Cnn.com/election/2020/results/house

303 "Senate Results." CNN News. Cnn.com/election/2020/results/senate

304 Ashley Parker, "'Results, not a revolution,' was Biden's promise. Covid changed everything," *The Washington Post*, "The First Hundred Days," April 28, 2021, AA3.

305 Politifact, The Poynter Institute, "Evaluating Joe Biden's First 100 Days in Office." Politifact.com/article/2021/apo/27evaluating-joe-biden's-first 100-days0off/

306 Harry Stevens and Naema Ahmed, "Vaccine Rollout Surpasses Early Pledge." *The Washington Post*, "The First 100 Days," April 28, 2021, AA5.

307 Grace Segers. "Biden Signs $1.9 Trillion American Rescue Plan into Law." CBS News, March 12, 2021. Cbsnews.com/bews/biden-signs-covid-releif-bill-amwerican-rescu-plan-into-law.

308 Ibid.

309 National Association of Counties. American Rescue Plan Act Funding Breakdown. Naco.org/resources/Feature/American-rescue-plan-act-funding breakdown.

310 Emily Cochrane. "Congress Clears $1.9 Trillion Aid Bill, Sending it to Biden." *The New York Times*, March 10, 2021. A1.

311 govtrak.us/congress/votes/117-2021/h72

312 James M. Kouzes and Barry Z. Posner, *The Leadership Challenge: How to Make Extraordinary Things Happen in Organizations*, 6th ed. New York, NY: John Wiley and Sons, 2017.

313 Ibid., 147.

314 Liz Halloran. "Michele Obama, 'Being President Reveals Who You Are,'" *It's All About Politics*. Political News from Political News NPR, September 5, 2012. https://www.npr.org/sections/itsallpolitics/2012/09/04/160581747/michelle-obama-being-president-reveals-who-you-are, 314.

315 Kouzes and Posner, *The Leadership Challenge*, 6th ed., 14.

316 Kouzes and Posner, *The Leadership Challenge*, 6th ed., 149.

317 For a discussion of "adaptive leadership," See Ronald A. Heifitz and Marty Linksy. *Leadership on the Line, with a New Preface: Staying Alive Through the Dangers of Change.* Cambridge, MA: Harvard Business Press, 2017, 318.

318 Kouzes and Posner, *The Leadership Challenge*, 6th ed., 152.

319 Howard Schultz, *Pour Your Heart into It: How Starbucks Built a Company One Cup at a Time.* New York, NY: Hachette Books, 1999, 205–210.

320 John Kotter. Leading Change. Cambridge MA: Harvard Business Review Press, 2012, 37–168.

321 Kouzes and Posner, *The Leadership Challenge*, 6th ed., 152.

322 Ibid., 152.

323 Ibid., 154.

324 Karl E. Wieck. "Small Wins: Redefining the Scale of Social Problems." *American Psychologist*, 39, No. 1, 1984, 43.

325 Kouzes and Posner, *The Leadership Challenge*, 6th ed., 173.
326 Douglas K. Smith. *Taking Charge of Change: Ten Principles for Managing People and Performance*. New York, NY: Basic Books, 1995, 9–10.
327 Donald Sull, Stefano Turconi, Charles Sull, and Jaems Yoder. "Turning Strategy into Results," MIT *Sloan Management Review*, vol. 59, Issue 3, Spring, 2018, 1–12.
328 Douglas Stone, Bruce Patton, and Sheila Heen. *Difficult Conversations: How to Discuss What Matters Most*. New York, NY: Penguin Books, 2010.
329 Jay A. Conger. *Winning 'Em Over: A New Model for Management in the Age of Persuasion*. New York, NY: Simon and Schuster, 1998, 40.

4

STRUCTURE, MANAGEMENT

Importance to Presidents and All Other Leaders

Structure refers to the management acumen and organizational skill a president must have to manage the vast federal executive branch of government of over 3 million people.

Questions a president might ask under this component include:

- How will I organize the White House?
- What management structure will I utilize?
- Will I have a chief of staff?
- Will I have an open or closed operation?
- Will I favor micro or macromanagement of White House staff?
- How will I assure the alignment of the management with my policy agenda?

There is nothing in the constitution that mandates an organizational structure for the presidency. Presidents have wide latitude in the kind of management design they choose, and, as of this writing, the 46 men who have served in the office have certainly taken full advantage of this flexibility. For example, presidents have taken dramatically different approaches to the chief-of-staff position, including whether to include one in their White House operation.[1]

To amplify, slightly, on the size and scope of the executive branch of government, and the president's awesome responsibility as its chief executive officer, we should consider the agencies that compose President Joseph Biden's (the 46th and most recent president) cabinet: Vice President Kamala Harris; the Secretaries of Agriculture, Commerce, Defense, Education, Energy, Health and Human Services, Homeland Security, Housing and Urban Development, Interior, Justice, Labor, State, Transportation, Treasury, Veterans Affairs; the White House Chief of Staff, the US Ambassador to the United Nations, the

DOI: 10.4324/9781003285229-4

Director of National Intelligence, the US Trade Representative; and the heads of the Environmental Protection Agency, the Office of Management and Budget, the Office of Science and Technology, and the Small Business Administration.[2]

How have presidents managed this huge bureaucracy and kept it aligned with his vision and attuned to his agenda? How have they dealt with the tension that can exist between the political appointees, whom the president appoints, and the much larger group of permanent civil servants, who stay in place after the president's term ends?

Jimmy Carter

Having campaigned as an "outsider," President Carter decided to challenge some of his predecessors' approaches to politics and management. For instance, during the transition, Carter decided to structure his White House staff without a chief of staff to set priorities among his ambitious set on initiatives. Carter would act as his own chief of staff.[3] In addition, according to Stuart Eizenstat, who served as President Carter's Domestic Policy Adviser, Carter sought to implement a "cabinet-style" government, which would empower each cabinet officer to choose the department's own top officials and initiate its own legislative agenda. The loyalties of subcabinet officials, then, would be to the cabinet secretary who appointed them.[4]

Carter specifically sought to avoid a Nixon-style administration of highly centralized control by the president's chief of staff, who, in the case of Nixon was H. R. Haldeman.[5] Instead, Carter sought to "denude" the White House staff and elevate the cabinet, while serving as his own chief of staff.[6] Haldeman had, indeed, amassed too much power relative to Nixon's cabinet, leading to disastrous results. Accordingly, when President Ford took office (after Nixon's resignation), he initially chose a "spokes of the wheel" White House structure, which had also been used by President Kennedy. In this model of management, four or five senior presidential aides—the bicycle spokes—would report directly to the president at the hub. But for Ford the spokes of the wheel White House management led to a serious lack of coordination, and he quickly abandoned it on favor of a chief of staff model. When Ford lost his bid for a second term to Carter, Ford's chief of staff, Dick Cheney, was given a going-away present at a staff party—a mounted bicycle wheel with all the spokes except one busted, bent, and twisted. Cheney, in turn, left the gift for the Carter folks with a note of warning about the "spokes of the Wheel."[7]

Carter eventually realized that he needed a chief of staff, and on several occasions offered the job to one of his closest aides, Hamilton Jordan. Ham finally agreed to assume the chief of staff position, but by then things had truly fallen apart in the Carter administration. "Frankly," said Stuart Eizenstat, "the president would have been far better off with a chief of staff from the beginning."[8]

Carter assembled a highly credentialed and skilled cabinet, including his Secretary of State, Cyrus Vance, who had served in several positions in the Departments of State and Defense in the Kennedy and Johnsons administrations; Secretary of Treasury W. Michael Blumenthal, a Ph.D. in economics, was a key trade negotiator in the Kennedy administration, and had led a major corporation; Defense Secretary Harold Brown had served at the Pentagon and had been the director of Livermore National Laboratory and President of the California Institute of Technology; Secretary of Health, Education and Welfare, Joseph Califano, had served as domestic policy adviser to President Lyndon B. Johnson; and the Secretaries of Labor and Commerce, Roy Marshall and Juanita Kreps, were well-respected economists. The Secretary of Housing and Urban Development, Patricia Harris, was a well-known Washington lawyer, urban activist, and the first African American woman ever named to the cabinet.[9] "But," according to Eizenstat, "precisely because his cabinet was composed of strong individuals, with their own agendas, this led to a dissonance and lack of clear message and priorities, when combined with Carter's refusal to allow strong White House Staff intervention."[10]

As I have written elsewhere, "Jimmy Carter was a detail-oriented person who prided himself on his ability to master the intricacies of public policy."[11] Political scientist Erwin Hargrove reached a similar conclusion, saying, "He wished to understand thoroughly the issues for which he assumed primary responsibility and he characterized his cognitive processes as those of an engineer."[12]

Carter's Vic President, former US Senator Walter Mondale (D, MN) saw the engineer in Carter. Mondale expressed the view that the president believed once policy

> was constructed and displayed it would carry its own weight and be understood, "that intelligent people would add up the numbers—it wasn't oratory. Oh yea, you and Humphrey like to speak. I don't do that."[13]

The engineer's habit of mind led Jimmy Carter to read every bill that came before the Georgia legislature when he was governor, and to also spend many nights reading draft bills.[14]

According to Stuart Eizenstat:

> Carter announced to the incoming cabinet that he would be available to them "at all times" and that he would be in his office by 6:00 am every morning; that he liked to read and would welcome receiving their memos. Blumenthal remembered thinking, I wonder whether he realizes what he means? He's going to be inundated. But he seems sincere.[15]

While Carter's engineering mindset resulted on the application of microman-agement of some details of White House operations (like Carter scheduling the White House tennis courts), it did not extend to the coordination of his cabinet agencies or to the disciplined vetting of presidential staff, most promi-nently Carter's Director of the Office of Management and Budget, Bert Lance. As we have seen earlier in this book, presidents can remain overly loyal to their friends, even when that loyalty comes at a high political price. Despite being easily confirmed as OMB Director by the US Senate, Lance's history of irregular banking practices came to the surface, and they presented a true embarrassment to an administration whose "raison d'etre" was to restore hon-esty and integrity to Washington. Carter and Lance had a friendship dating back to their days in Georgia, and the president was highly reluctant to ask Lance to leave the administration, despite entreaties to do so from several close staff members. Lance finally resigned, and by the time President Carter accepted the resignation, his popularity, as measured by the Gallup Poll, had fallen by 20 percent![16]

There were other signs that the Carter administration was not united, and in some ways, was sending mixed signals about its policy intentions. Andrew Young, the US Ambassador to the United Nations, traveled around the coun-try making nondiplomatic statements. For example, in May 1997, he told reporters on a trip to London that "the old colonial mentality is still strong in Britain," and that "The Russians and Swedes are racists."[17] Yong finally went too far when he held an unauthorized meeting with Palestinian Liberation Organization (PLO) representative Zuhdi Labib Terzi. He was forced to resign shortly afterwards.[18]

By May 1979, a CBS/*New York Times* poll found that only 30 percent of Americans approved of Carter's presidency, a level reached by no other pres-ident, including Richard Nixon during Watergate.[19] The president contem-plated the actions he might take to ameliorate the situation, and at this time he conceded to the idea of naming a chief of staff and revealed that his choice for the job would be Hamilton Jordan.[20] In the meantime, Carter began to pay serious attention to a series of memos from his pollster, Patrick Caddell, that described fundamental problems with the country requiring a dose of "trans-formational" leadership from Carter. Caddell argued that the president had more serious problems than gas lines and high inflation: that there was a loss of confidence among the American public about the future of their own lives, and the life of the country, magnified by Carter losing touch with the mes-sages that led to his election.[21] Carter's close advisers, especially Vice President Mondale, cautioned the president against embracing the Caddell thesis too seriously, and instead focus on taming inflation and dealing with the gas lines. But Caddell's messaging struck a chord with Carter, and in consultation with the First Lady, he decided to convene a presidential retreat at Camp David in July 1979, and invite mayors, governors, civil rights, and business leaders, and seasoned Washington insiders to glean their views on his presidency and on solutions to domestic problems.

According to Stuart Eizenstat, "I doubt any other American president has subjected himself to such intense scrutiny, soul-searching, and criticism as Carter did during that week—and for good reason."[22]

Carter learned a great deal during these conversations, about how the "Georgia Mafia" was inadequate in carrying out the awesome duties of White House staff, about how divided Carter's cabinet appeared to be, and about how Ham Jordan was NOT the right person for the chief of staff position. Eizenstat notes that one "particularly impressive" participant was the 32-year-old Governor of Arkansas, Bill Clinton, who proposed the idea that a percentage of public service jobs be tied to energy conservation. While some of the advice of other participants did not truly influence Carter, Clinton's did, especially when he told the president, "Don't just preach sacrifice but liberation—that it is an exciting time to be alive. Say your program will unleash a burst of energy."[23]

Carter built his July 15, 1979, Oval Office speech to the Nation, "A Crisis of Confidence" around many of the ideas and insights he had heard at Camp David. He discussed the rise of pessimism in the country, agreeing with Caddell's findings, urged that Americans renew their faith in each other, and in "our ability to govern ourselves," and to restore American values. He then discussed the energy problem and attacked OPEC as the enemy, and asked the help of all Americans to develop solid energy and social programs for the future.[24] Carter was not known for his great oratory, but this one flawlessly delivered from his desk in the Oval Office hit a home run. In one night, Carter's approval rating jumped 17 points as measured by the Gallup poll.[25]

And then, with 18 months left in his presidency, Carter did something remarkable: he asked for the resignations of his entire cabinet, and allowed some of them—Califano, Blumenthal, and Schlesinger—to be permanent. The rest were hired back. He also announced the appointment of Hamilton Jordan as chief of staff. And he did not make any other changes to the White House staff, contravening a good deal of advice he had been given at Camp David.[26]

According to Eizenstat, "The wrong heads rolled."[27]

Looking back on his experiences in the Carter White House, Hamilton Jordan shared the following reflections:[28]

> We also overreacted to some of the excesses of the past. As a result of the Nixon experience, it became a campaign statement that we would not have a powerful chief of staff in the White House. "I'm going to be the President, and I'm going to make decisions and run things. We never sat down and talked about whether Jimmy Carter should make that statement or not. That was a political reaction to the excesses of the Nixon

administration. It was also the kind of hands-on president he thought he should be."

TAKEAWAYS FOR ALL LEADERS

- A busy executive with an elaborate agenda will really benefit from the assistance of a chief of staff, or a similar position, to help control the flow of people and information.
- Another function a chief of staff can play is to sustain alignment of the agencies, departments, or divisional offices with the chief executive's key programs and goals.
- A chief executive, especially the president of the United States, should focus on strategic matters and not get drawn into narrow and often tactical issues.

Ronald Reagan

In terms of managing the White House and the executive branch of government, President Reagan relied on the approach he had successfully used as Governor of California: "macro-management." As explained Ed Rollins, an aide who worked for Reagan in California and DC, Reagan focused only on the big picture, the large objectives and general direction of his administration, and left the details of implementation to others. In an interview with his biographer, Lou Cannon, Reagan said, "You get the people that you believe in and can do things that need doing. The decisions about policy are mine, and I make them."[29]

According to Lou Cannon, this "macro" managerial approach worked quite well in Reagan's first term, because the president's 1980 campaign had clearly laid out an agenda of lowering taxes, cutting social welfare spending, and increasing defense spending. Because Reagan's team was closely aligned around executing on these goals, the president could be a "9-to-5" chief executive.[30] Reagan explained his management philosophy to *Fortune* Magazine by saying that "A president should surround yourself with the best people you can find, delegate authority, and don't interfere as long as the policy you've decided is being carried out."[31]

Reagan chose a "cabinet council" model to oversee his cabinet. This approach had been used by Governor Reagan's assistant, Ed Meese, in California. Meese had assigned a small "super cabinet" at the top of the hierarchy, presiding over policy to be carried out by individual departments. As envisioned for the federal government, the "top tone" would consist of the three or four most senior cabinet officers—perhaps state, defense, treasury, and justice—and a similar number of White House aides. This group would be aboard of directors, over which President Reagan would preside as chair.[32]

Reagan's chief of staff, James A. Baker, was skeptical of the idea, insisting that Meese's proposed cabinet structure would result in administrative gridlock. He was equally dubious about the secretaries of state and defense spending long hours deliberating issues pertinent to Interior, Labor, or Education. Instead, Baker developed a model of "modified cabinet councils," or subcommittees of the cabinet, where heads of departments with related concerns would refine options for President Reagan. Similar to the working of the National Security Council (NSC), each body would comb information and tease out proposals for the president, who would be spared the details of analysis.[33]

In the end, the White House established six cabinet councils:[34]

- Economic Affairs—chaired by the treasury secretary
- Natural Resources and the Environment—chaired by the commerce secretary
- Human Resources—chaired by the secretary of health and human services
- Food and Agriculture—chaired by the secretary of agriculture
- Legal Policy—chaired by the attorney general
- Management and Administration—chaired by Ed Meese (White House Counsel)

More important than the management structure that the Reagan team developed, however, was the focus and alignment of the White House staff and cabinet secretaries around the twin Reagan goals of restoring economic prosperity and military strength to the Unites States. Unlike the Carter cabinet, the Reagan cabinet worked mostly in unity, in spite of temporary setbacks and lively disagreements. They were committed to helping Reagan implement his vision.[35]

In fact, Reagan's cabinet members and political lieutenants were frequently more loyal to "Reaganism" and its policy aspirations than they were to the specific missions of the agencies they headed. As would be true later, in the Trump Administration, some of Reagan's cabinet secretaries were historically or ideologically opposed to the goals of the agencies they now managed. A glaring example from Reagan's cabinet was his Interior Secretary, who was an "ardent promoter of private development of public lands" and an opponent of government regulations.[36]

In his second term, Reagan showed the limitations of "Macro" management, however, when he easily accepted a switch in positions between James A. Baker, his first-term chief of staff, and Donald Regan, his first-term Secretary of the Treasury. For the men involved, the switch made sense. Baker was fatigued from the overwhelming responsibilities of the chief of staff position, and also wanted more exposure to global affairs, which would happen at Treasury. Regan, a former corporate CEO, simply wanted to be closer to the presidency and to the power center of the government. But the switch did not really make sense for President Reagan, as Lou Cannon explained:

> No presidency has ever undergone such a thorough transformation in management style as Regan's did under his new chief of staff Baker's and Reagan's styles were totally contrasting. Where Baker was collegial, Reagan was directive. Where Baker was cautious, Reagan was bold. Baker preferred to operate behind the scenes, forging a political consensus and framing it in terms that Reagan could endorse. Reagan charged ahead, dismissing arguments he disagreed with …[37]

As chief of staff, Baker had been aware of Reagan's blind spots and had taken effective measures to mitigate the harm they could cause to the president. Reagan was not attuned to the fullness of Ronald Regan's character and felt it was best to let Reagan be Reagan! With his admiring indifference to Reagan's shortcomings, Regan allowed poor decisions to forward without debate or analysis. For example, Ronald Reagan was silent on the plan hatched by German Chancellor Helmut Kohl, in early 1985, to have President Reagan lay a wreath at the German military cemetery at Bitburg. Among the fallen buried at Bitburg were 49 Waffen SS troops. The thought of Ronald Reagan effectively honoring Nazi SS soldiers provoked a strong outcry from the American Jewish community. One of the most prominent Holocaust survivors, Nobel Prize winner Elie Wiesel, begged President Reagan not to accepted Kohl's invitation.[38]

But the president was determined to solidify his relationship with Kohl. According to biographer Lou Cannon, the visit "inflicted needless political damage on his presidency in the opening months of the second term."[39] Cannon also noted that Bitburg revealed the weakness of Don Reagan's premise "that the Reagan presidency operated best if Reagan were left to his own devices."[40] In addition, Don Regan's and Regan had shown himself lacking in the skills of political damage control that had distinguished his predecessor.

Shortly after Bitburg, President Reagan confronted another major scandal called Iran–Contra. Operating initially in cooperation with the Israelis and subsequently through a covert US program by Oliver North, the Reagan administration, from the late summer of 1985 through the mid-fall of 1986, supplied antitank and antiaircraft weapons to Iran in violation of its official policy of withholding weapons from states that sponsored terrorism and of a specific ban on weapons sales to Iran. President Reagan had envisioned that these actions would influence the Iran to help free US hostages being held in Lebanon. The Iranians were overcharged for the weapons they purchased, and some of the proceeds from the arms deals were diverted to assist rebel forces in Nicaragua, known as the "contras." This action was also prohibited by law through the Boland Amendments.[41]

Many questions about Iran–Contra, and the extent of President Reagan's involvement in it were never fully answered, due to the death of the then CIA director, William Casey, on May 12, 1987. The Tower Board, appointed by Congress to investigate and chaired by former US Senator (R, TX) John Tower, concluded that Reagan's adviser had traded arms for hostages in violation of administration policy and singled out Chief of Staff Donald Reagan for criticism.[42] The Tower Commission also subjected President Reagan to criticism for his conduct in the Iran–Contra episode: The President's management style is to put the principal responsibility of policy review and information on the shoulders of his advisers. Nevertheless, with such a complex, high-risk operation and so much at stake, the president should have ensured that the NSC system did not fail him. As summarized by the Tower Commission, "He did not force his policy to undergo the most critical review of which the NSC participants and the process were capable ... the most powerful functions of the NSC system—providing comprehensive analysis, alternatives, and follow-up—were not utilized."[43]

According to Reagan biographer, Lou Canon, the Iran initiative would have been "inconceivable" during President Reagan's first term, when he was surrounded by aides who guarded his approval ratings and by associates from California used to protecting Reagan from himself. But Reagan had "almost casually" cut himself loose from the political moorings that had secured his power and credibility during the first term. He continues, "Gone were Baker, Deaver, and Darman, the trio of pragmatists associated with most of his political successes .... The pragmatists would have recognized the political risk of selling weapons to Iran ..."[44]

TAKEAWAYS FOR ALL LEADERS

- Macromanagement can be an effective leadership tool when the leader has carefully selected his or her executive team and knows they are aligned with his or her vision.
- Macromanagement can help other members of the executive team, and even beyond, feel trusted and empowered.
- Like micromanagement, macromanagement can have its own pathologies, as the leader loses touch with important events and developments in the organization.
- High level officials cannot be moved around like chess pieces; they are not easily interchangeable.

George Herbert Walker Bush

President Bush was certainly a more hands-on leader than Reagan was. Instead of following Reagan's 9-to-5 White House schedule, Bush adopted a 7-to-6 pattern. Bush promised reporters that he would stay in touch and not allow himself to be isolated by White House staff.[45] Given the considerable public service experience of his top aides, Bush was not in favor of a heavily managed White House and attempted to downplay the pomp and circumstance of the office. The modest approach to leadership paralleled the narrow policy objectives and, perhaps, also reflected the disdain for self-importance that Bush's mother had imparted during his younger years.[46]

To amplify on the level of experience and professionalism of the Bush's White House, 24 of the 29 key White House positions were held by people who had previous White House experience.[47] He quickly named John Sununu as his chief of staff. Sununu's experience as governor of New Hampshire from 1983 to 1989 profoundly influenced his White House career. Andrew Card, who served as assistant to the president and deputy chief of staff (and would serve as chief of staff in the first Bush 43 administration) noted that "Governors, in my opinion, always have a difficult time being staffers."[48]

Technically Sununu was a staffer in the young Bush administration; nevertheless, he kept reverting to the role of executive decision maker.

Sununu's performance as chief of staff resembled the performance of Ronald Reagan more than it resembled the behavior of James A. Baker during the Reagan years. He was abrupt, demanding, and impatient with those who disagreed with him. On the other hand, given President Bush's reluctance to confront people with whom he disagreed, always preferring polite discourse, he needed someone like Sununu who would be loyal to him and give him cover when he needed it.

Bush and Sununu made an interesting pair. According to authors Duffy and Goodgame:

> Like Arnold Schwarzenegger and Danny DeVito, Bush and John Sununu were about to become the stars of a real-life buddy film: one was tall, well built, and handsome; the other was short, pear-shaped, and homely. One was polite, graceful and courteous, even when angry; the other was hostile, brash, and rude, even when perfectly happy .... One had been blessed with a fortune, a famous name and a powerful father on a first-name basis with presidents, CEO's and other power brokers. The other was born in Havana, the son of a foreign film distributor, who bequeathed to his children a funny-sounding name and a polyglot Lebanese, Greek, and Salvadoran heritage.[49]

Sununu proved to be a highly loyal chief of staff. He took many arrows on behalf of his boss—fired by groups of environmentalists who felt betrayed by Bush's timidity, in perception, on environmental protection and by teachers who were disappointed on what they perceived to be Bush's inadequate passion as their advocate. Those who felt double-crossed rarely blamed Bush; instead, they blamed Sununu.[50]

According to Duffy and Goodgame,

> Sununu could run interference when Bush needed to shuffle to the right on issues such as judicial appointments or abortion, Sununu's ties to the conservatives were also strong enough to mollify them when Bush had to appease the moderates on taxes or other issues.[51]

On the other hand, John Sununu created problems for some of Bush's other appointees and advisers. For example, during the drafting of the Americans with Disabilities Act, which President Bush strongly favored, Sununu proved to be an obstacle to getting the bill to the finish line. The ADA was a landmark bill, and Bush had balanced the interests of activists, Democrats, and businesses to craft legislation that would grant the disabled access to jobs and buildings without creating a regulatory nightmare.[52] To Bush, it was not fair that someone in a wheelchair or someone who was deaf did not have the same exact rights—of access and employment—as anybody else.[53] Accordingly, he became directly involved in the process and met with Democratic Senator Tom Harkin (Iowa), who was also a champion of ADA, at the White House to discuss ADA, among other issues. Harkin confided to Bush that John Sununu was creating difficulties in the negotiations to get the bill passed. Bush immediately tapped his White House Counsel, Boyden Gray, to take over for the administration in the ADA legislative process. Gray handled Harkin's concerns, the talks proceeded more smoothly, and the bill was ready for Bush's signature in the last week of 1990. In signing the bill on the South Lawn of the White House, Bush equated the ADA with the fall of the Berlin Wall, noting that barriers had been broken down in both cases.[54]

Ultimately, Sununu was dismissed from his position for running afoul of white House travel regulations by taking taxpayer-financed planes and free Gulfstream jets on 99 official political and personal trips, including visits to his dentist in Boston and ski resorts in the West. Instead of simply apologizing and reimbursing the Treasury, Sununu displayed his usual arrogance and designated all but a few of his trips as official business. As the president's popularity began to sag under the pressure of an economic recession, he could not afford the added burden of an irascible chief of staff. Bush sent his son George—the future president—to deliver a note to Sununu saying his services would no longer be needed.[55]

In terms of the cabinet, Bush chose a group of highly credentialed, mostly nonideological professionals. As discussed in the previous chapter, he named James A. Baker as his secretary of state. According to historian Jon Meacham, longtime friends Bush and Baker seemed connected "telepathically," with each man appearing to be personally aware of what the other was thinking and doing.[56] He chose Dick Cheney as his secretary of defense, after the failure of his first nominee, John Tower; Nicholas Brady as his Treasury Secretary.

He named Brent Scowcroft as National Security Adviser and Richard Darman as Director of the Office of Management and Budget. As I have written elsewhere,

> Bush was a seasoned political professional in charge of a network of similarly credentialed professionals. Those who worked for him were competent managers and experienced public servants; however, they were not particularly animated by a sense of purpose or a guiding vision. They proved to be loyal to the president and his executive team. But the team had elements of dysfunction and conflict that Bush failed to confront. Problems were particularly evident in the domestic policy area.[57]

TAKEAWAYS FOR ALL LEADERS

- A leader needs to react quickly when a chief of staff or a high-level member of the executive team creates tension or conflict with internal teams or key stakeholders.
- A leader with a highly experienced and professional executive team still needs to periodically revisit shared vision or collective purpose with them.
- A leader must confront ethical lapses among his team quickly and decisively.

Bill Clinton

Based on his observations of the early days of the Clinton presidency, presidential scholar Fred Greenstein concluded that Clinton "seemed insensitive to organization."[58] According to Greenstein, Clinton tended to take on many personal responsibilities and delegate little. Greenstein added that Clinton himself acknowledged that he entered the White House without a plan for organization and staffed major White House positions with aides who had little experience.[59] Clinton demonstrated an awareness of the management issue in his autobiography, where he reflected on what he had learned as governor that would inform his White House strategies: "I would have to delegate more and have a better-organized decision-making process than I had as governor."[60] Apparently, he did not follow his own advice.

Clinton and his transition chief, Warren Christopher (who would serve as Clinton's secretary of state) paid far greater attention to staffing the cabinet than they did to choosing White House staff. They put a great deal of effort into building a cabinet that "looked like America," but as Michael Waldman, Clinton's speechwriter observed, "The cabinet included Citizens of Berkley,

Cambridge, and Madison (WI), but none came from swing states like Illinois, Ohio, Michigan, or Pennsylvania."[61]

Clinton concentrated initially on the economic team for the cabinet, choosing Lloyd Bentsen, a pro-business former US Democratic Senator (TX), as his Treasury Secretary. Bentsen's deputy would be Roger Altman, vice chairman of the Blackstone Group investment firm; Altman was a life-long Democrat and financial wizard. Clinton also named Larry Summers as the Treasury Department deputy undersecretary for international affairs. Summers' was the youngest tenure professor at Harvard, at the age of 28.[62] Clinton named his friend from Oxford, Robert Reich, as Labor Secretary; Reich had authored books on labor-management cooperation. He designated University of Wisconsin Chancellor Donna Shalala as secretary of Health and Human Services and Carol Browner, the state of Florida's environmental director, to head the Environmental Protection Agency; Henry Cisneros, former mayor of San Antonio, to lead the Department of Housing and Urban Development. And he named Hazel O'Leary, an African American utility executive in Minnesota, as Secretary of Energy, and Dick Riley, an educator, and former governor, as head of the Department of Education.[63]

For his foreign policy team at the cabinet level, he named Warren Christopher, who had considerable experience at the state and defense departments, as secretary of state, and Les Aspin, former chairman of the House Armed Services Committee, as secretary of Defense. He chose Georgetown University professor Madeleine Albright as our ambassador to the United Nations, and Leon Panetta, former Democratic member of Congress from California, to be director of the Office of Management and Budget.[64]

Clinton chose his longtime friend and loyal Democratic activist, Mack McLarty to be his chief of staff. Author Chris Whipple correctly analyzed the McLarty appointment by saying "Clinton's selection of McLarty was a last-minute, seat-of-the-pants decision, but also a telling one: In the White House, Bill and Hillary Clinton would hold their friends close and keep their enemies at a distance."[65]

McLarty was not the right person to help an undisciplined president restore order to an increasingly chaotic White House, as will be explained below. The McLarty appointment reveals the limitation of a leader relying too heavily on friendships to fill key staff positions. Here is how Secretary of Labor Robert Reich saw the situation:

> The chief of staff cannot be a dear old friend. It's too difficult for the chief to tell the president no. It's also difficult for the chief of staff and his boss to see and understand their respective roles and not to let the past intrude on the present.[66]

There were problems and complications in the early days of Clinton's White House, including poorly run meetings, chaotic scheduling, and a scandal in the White House travel office; an FBI probe revealed financial improprieties and embezzlement by the supervisor.

In his autobiography, Clinton attributed these problems to an inexperienced White House staff having too few connections to the Washington establishment power centers. He added that he was trying to do too many things at once and that he and his team were creating an image of "disarray."[67] Compounding the internal managerial issues was the defeat of the president's proposal to allow LGBTQ individuals to freely enlist in the military.

As Clinton acknowledged in his autobiography, the president's outreach to David Gergen to ask for his assistance resulted in positive change. Clinton designated Gergen as Counselor to the President, and as Clinton recalls, Gergen had a "calming" influence on the White House. He moved quickly to improve relations with the press by restoring their direct access to the communications office.[68]

There were a few anomalies to the structure of the Clinton White House. Unlike previous presidents, Clinton installed the first lady and vice president in the West Wing of the White House. No other first lady had been there before.[69] The physical arrangement foreshadowed the unusually large influence of the first lady and the vice present in the Clinton administration.

When Gergen joined the White House staff in 1993, he asked chief of staff Mack McLarty to summarize the White House organization. "Every White House has its own personality," replied McLarty. "In this White House as you will find, we usually have three people in the top box: the President, the Vice President, and the First Lady. All of them sign on big decisions. You'll have to get used to that."[70]

Hillary's influence was so pervasive that Gergen mused about a co-presidency. He believed that the Clintons worked well when they were "in balance." In his view,

> She was the anchor, he the sail. He was the dreamer, she the realist. She was the strategist, he the tactician … She helped him gain office, he helped her gain power. He leaned to the center, she leaned to the left. She was composed, he flew off the handle. He liked to laugh. She was serious.[71]

Yet Gergen also expressed concern about the political/leadership partnership, and opined that "no matter how talented, two people cannot occupy the space jointly making decisions."[72]

Conflicts did arise between them on several policy issues, including healthcare reform. But she was also concerned about the chaos and drift of the White House from a management perspective. Six months into the presidency, Hillary was at the "end of her rope."[73] She concluded that the burden of carrying out the administrative policies was overwhelming her husband. He was, in the words of Washington Post reporter Bob Woodward, "the chief congressional lobbyist, the chief message person, the policy designer, the spokesman—he carried out all the functions. Too many senior people in the administration and on the staff were stopping short of full preparation."[74]

Hillary did not hesitate to sound off to McLarty, who as chief of staff, she believed, needed to improve White House management, and strive for more order and routine. She wanted to set up the governing equivalent of the War Room—the brutally efficient campaign headquarters run by Carville and Stephanopoulos out of Little Rock, Arkansas.[75] By the middle of 1994, it was clear that McLarty was not going to be able to complete the necessary repair work, and President Clinton reached out to his Director of Management and Budget, former California (D) Congressman Leon Panetta to take over as chief of staff. Panetta accepted the job with conditions that he articulated as follows:

> (1) that I have the trust of you and the first lady; (2) that you give me some authority to do some reorganization if I think it's needed to make the place work; and (3) that we really be honest with each other—that we tell each other what we feel and what we're thinking.[76]

As his deputy, Panetta installed Erskine Bowles, who had left a lucrative business to run the Small Business Administration and had formed a bond with Bill Clinton during the 1992 presidential campaign. Bowles told Clinton that he needed a better approach to manage his time and convinced the president to allow Bowles to conduct a time and motion study on Clinton's use of time. The results persuaded President Clinton to stop pulling all-nighters and to use his time more efficiently, allowing him time to think.[77] Bowles would replace Panetta as Clinton's third chief of staff.

As chief of staff, Panetta helped the president's time management by performing the role of gatekeeper. As he said, "The first order of business was … to make very clear that I was going to be a chief of staff that would in fact control the staff, that if the wanted to go to the president, they would have to go through me."[78] There would be no more uninvited guests dropping in on the Oval Office.

As described earlier in the chapter, Bill Clinton saw himself as a "New Democrat," willing to break free from orthodoxies of the party. He used terms like a "New Covenant" to capture his expectations that government would move from the business of giveaways to the business of investment. In his Second Inaugural Address, which he described as the "last Presidential Inauguration of the 20th century," he called for a "New Government for a New Century," one that was "humble enough not to try to solve all our problems for us" and one that was "smaller, lives within its means and does more with less."[79]

But if the era of "big government" was over, the ear of better government was in view. Despite his lack of deep insight into the organizational needs of his own White House operation, Bill Clinton possessed a deep faith in the power of technology to make government more efficient and more accessible.

In March 1993, he designated Vice President Al Gore to lead an effort to reinvent government. In announcing the program, Clinton declared that the goal was to make the federal government less expensive to run and more efficient, and to "change the climate of your national bureaucracy away from entitlement and toward innovation and impact." He added that "We intend to redesign, to reinvent, to reinvigorate the entire national government."[80]

Unlike past federal government reform initiatives, The National Performance Review (later called the National Partnership to Reinvent Government) was staffed by experienced federal managers and employees at all levels of the government, not by outside experts.[81]

Gore organized experienced government managers into teams to analyze problems and develop solutions in areas, like budget, procurement, information technology, and personnel. The NPR proposed to create a more efficient, less costly government by cutting red tape, perfecting "customer service" for government, empowering federal employees to innovate, and eliminating wasteful programs.[82]

In his autobiography, President Clinton gave the NPR high marks, "helping us by 300,000, making this the smallest federal government since 1960, and to save $136 million in tax money."[83]

TAKEAWAYS FOR ALL LEADERS

- A leader must develop a strong management structure, and if he or she is not proficient in organizational skills, they must recruit a skillful chief of staff or similar position to help.
- Management efficiency will help move the leader's agenda along and will be of tremendous value in protecting the leader from micromanagement and burnout.
- Campaigning is significantly different from governing, and people who excel at one will not automatically excel at the other.

George W. Bush

As the nation's first MBA president, George W. Bush preferred to set a bold direction, Within a clearly limited agenda, and delegate administrative matters to his executive team, led by Vice President Dick Cheney and Chief of Staff Andrew Card.[84] Bush's management style was characterized by speed, secrecy, and top-down control,[85] making him substantially different as a leader than Bill Clinton was. Bush envisioned his role as a chief corporate executive; he would be tough-minded and decisive and leave the details of execution to others. He also emphasized message discipline and had a particular disdain for unauthorized leaks.[86]

What made the Bush 43 administrative structure somewhat unique was the unusually large portfolio and influence enjoyed by Vice President Dick Cheney. Several scholars, journalists, and even comedians exaggerated the extent of Cheney's influence musing about a "co-presidency" situation.[87] But this commentary misses the reality of the relationship, according to NY Times White House reporter Peter Baker.

Although Baker admits that Cheney was "unquestionably the most influential vice present in American history," Cheney subordinated himself to Bush in a way that no other vice present in modern times has done, "by forgoing any independent expectation to run for president himself in order to focus entirely on making Bush's presidency successful."[88]

Of course Bush reciprocated by giving Cheney access to every meeting and decision.[89] Dick Cheney's overwhelming presence in the Bush 43 White House did present challenges to the chief of staff, Andrew Card. With a long history in Republican politics, including an unsuccessful run for governor of Massachusetts, Card joined Bush 41's 1980 presidential campaign, and eight years later served as his deputy chief of staff and transportation Secretary.[90]

George W. Bush invited Card to join his administration as chief of staff, and like Leon Panetta before him, Card said he would do it on two conditions:

- He told Bush, "we have to have a candid relationship. You have to be comfortable with me saying anything to you-and I will be comfortable with you comfortable with you saying anything to me."
- "As long as I'm going to be your chief of staff, I can't be your friend." And he added, "if you're looking for more than one chief of staff at the same time, I won't be one of them."[91]

The other members of Bush's inner circle or team were:

Karen Hughes, Counselor to the President. Hughes had been a member of Bush's staff when he was governor of Texas. Previously, she had been a television reporter and executive director of the Texas Republican Party. As counselor to the president, Hughes supervised the Communications Office, the Office of Media Affairs, and the Office of Speechwriting.[92]

Karl Rove, Senior White House Adviser. Close observers described Rove as "Bush's brain" for his deft political instincts and influence on Bush's political strategy. Rove had headed an Austin-based public affairs firm and masterminded Bush's gubernatorial wins.[93] Rove supervised several offices, including the Office of Strategic Initiatives, the Office of Political Affairs, and the Office of Public Liaisons.

In contrast to the Clinton White House, Bush's would be a tightly run ship. Chief of Staff Andrew Card listed the following rules for White House staffers:[94]

- *Attire*: Suit and tie were required for men and equivalent business attire for women. The casual dress code of the Clinton years was over.
- *Brevity is vital*: Bush demanded that briefing papers be limited to one or two pages.
- *Punctuality*: Bush was ruthless in starting and ending meetings on time, another dramatic contrast to Clinton.
- *Treat everyone with respect*: The president demanded that staffers return each other's phone calls promptly.
- *Develop healthy work habits*: Bush stressed the importance of life balance and encouraged his staff to spend time with their families. Like Reagan, and unlike Clinton, Bush expected most work to be completed during the normal workday.

To fill his cabinet, Bush 43 chose many figures from his father's administration, including Colin Powell as Secretary of State, Condoleezza Rice as National Security Adviser, and Donald Rumsfeld as Secretary of Defense. But he also chose members of the cabinet who would add to the diversity of the administration, including Elaine Chao as Secretary of Labor, Rodney Paige as Secretary of Education, Norman Mineta as Secretary of Transportation, and Ann Veneman as Secretary of Agriculture.

From the beginning of his presidency, Bush 43 demanded better management and performance from the federal government. The President's Management Agenda (PMA) established five priorities for all federal agencies:

- Strategic management of human capital
- Competitive sourcing
- Improved financial management
- Expanded use of E-government
- Budget and performance integration.[95]

The administration assigned four political appointees in OMB and one in the Office of Personnel Management (OPM) as "owners" of each initiative, holding them responsible for implementing change. The "owners" asked each agency to develop plans, identifying the responsible officials and securing resources to achieve organizational improvements.[96]

In addition, the Bush administration developed an Executive Branch Management Scorecard to track the execution of PMA. The scorecard used a "traffic light" grading system to assess the progress of each agency. A "green" signal meant the agency had met all the elements of the standards for success, "yellow" signified an intermediate level of achievement, and "red" meant the agency had one or more serious flaws.[97]

When PMA was launched, 110 of the 130 scores (based on 26 participating agencies on 5 separate initiatives) were "red." Almost none of the agencies scored were acceptably managing their people, program costs, or IT investments. As of June 30, 2006, the US Department of Labor was found to be the most successful in using management disciplines that comprised the PMA, with five "green" scores.[98]

Bush also introduced legislative proposals to improve management; however, he was unable to secure congressional passage for them. One proposal was the Freedom to Manage Act of 2001, which was the first bill Bush sent to Congress.[99] The proposed bill established a procedure to allow heads of agencies and departments to identify statutory barriers to good management and recommend that Congress remove them. The Managerial Flexibility Act would have provided federal managers with tools and increased managerial flexibility in areas like budget, personnel, and property management and disposal.[100] Members of both parties in Congress hesitated about ceding any legislative power to the White House. In addition, the proposals met stiff resistance from the American Federation of Government Employees. Nevertheless, several of the ideas contained in the failed pieces of legislation found their way into subsequent legislative proposals, most notably the Bush administration's bill to create the Department of Homeland Security.[101]

A third management reform initiative undertaken by the Bush administration was the Program Assessment Rating Tool (PART), developed to apply performance metrics to the budgeting process. PART was centered on 25 diagnostic questions focused on (1) program purpose and design, (2) strategic planning, (3) program management, and (4) program results. The PART came up with "scores" for agencies based on their performance in the four aforementioned areas.[102]

Although the PART ratings did not automatically affect agency funding, they helped surface ideas for needed improvement in program design, planning, and management.[103] As of February 2002, the administration has assessed 794 programs, representing 80 percent of the federal budget, with the use of PART.[104] Over time, according to analyst Jonathan Bruel, there was a substantial increase in the number of programs rated "effective," "moderately effective," or "adequate." In the first year, 45 percent of the programs received such scores; by 2006, the percentage had grown to 72 percent.[105]

In 2005, PART won the Prestigious Innovation in American Government Award, a program jointly sponsored by the Ash Institute at Harvard's John F. Kennedy School of Government and the Council for Excellence in Government. According to Bruel, "taken together, the Bush management reforms represent a highly disciplined, diplomatic, transparent, and sustained approach to reforming the inner workings of government."[106]

As previously mentioned, Bush also decided to create a new federal agency, called the Department of Homeland Security. In reaction to the September 11 terrorist attacks, Bush, in his January 2002 State of the Union Address to Congress, named Pennsylvania Republican Governor Tom Ridge as the director of a new federal effort to protect the homeland from future attacks. Bush did not contemplate elevating Ridge to cabinet status or creating a new cabinet agency initially; however, advocates like Senator Joe Lieberman (D, CT) and chief of staff Andrew Card pushed him that direction,[107] and on November 25, 2002, Bush signed legislation that merged 22 federal agencies (including the US Customs Service, the Coast Guard, the US Secret Service, the USA Immigration and Customs Enforcement) with more than 170,000 employees, into a new Department of Homeland Security.[108]

A few days earlier, in a November 19 statement, President Bush commended Congress for passing legislation creating DHS "to help meet the emerging threat of terrorism in the 21st century."[109]

Although the nation needed a consolidated approach to homeland security, the department was created hastily and without adequate planning for melding disparate organizational visions and cultures into a new Department of Homeland Security. For instance, the placement of the Federal Emergency Management Agency within this vast bureaucratic framework reduced its visibility and possibly its effectiveness in dealing with future national emergencies, like Hurricane Katrina.[110]

Bush was not a purist around scientific management either. His administration, like others, was infused with politics. Like Reagan before him, Bush proved to be adept at populating the executive agencies with conservative ideologues.[111]

As previously mentioned, Vice President Cheney played a key role in staffing the administration, and he made sure that the appointees shared the president's (and his) views. When he needed someone to manage surface mines, he turned to the mining industry. When he needed someone to manage the national parks, he selected someone from the logging industry. And when he needed someone to manage environmental policy, he drew from the energy industry.[112]

Although he professed allegiance to the MBA style of professional management, then, Bush's true allegiance was to his conservative principles and political success. Program outcomes were periodically subordinated to political and ideological calculations, as dramatically illustrated in the Bush administration's replacement of large numbers of US attorneys (who work in the Department of Justice because they were not ardent Bush loyalists).[113]

Rounding out the assessment of "structure" in the Bush 43 administration also requires an acknowledgment of the Bush and Cheney belief, especially Cheney, that it was imperative to restore the presidency as an institution to a more prominent, if not dominant, role in American government. Cheney had been concerned for many years with the post-Watergate shrinkage of the presidency and the concomitant power grabs by Congress and the courts that, in his mind, intruded on the dominion of the executive.[114] Cheney wanted the president's authority to be as close to absolute as is constitutionally possible, and frequently advocated for a "unitary" executive.

TAKEAWAYS FOR ALL LEADERS

- A public sector leader can make management improvements by relying on ideas from the private sector.
- A leader who wishes to reduce the role of politics on public administration must resist the temptation to abandon this posture for political gain.
- Forming a capable executive team will greatly assist a leader in carrying out his or her agenda and reduce the need for micromanagement.

Barack Hussein Obama

Obama entered the White House without a long history of executive experience. True, he had managed a statewide political campaign, a US Senate office staff, and the *Harvard Law Review; however* none of these experiences would adequately prepare him to manage a federal workforce of 3–4 million people.[115]

In addition, the White House staff faced the same challenge; most of them had been recruited from the world of politics and not from large public sector agencies or business corporations. The only White House official who had accumulated significant management experience was Jeffrey Zients, a successful entrepreneur whom Obama designated as chief performance officer in 2009.[116] (Later, in the Biden administration in 2021, Zients served as the White House Coronavirus Response Coordinator.)

Obama's first choice for the White House staff was Rahm Emanuel as chief of staff. At the time he agreed (with some reluctance) to serve in this capacity, Emanuel was serving as a Democratic Congressman from Chicago's north side. In fact, one of the reasons for Rahm's reluctance was that he believed he might become the first Jewish Speaker of the House.[117]

But President Obama understood the strengths Emanuel would bring to his team, as he described in his autobiography, "Rahm, knew policy, knew politics, knew Congress, knew the White House and knew financial markets from a stint working on Wall Street."[118]

Rahm had also served in the Clinton White House and, no one doubted his ability to tell the president what he needed to hear.[119] Few doubted that Emanuel would be the right person to help President Obama translate his vision into reality.

When Rahm Emanuel decided to resign as chief of staff to run for mayor of Chicago in the fall of 2010, Obama temporarily designated Peter Rouse, who had been chief of staff in Obama's Senate office, to serve in this capacity, and then in early 2011 assigned the position to William Daly, the Midwest Chair of JP Morgan. Daly had been Secretary of Commerce in the Clinton years and chairman of Al Gore's presidential campaign. As chief of staff with corporate connections, Daly insisted on an orderly and hierarchical decision-making process in the White House; he canceled the daily 8:30 am gathering of White House departments, and severely limited the people who could attend various meetings.[120]

Obama chose several other high-level campaign staff as his White House aides: David Axlerod, who was a chief campaign strategist, was named Senior Adviser to the President; Valerie Jarrett, a campaign activist and longtime friend of First Lady Michele Obama, was named Assistant to the President; David Plouffe, a senior campaign strategist, was also designated Senior Adviser to the President. Obama named Robert Gibbs as White House Press Secretary. Gibbs had served as global chief of communications for McDonald's.[121]

Obama's cabinet picks were described in the "Politics" chapter of this book, but one additional choice is worth noting. President Obama chose Robert Gates as his defense secretary. Gates had served several Republican presidents, most recently as secretary of defense for Bush 43; but Obama chose him for a few compelling reasons, as he explained in his autobiography:

- "... With 180,000 US troops deployed on Iraq and Afghanistan, any wholesale turnover in the Defense Department seemed fraught with risk."[122]
- "... I had promised to end constant political rancor, and Gates' presence in my Cabinet would show I was serious about delivering on that promise."[123]

Obama's White House executive experience shows signs of leadership strength as well as weakness. On the positive side, President Obama followed the sagacious advice of Vice President Biden, who suggested a point person for the implementation of the $787 billion Recovery Act. According to Michael Greenwald,

> Biden thought the Recovery Act had the potential to make the administration look silly. It would fund more than 10,000 projects—275 programs at 28 federal agencies. Tax dollars could get wasted, spending deadlines missed ... Had anyone ever doled out $787 billion without some of it getting squandered?[124]

At a February 12, 2010, lunch with President Obama, Biden described the need for a stimulus manager to the president and added that the chosen person would have to "ride herd" on the stimulus to make sure the money was spent quickly and effectively. The person, said the vice president, would have to be an energetic senior official with easy access to the president, and someone who could cajole and persuade cabinet secretaries. When Biden handed Obama a written memo outlining the position and qualities needed by its occupant, the president glanced at it quickly and said, "Great, do it!"[125]

Over the next two years, Biden would convene 22 cabinet meetings on the Recovery Act and visit 56 stimulus projects. He would host 57 conference calls with governors and mayors, and block 260 Recovery Act projects that failed to meet the "smell test."[126] As well, Biden recruited Earl Devaney, who had 40 years of law enforcement experience, to manage a Recovery Accountability and Transparency Board. Devaney organized a centralized reporting system to track spending activities associated with tens of thousands of stimulus contracts. He also installed software to detect and prevent fraud. The efforts were effective, as Recovery Act fraud was found to be near zero.[127]

On the other hand, Obama did not display the same level of management acumen in the roll-out of Obamacare, especially in terms of the launch of the HealthCare.gov website, which everyone—including Obama—said was a disaster. In early 2013, the Congressional Budget Office estimated that once the Affordable Care Act (ACA) got going, 7 million Americans would enroll in the new national healthcare exchanges the first six months. But in the weeks following ACA's October 2014 launch, only a few thousand were able to do so. More than a quarter of a million more were prevented from even beginning to enroll by technical glitches and error messages on the Healthcare site. Worst of all, on several occasions in October and November, the system crashed entirely.[128]

How could this happen? To begin with, Obama had entrusted the implementation of the ACA to the person who had been instrumental in moving the bill through Congress, Nancy-Ann DeParle. Then president's admirable sense of loyalty to a valued team member led him to underestimate the difficulties of implementation, according to Brookings Institution scholar, Elaine C. Kamarck.[129]

In addition, instead of following the successful practices of the stimulus program, including oversight of the program by the White House, Obama delegated responsibility for health-care implementation to the executive bureaucracy. He placed most of the responsibility on a powerful but little-known agency spread over several locations in Washington DC and Maryland, named the Centers for Medicare and Medicaid Services (CMS). In September 2011, CMS hired a large Canadian firm, CGI Federal, as the lead contractor on the ACA website. Due to a series of management problems, CMS was on a list of high-risk agencies developed by the Government Accountability Office.[130]

In the effort to launch the website, there were warning signs as early as late March, when a report prepared for the Department of Health and Human Services (HHS) by the McKinsey consulting firm criticized the "insufficient time and scope for end-to-end testing."[131] By the summer of 2013, experts in building large, complex websites knew there were problems. GAO reported that "the large number of activities remaining to be performed suggest a potential for implementation challenges."[132] On August 17, CGI Federal told CMS that its part of the system was only a little more than half finished. With less than six months to go before launch, "this should have rung alarm bells."[133]

By March 2014, six months after the deeply flawed roll-out, the problems with HealthCare.gov had been fixed, and during the early part of March, 11 million people were able to sign up for coverage through the federal and state-operated online exchanges.

Still, the numbers were lower than had been predicted.[134] And the political damage that HealthCare.gov had created for Obama during the last three months of 2013 was increasingly evident: His approval rating fell to the lowest point ever, with only 39.8 percent approval of the job he was doing as president.[135] According to Elaine Kamarck, "Obama's inattention to the capacity of the government he was in charge of cost him dearly."[136]

And just as he was recovering from the HealthCare.gov fiasco, another executive agency disaster came to light. Media revelations in 2014 revealed a serious level of malfeasance in the US Department of Veterans Affairs, commonly known as the VA. A 2014 congressional oversight committee reported that veterans were waiting an average of 115 days to get primary medical care—in contrast to the VA records of 24 days—while 1,700 people seeking medical appointments were not on lists at all. Moreover, the report found that it was taking over 700 days for the VA to fire senior level employees who oversaw the operations of the agency; that the agency had received large budgetary increases during the Obama years; and that, despite some improvements, over 500,000 appointments still had a wait time of a month or more.[137]

Finally, the *Washington Post* reported that medical errors on VA facilities had risen by 8 percent in recent years.[138] The scandal would cost Eric Shinseki, a respected former army general, his job as secretary of the VA, and would become another blot on Obama's career as chief executive. According to Elaine Kamarck,

> Once again, an American president looked like he was not in charge of the Government he was supposed to run. In one instance, implementation of the Affordable Care Act, the Obama administration's biggest domestic policy achievement, was handed over to an agency that had been starved of resources for decades as its mission had grown, and that was ill-equipped to take on yet another large task. In the second instance, the ongoing problems at the Department of Veterans Affairs were well known but went unaddressed.[139]

It is apparent that President Obama did not excel in the area of management (or "structure"). He did not sufficiently appreciate the complexity of the executive branch of government, or the need to have capable assistance in the implementation of new, complex public policies and the monitoring of existing ones. According to journalist Jonathan Alter:

> Had he served even briefly in the executive branch of the federal government, Obama might have been more equipped to manage the government. He was sophisticated enough to grasp the games that bureaucrats play to stymie presidents and their political appointees but not yet experienced enough to navigate expertly around the impediments.[140]

TAKEAWAYS FOR ALL LEADERS

- While less glamorous than other aspects of leadership, execution is one of the most important jobs of leaders.[141]
- While every organizational project is unique, when a leader discovers a successful management approach, he or she should use it again, with modification.
- A leader can benefit from a diverse team in managing a large organization with multiple responsibilities and stakeholders.

Donald John Trump

President Donald Trump once described himself a "singularly talented chief executive with an uncanny ability to spot and cultivate talent."[142] On the other hand, he did little to prepare himself for the awesome responsibility of managing 3–4 million people in the executive branch of government, and proved to be unusually uninterested in learning about the details of the government he was about to inherit.

The Trump transition process was chaotic, when compared to the transition of Obama, Trump's most immediate predecessor. Chris Christie, the former Governor of NJ, volunteered himself for the job after abandoning his own 2016 presidential campaign.[143] Trump told Christie that he was not interested in a transition process, and Christie reminded the president-elect that it was legally required and could be funded by Trump himself or by campaign funds. Trump grudgingly agreed to the idea and empowered Christie to raise a separate fund to pay for the transition.[144]

The president's son-in-law, Jared Kushner, still harbored ill will toward Christie, because when Christie was US Attorney for the district of NJ, he had prosecuted and jailed Jared's father, Charles, for tax fraud. Jared inserted himself into an oversight role over the transition operation, along with his wife, Ivanka, Trump's two sons, Eric and Donald Jr., Paul Manafort (Trump's campaign manager for a brief period), and Steven Mnuchin (who would be named Trump's Treasury Secretary).[145]

By August 2016, 130 people were showing up daily, with hundreds more working part-time, to help staff the Trump presidency. Under Christie's supervision, the team developed lists of suggested candidates of Republicans who had worked in government, for some 500 jobs. At the end of each week, Christie handed over binders with names of potential candidates to Jared, Ivanka, and the rest of the "executive committee."[146]

But when Trump learned that the transition operation was costing him money, he ordered Steve Bannon to shut it down. Christie and Bannon were able to push back and convince Trump that shuttering the transition operation would be a public relations nightmare, Trump backed off from the demand.[147]

Nevertheless, it became clear that the advice of Christie's transition team could not compete with Trump's personal opinions and leanings. For example, the transition team was quite wary about assigning a high-level national security position to retired Army General Michael Flynn, who had been a close adviser to Trump during the campaign. Flynn had previously served as head of the Defense Intelligence Agency in the Obama administration, only to be fired from the position by President Obama. In their one-on-one discussion in the White House, Obama specifically warned Trump against hiring Flynn, advice Trump ignored.[148]

Shortly after inviting Flynn to join the administration, Trump told Bannon that it was time to relieve Christie of his duties. Bannon did so, and when Christie pressed him for a reason, Bannon blamed the decision on Jared Kushner.[149] Bannon visited the transition headquarters after he'd given Christie the news and made a show out of tossing the work of Christie's team into the trash. Trump would handle the transition more or less on his own.[150]

And so, left to his own devices, Donald Trump, with input from Steve Bannon, Jared and Ivanka, and a few others, assembled a cabinet that was 85 percent white, generally very wealthy, with an average age of 62.[151] The cabinet included the following individuals, among others:

Wilbur Ross, Secretary of Commerce. A very wealthy man, who had accumulated his fortune by buying troubled companies, restructuring them, and selling them at a great profit. In 2009, Ross had invested $100 million in Longyuan Power, a Chinese wind operator. He was also an investor in Diamond S Shipping Group, Inc., a Chinese concern that would benefit from continued trade with the United States.

In his congressional confirmation hearing, Ross promised to be "quite scrupulous about recusal and any topic where there is the slightest scintilla of doubt." Ross, like her cabinet secretaries, tried to curry favor with Trump by attaching a citizenship question to the questionnaire people would fill out to complete the 2020 census survey. Ross and Trump both knew that this move, ultimately declared unconstitutional by the US Supreme Court (2019), would lead to a population undercount in heavily blue states, and hence to fewer members of Congress there.[152]

> **Steven Mnuchin, Secretary of the Treasury.** A very wealthy Santa Monica banker, who was quite active in Trump's campaign. According to author Alexander Nazaryan, "His riches were about as ill gained as riches cloud get, predicated on his 2009 purchase of IndyMac, the California bank in part responsible for driving the foreclosure crisis."[153]

In his congressional confirmation hearings, it was revealed that Mnuchin had failed to disclose around $100 million in asset, which he claimed was a mere oversight. Nonetheless, he was confirmed. As Nazaryan said, "Democrats wanted badly to sink Mnuchin's nomination, but got no help from their GOP counterparts, who praised Mnuchin for a nonexistent commitment to ordinary Americans."[154]

Mnuchin was one of the few high-level Trump administration officials to last the entire term.

> **Ben Carson, Secretary of Housing and Urban Development.** Previously, he was a highly successful Johns Hopkins University neurosurgeon. Carson had expressed unusual political and social theories, including the idea that perhaps the Holocaust could have been avoided if European Jews were better armed.[155]

Carson himself remarked that he was not truly qualified to lead HUD, and he did not accept a proposed meeting with Obama's outgoing Secretary, Julian Castro.[156]

And like others in Trump's Carson preached parsimony but did not practice it himself. To re-decorate his office at HUD headquarters, Carson purchased a $31,000 mahogany dining room set (Cabinet secretaries are allowed $5,000 to re-decorate).[157]

> **Tom Price, Secretary of Health and Human Services.** A former member of Congress from Georgia's 6th congressional district, who had strongly opposed Obamacare. In the spring of 2016, he became chair of the House Budget Committee and joined eight other House committee chairs who endorsed Trump for president. He promised Trump to help end Obamacare.

During the confirmation process, it came out that as a member of the House Ways and Means Committee, Price had made legislative decisions that bene-fitted companies in which he had invested.[158]

Democrats on the Senate Finance Committee boycotted the vote on Price's nomination (as well as Mnuchin's), but committee chair Orrin Hatch changed the rules so the vote could proceed with no Democrats present. The full Senate confirmed his appointment by a 52–47 vote, reflecting a pure partisan split.[159]

Shortly after the unsuccessful attempt by Republicans to kill Obamacare, *Politico* published a story on how Price had abused his office by taking several private trips on government-funded aircraft, and that he spent some $341,000 doing so. Shortly after these revelations, he resigned.[160]

> **Ryan Zinke, Secretary of the Interior.** Zinke served one term as the sole member of the House of Representatives from Montana. He was conformed for a position that oversees 58 national parks, 566 wildlife refuges, and 250 million acres of open space across the West under the control of the Bureau of Land Management. The jurisdiction of the Department of Interior also includes the Bureau of Indian Affairs, the National Park Service, the US Geological Survey, and the Fish and Wildlife Service.[161]

No one would try harder to project the image of an outsider. On his first day as secretary, March 2, 2017, Zinke rode a horse to the Department of Interior in downtown Washington DC, attired in cowboy hat and jeans, and a rodeo windbreaker instead of a suit coat.[162] Zinke had publicly questioned the role of President Obama in the demise of Osama-bin-Laden.

As secretary, Zinke's agenda was to make it easier for energy companies to access oil and gas on public lands. Zinke took an $8,000 helicopter ride to Shepherdstown, WV, to attend an energy management exercise, and another $6,250 one from VA to Washington, DC, so he could go horseback riding with Vice President Mike Pence.[163]

Like Trump, Secretary Zinke distrusted the federal workforce, and in a September 2017 speech to the National Petroleum Council, said "I got 30 percent of the crew that's not loyal to the flag."[164]

In April 2017, Trump signed an Executive Order mandating that the Department of Interior "review" 27 national monuments designated during the previous 20 years. Zinke praised Trump's action and recommended that 10 national monuments be reduced in size, including Bears Ears, which Obama had signed into existence to protect land spiritually significant to the Navajo and Hopi Native American tribes.

In December 2017, Trump became the first president since Kennedy to shrink national monuments dedicated by his predecessors.[165]

Zinke also proposed raising entry fees of 17 of the nation's most popular national parks. In August 2018, *Politico* reported that Zinke entered an ostensibly illegal arrangement with the chair of Haliburton, who wanted to build a brewery on land Zinke owned in Whitefish, Montana. In a tweet, Trump informed Zinke that he was relieved of his duties, and subsequently quipped that the president was supposed to be the news, not a cabinet member![166]

> **Betsy DeVos, Secretary of Education.** A wealthy woman who had married into the Amway fortune on Michigan and had been an education activist. None of the four DeVos children attended public school.[167]

She and her husband fought to introduce and expand school choice in Michigan and helped sustain an unregulated market for the operation of charter schools in that state. DeVos was confirmed by a 50–51 vote, with Vice President Mike pence casting the deciding vote. As secretary, DeVos worked to undo the Obama administration's prosecution of for-profit colleges, protection of transgender students' rights, and insistence that colleges take students' allegations of sexual assault more seriously.[168] DeVos lasted through the Trump term in office.

> **James N. Mattis, Secretary of Defense.** A retired Marine Corps General, who had been commander of US Central Command, known as CentCom, from 2020 to 2013, and in this capacity oversaw the wars in Iraq and Afghanistan.[169] He was fired by Obama for being overly aggressive toward Iran while the Obama administration was negotiating the nuclear deal.[170] A true professional, Mattis was frequently required to provide information to Trump, such as about the vital role in our collective security NATO played, and why we should continue to support it.[171]

During his tenure in the Trump cabinet, Mattis was frequently caught off guard by abrupt, impulsive defense policy moves made by President Trump, including his declaration that transgender individuals would no longer be welcomed in the military, his sudden cancellation of joint military exercises in South Korea, his deployment of thousands of troops to the US-Mexican border, and his decision in December 2018 to withdraw US troops from Syria after declaring victory over ISIS there. The Syrian decision was the straw that broke the camel's back, and Mattis submitted his resignation shortly afterwards.[172]

Interestingly, when Mattis had called his mother after Trump offered him the position, Mattis' mother said, "How can you work for that man?" Mattis replied, "Ma, last time I checked, I work for the Constitution ..."[173]

> **Rex Tillerson, Secretary of State.** He was the CEO of Exxon Mobil, on the verge of retirement, and had experienced a wide variety of international contacts, especially with Russia. Oil and gas amounted

to over 60 percent of Russia's exports, and Russia was Exxon's biggest oil exploration in the world, with holdings of more than 60 million acres.[174] Trump, who could be somewhat superficial in the way he sized people up, believed Tillerson looked the part of secretary of state, with his swept back mane of gray hair and his pinstriped, tailored suits.

In his interview with Trump at Trump Tower, Tillerson told the president-elect that he could deal with Putin in ways that Obama could not. He also spoke to Trump about America's "strength" stemming not only from military strength but also from economic strength and from democracy and freedom. According to Bob Woodard, Trump showed little interest in these points. But he showed great interest and awareness about the fact that Tillerson was three months away from retirement at Exxon.[175]

After consulting with Condoleezza Rice, James A. Baker, and George Schultz, Tillerson told Trump he would accept the position on three conditions: (a) he could choose his own staff; (b) he had assurance that Trump would not withdraw the nomination, even during a tough confirmation process; and (c) that they would not have a "public dispute."[176]

Tillerson experienced some of the same disappointments in working with Trump as Mattis did—slight differences in policy, exacerbated by significant differences in style. The ostensibly precipitating event was the public criticism Tillerson leveled at Russia for a nerve gas attack on a former Russian spy in England. In March 2018, Trump fired Tillerson on twitter and immediately replaced him with Mike Pompeo.[177]

Scott Pruitt, Administrator of the Environmental Protection Agency. Pruitt's political career began in 1998, when he successfully challenged a 16-year incumbent to gain a seat in the Oklahoma state senate.

He quickly ascended to the position of Republican floor leader in 2003, and his religious fervor earned him the title of "Pastor Pruitt," from the Tulsa newspapers. Pruitt attempted to curb the teaching of evolution in public schools and proposed a highly restrictive abortion measures failed.[178]

When he became Attorney General of Oklahoma, one of Pruitt's first steps was to file suit against Kathleen Sebelius, Obama's HHS Secretary in an attempt to stop the federal government from issuing tax credits for health insurance. He also closed his office's Environment Protection Unit and established a Federalism unit whose purpose was to fend off the federal government.[179] He sued the EPA 14 times during his tenure as Oklahoma A-G.

Democrats strenuously opposed his nomination to head EPA, but they were powerless to stop it. By late spring 2017, Pruitt had assembled a "team of oil and gas lobbyists, climate change deniers, and conservative ideologues" to run the agency.[180] EPA staffers were not permitted top answer letters that poured into the agency about climate change.[181]

Pruitt also liked to fly around the country at government expense and saw no problem spending nearly $10,000 decorating his office, including $2,963 for a standing desk. He also had part of his office torn out to install a private communications booth and hired a private security detail to accompany his and his family on trips.

In January 2018, shortly before he was fired, the EPA published a list of 67 environmental safeguards Pruitt had either roiled back or was on the process of undoing. These included the 2015 Waters of the United States rule and the Clean Power Plan, which established nationwide carbon emissions standards for power plants.[182] Although many of Pruitt's regulatory cutbacks were reversed by the federal judiciary, the legacy he left as an opponent of environmental reform was quite clear.

Usually, an incoming presidential administration shows great interest and curiosity about the operation of the government they are about to inherit. This was not the case with the Trump administration, as intimated above. For example, on the morning of November 9, 2016, Obama administration Department of Energy officials had thoroughly prepared an orientation for the Trump folks, going so far as to reserve 30 parking places for them at DOE headquarters.[183] The Trump people never showed up, and the same situation was replicated across the government.

An experienced civil servant from the Department of Energy, who had watched four different administrations assume the responsibilities of governance remarked, "You always have the issue of maybe they don't understand what the department does."[184]

To address the issue of the transfer of the transfer of power, President Obama, a year before he left office, instructed several knowledgeable people across the government, including 50 in the Department of Energy, to gather the information his successor would need to understand the functions and operations of government on the ground. The Bush team had done the same for Obama.[185]

Obama's request resulted in thousands of people inside the federal government spending the better part of a year drawing a vivid picture for the benefit of the incoming administration. After all, observed author Michael Lewis, "The United States government might be the most complicated organization on the face of the earth. Its two million federal employees take orders from four thousand political appointees. Dysfunction is baked into the structure of the thing …"[186]

Many of the problems a new administration inherits are technical, not ideological—how to stop a virus, how to take a census, how to determine if a foreign country is attempting to develop a nuclear weapon. The people appointed by a new president have 75 days to learn from their predecessors, as shortly after the inauguration, many highly knowledgeable people will scatter to the four winds![187]

Two weeks after Trump's election the Obama team inside of the Department of Energy learned that Trump had created a "landing team," led by Thomas Pyle, president of the American Energy Alliance. Pyle previously served as a Koch Industries lobbyist; Koch is one of the richest right-wing lobbying groups. Pyle also ran a side business writing editorials attacking DOE's attempts to reduce American dependence on carbon sources of energy. Pyle arrived for an appointment with Obama's Energy Secretary, Ernie Moniz, an MIT nuclear physicist who had assisted in the Iran nuclear deal negotiations, and two of his deputies.

According to author Michael Lewis, Pyle appeared to have no interest on anything Moniz had to say.[188] According to Deputy Secretary Sherwood-Randall, "He didn't bring a pencil or piece of paper. He didn't ask questions. He spent an hour … and never asked to meet with us again."[189] Pyle displayed little interest in an agency that spends $30 billion a year and has 110,000 employees and industrial sites across the country.[190]

Pyle eventually sent a list of 74 questions to the Energy Department that he wanted answers to. His list covered some of the briefing subjects, but focused mostly on the following kinds of questions:

- Can you provide a list of all DOE employees or contractors who have attended any Interagency Working Group on the Social Cost of Carbon Meetings?
- Can you provide a list of DOE employees or contractors who attended any Conference of the Parties (under the United Nations Framework Convention on Climate Change) in the last five years?[191]

Subsequently, Pyle disappeared and was replaced by a group of young ideologues who called themselves the Beachhead Team. They planted a Trumpian flag in the department by treating outgoing employees with disdain and belittling the role of government. They wanted to know the names and salaries of the 20 highest paid people at the national science labs overseen by the Department of Energy. They never asked for an introductory briefing.[192]

Perhaps most alarming of all, the Trump Beachhead Team never asked for a briefing from the Energy Department's Chief Financial Officer, who could have alerted them to the terrifying risks they would be asked to manage:

- Roughly half of DOE's annual budget is spent on maintaining and guarding the US nuclear arsenal.
- Two billion of the $30 billion Energy Department budget goes to hunting down weapons-grade plutonium and uranium lose in the world, so

it doesn't fall into the hands of terrorists. In 8 years alone—from 2010 to 2018—the DOE's National Nuclear Security Administration collected enough material to make 160 nuclear bombs.
- The department trains every international atomic energy inspector.[193]

> In the run up to Trump's inauguration, the man inside DOE responsible for the nuclear weapons program, Frank Klotz, was asked to submit his resignation, along with the department's other 137 political appointees. Klotz was a retired 3-star air force lieutenant with a Ph.D. in politics from Oxford. He had boxed up his books, notes, and memorabilia and had walked out the door. Only after outgoing Secretary Moniz called US Senators and alerted them to the disturbing vacancy and the senators phoned Trump Tower and sounded an alarm, did the Trump people call General Klotz—on the day before Trump's inauguration—and ask him to return to his office with his materials.[194]

The greatest management failure in the Trump years was the president's deeply flawed response to the coronavirus pandemic that began in January 2020 and continues to this day. On January 28, 2020, during the President's Daily Brief, discussion in the oval office turned to a mysterious pneumonia-like virus outbreak in China. Trump's fourth national security adviser, Robert O'Brien, said to the president "This will be the biggest national security you face in your presidency."[195]

At the time, Trump was in the model of his first impeachment trial in the Senate. The deputy national security adviser, Matt Pottinger, concurred with O'Brien's assessment. His views carried weight; Pottinger had lived in China for seven years and had been a *Wall Street Journal* reporter there during the SARS outbreak. He was a China scholar and spoke Mandarin. Pottinger asked his China contacts if the current virus would be like SARS 2003, and they responded "Don't think SARS 2003, think influenza pandemic 1918!"[196]

Pottinger's contacts emphasized factors that were accelerating the transmission of the new disease: (a) people were getting the disease from other people, and the disease was being spread by people who did not show any symptoms, and (b) the Chinese government had quarantined Wuhan, a city of 11 million people.[197]

In a January 30 phone call, the health and human services secretary, Alex Azar, directly warned President Trump of the possibility of a pandemic hitting the United States. The president, who received the phone call on Air Force One, said Azar was being alarmist.[198]

Nevertheless, on January 31, the president imposed restrictions on travelers from China, and then reassured the public they faced little risk.[199]

Two days later, nearly 40 million Americans tuned in to watch the president's state of the union address. About halfway through the speech, Trump mentioned coronavirus, saying "Protecting Americans' health means fighting infectious diseases. We are coordinating with the Chinese government and working closely together on the coronavirus Outbreak in China."[200]

When pressed by Bob Woodward on why he chose to reassure, instead of educating the public, Trump responded, "I wanted to play it down. I still like playing it down, because I don't want to create a panic."[201]

Trump clearly understood the severity and danger posed by COVID-19. In a February 7, 2020 interview with Woodward, Trump confessed that the issue was "tricky." "What made it tricky?," asked Woodward. "It goes through the air. That's always tougher than the touch. … you just breathe the air and that's how it's passed. And so that's a very tricky one. … It's also more deadly than even your strenuous flu."[202]

By the last week of February, it was clear to the administration's public health team that schools and businesses in hot spots would have to close. But it took the team, and others, three issue more weeks to persuade the president that failure to take decisive action to control the spread of the virus would be disastrous.[203]

When Dr. Robert Kadlec, the top disaster response official at the Department of Health and Human Services, convened the White House coronavirus task force on February 21, his agenda was urgent. There were deep cracks in the administration's strategy for keeping the virus out of the United States. There had already been an alarming spike in new cases around the world. As well, the administration had failed to roll out an effective testing and tracking system in the United States. The president was not worried, predicting that "by April when it gets a little warmer, it miraculously goes away."[204]

Kadlec, meanwhile, assembled a group of experts, including Dr. Anthony Fauci of the National Institute of Health, Dr. Robert Redfield of the Centers for Disease Control and Prevention, and Azar for a tabletop exercise on how the disease could spread through the United States.

The group unanimously concluded that the United States would have to move quickly toward aggressive policies of social distancing at the risk of severe disruption to the nation's economy and daily lives of millions of American.[205]

Kadlec and others decided to present Trump with a plan titled "Four Steps to Mitigation," summarizing the steps the United States would have to take to control the spread of COVID-19. Kadlec's group wanted to meet Trump in person, but the president was in India, and the meeting was delayed. A memo dated February 14, prepared in coordination with the NSC and titled "US Government Response to the 2019 Novel Coronavirus," detailed what dramatic measure would be needed: "limiting public gatherings and cancellation of almost all sporting events, performances … considering school closures. Widespread 'stay at home' directives from public and private organizations."[206]

But their plan was disrupted by circumstance. Trump was walking up the steps of Air Force One to return home from India on February 25 when Dr. Nancy Messonnier, director of the National Center for Immunization and

Respiratory Disease, publicly issued the blunt warning the group had been contemplating: she "had jumped the gun." On the 18-hour plane ride home Trump was furious as he watched the stock market crash after Messonnier's comments. The meeting with Kadlec's group was cancelled, and the president announced that the White House response would be put under the command of Vice President Mike Pence.

It would be more than three weeks before President Trump would announce serious social distancing efforts, a lost period during which the number of coronavirus cases in the United States grew from 15 to 4,226![207] Finally, on March 16, President Trump, at the urging of veteran AIDS researcher, Dr. Deborah Brix, who had joined the task force, announced new social distancing guidelines, saying they would be in place for two weeks.[208]

According to a *New York Times* report:

> These final days of February, perhaps more than any other moment during his tenure in the White House, illustrated Mr. Trump's inability or unwillingness to absorb warnings coming at him. He instead reverted to his traditional political playbook on the midst of a public health calamity, squandering vital time as the coronavirus spread silently across the country.[209]

As of this writing, the coronavirus has killed over 1 million Americans. There is little doubt that a more aggressive and engaged White House response, and a serious crisis management strategy, could have reduced this number substantially. According to the *New York Times*:

> From the time the virus was first identified as a concern, the administration's response was plagued by rivals and factionalism that routinely swirl around Mr. Trump, and, along with the president's impulsiveness, undercut decision making and policy development.
>
> Faced with the relentless march of a deadly pathogen, the disagreements and a lack of long-term planning, had significant consequences. They slowed the president's response and resulted in problems with execution and planning, including delays in seeking money from Capitol Hill and a failure to begin broad surveillance testing.[210]

On the other hand, President Trump deserves credit for effectively leading and managing the development of an effective COVID-19 vaccine in record-breaking time. No less a critic than President Joe Biden, in a December 22, 2021, speech, praised Trump for developing and manufacturing the vaccine.[211]

The process of developing and manufacturing the COVID-19 vaccine, encouraged and funded by the Trump administration, was called *Operation*

Warp Speed, and was the brainchild of Dr. Peter Marks, the top vaccine regulator at the Food and Drug Administration.[212]

As defined by the US Department of Health and Human Services, "Operation Warp Speed was a public private partnership initiated by the US Government to facilitate and accelerate the development of COVID-19 vaccines, therapeutics, and diagnostics."[213]

Dr. Marks envisioned a collaboration between the Pentagon and HHS to support pharmaceutical and biotechnology companies, with the full support of the government's expertise in areas like clinical trials and logistics, to bring a vaccine to US citizens.[214]

The operation funded several drug companies, notably Pfizer and Moderna, to the tune of $14 billion, to study and develop an mRNA vaccine. Normally, vaccine development takes at least 18 months, but the urging of President Trump and the scientists' strong motivation to find a cure, the companies were able to cut the time to eight months, and by early 2021, Americans could get vaccinated.

TAKEAWAYS FOR ALL LEADERS

- Leaders must staff their governments or organizations with the most highly qualified people available.
- Men and women who constitute an executive team will appreciate being trusted by the leader and will deeply resent being undermined by him or her in public.
- During a crisis, a leader must "fire on all cylinders" and must be "brutally optimistic" with stakeholders and followers.[215]
- A leader who ignores clear warning signs about a coming crisis does so at great peril.

Joseph Robinette Biden

During the 2020 presidential campaign, Joe Biden frequently challenged the incumbent president on the subject of competence. In the first presidential debate, on September 29, 2020, Biden laced into Trump's leadership ineptitude in managing the pandemic. He noted Trump's underplaying the seriousness of COVID-19 so as not to cause panic; stressed the president's irresponsibility in mounting an effective response, leading to the fact that with 4 percent of the world's population, the United States at the time had 20 percent of COVID cases; and mocked Trump's proposal of swallowing bleach as a cure for the disease.[216]

In contrasting himself with Trump as a presidential candidate, Biden emphasized his own experience as a US senator for 36 years, and his service as President Obama's vice president for eight years. He also noted his widespread political networks and connections, including members of the US Congress and executive branch, as well as foreign leaders. Biden trumpeted (no pun intended) his ability to bring people together and to find common ground.

Once he secured his place as the presumptive democratic presidential candidate, Biden signaled his intention to introduce change to the political system and larger society by choosing Kamala D. Harris as his running mate. Harris, the black daughter of a Jamaican father and Indian mother, alumna of Howard University, and former California prosecutor and member of the US Senate from that state,[217] would be the first woman to hold the office of Vice President, following 48 white men. In all of her previous positions, Harris took great pride in "opening the doors of American leadership to more people who look like her."[218] Biden assigned Harris specific leadership responsibility in the areas of dealing with the border crisis and securing voting rights legislation.[219]

For his chief of staff, Biden selected an experienced hand named Ron Klain. An active democrat who had held responsible positions on Capitol Hill, Klain served as chief of staff to Vice President Al Gore (1995–1999) and to Vice President Biden from 2009 to 2011. During the Obama years, he served as the White House Ebola Response Coordinator from 2014 to 2015.[220]

In his cabinet selections, Biden included White House and political veterans, and notably, several "firsts." When confirmed, his cabinet was more racial and gender diverse than not only Trump's cabinet but also Obama's.[221]

General Lloyd J. Austin, III, Secretary of Defense. Austin rose to become a four-star Army general before retiring in 2016 as Chief of the US Central Command. Once confirmed, he was the first African American in history to head the Department of Defense.

Pete Buttigieg, Secretary of Transportation. A former Navy officer and McKinsey consultant, Buttigieg was also a two-term mayor of South Bend, Indiana. He was also the first openly gay major party candidate to win delegates in a bid for the White House, in the 2020 presidential election. Once confirmed he would serve as the first openly gay cabinet member in history.

Alejandro Mayorkas, Secretary of the Department of Homeland Security. A former federal prosecutor and attorney at the DC law firm of Wilmer Hale. He previously served as director of the US Citizenship and Immigration Services in the Obama years, and later as DHS deputy secretary. Once confirmed, Mayorkas was the first Latino and first immigrant in charge of DHS.

Janet L. Yellen, Secretary of the Treasury. Yellen previously served as chair of the Federal Reserve Board, president of the

Federal Reserve Bank of San Francisco, and as a top economic adviser to President Clinton. She was the first female chair of the Fed, and once confirmed the first female treasury secretary of the United States.

Representative Deb Haaland, Secretary of the Department of the Interior. Haaland, a congresswoman from New Mexico, fought for conservation efforts and restrictions on fossil fuel extraction from public lands and water. As an enrolled member of the Laguna Pueblo, she was, once confirmed, the first Native American to run the Department of Interior.

Cecilia Rouse, Chair, Council of Economic Advisers. Rouse, a Princeton University labor economist, frequently spoke about the need for an urgent government response to the pandemic. She was a member of the Council of Economic Advisers, and once confirmed she was the first woman of color to Chair the council.

Avril Haines, Director of National Intelligence. Haines previously served as deputy national security adviser, and prior to that as the first female deputy director of the CIA. Once confirmed she was the first female DIN.

In terms of fulfilling campaign promises, Biden moved early and aggressively on the distribution of COVID-19 vaccines and on getting Americans vaccinated, as described in the previous chapter. But the competence issue flared during the summer of 2021, especially with regard to the withdrawal of US troops from Afghanistan. In April 2021, Biden announced that the United States would withdraw all remaining troops from Afghanistan by September 11, 2021, saying that, "It's time to end America's longest war," and that we had accomplished our objectives there: bin Laden was dead, and Al Qaeda was degraded.[222] Subsequently, President Biden advanced the pullout date to August 31, as the European powers were already in the process of withdrawing their troops, and the internal satiation was looking increasingly unstable.[223]

Both the Afghan government and military collapsed quickly, as the US withdrawal accelerated. Thousands attempted to flee a country that was increasingly dominated by the Taliban, who promised to reimpose strict adherence to Islamic law, while protecting the rights of minorities and women.[224] Images of Afghans running after US aircraft on airport runways, desperately trying to leave the country, underlined the tragedy unfolding for President Biden. The president, a few weeks later, compounded the problem by declaring that his military advisers never counseled him to retain a small force in Afghanistan, only to be contradicted by his generals in congressional testimony. The generals told members of Congress that they recommended keeping 2,500 troops there for a limited period.[225]

Furthermore, there was criticism of the slow pace of filling high-level executive vacancies in a White House populated by experienced staffers. As of December 2021, of 1,200 appointments requiring Senate confirmation, 400 had not yet been filled, with 141 even lacking a Biden nominee.[226]

Application to Other Sectors

For many years, leadership and management gurus advised business leaders to develop a vision, craft a strategy, and articulate organizational goals. All these ideas are valuable, as elaborated in the "policy" chapter of this book.

But in 2002, Larry Bossidy and Ram Charan, in an important book titled, *Execution: The Discipline of Getting Things Done*,[227] reminded leaders of the importance of execution as a needed executive skill. Bossidy, Chairman and CEO of Allied Signal (later Honeywell), and Charan, an adviser to CEO's and widely published management expert, explained their argument this way: "Many people regard execution as detail work that's beneath the dignity of a business leader. That's wrong. To the contrary, it's a leader's most important job."[228]

Bossidy and Charan argued that leaders can create an "execution culture" that helps assure organizational vision will be translated into reality. To create an execution culture, leaders need to unify their organizations around a common purpose and a coordinated effort. When Bossidy became CEO of Allied Signal, he quickly noticed the absence of an execution culture. He said "We had a chemical culture, an automation culture, and an aerospace culture, and they did not like each other."[229]

As we have seen, US presidential staffs are not immune from personal animosities toward one another, or from pretty jealousies as to who has the best access or relationship to POTUS. Exemplary leaders are aware of these human dynamics and work hard to address these issues and create strong teams that can be sustained over time. Stanford University Business Professor Jeffrey Pfeffer suggests that organizations succeed when leaders envision the team sport of football instead of the more solitary game of golf.[230]

One of the cornerstones of building an effective organizational team, to advance the execution culture, according to Bossidy and Charan, is "having the right people in place."[231]

In one of the best-selling business books of all time, author Jim Collins reinforced the idea of "getting the right people on the bus" as a factor contributing to leaders being able to move companies from "good" to "great."[232]

The question animating Collins' exhaustive, multiyear study was: How does a company that was good become great? Just as Collins had previously done with his co-author, Jerry Porras, in *Built to Last*, he paired great companies with their less successful counterparts for a comparative analysis: Kimberly Clarke was matched with Scott Paper, Kroger with A+P, and Walgreens with Eckerd. Collins outlined several research findings, a few of which are particularly germane to the development of an execution culture:

- The great companies did not focus obsessively on developing the right strategy; they chose to focus on hiring the right people under conditions of limited opportunities to hire.
- The great companies achieved success by considering not only what to do, but also what to STOP doing.[233]

Another leadership characteristic that underlies great teams and an execution culture is trust. Authors Jim Kouzes and Barry Posner, drawing from 112 studies representing over 7,000 teams, concluded that the extent to which team members trust each other made an important difference in the teams' performance.[234]

> The veracity of this conclusion was also verified by another leader Kouzes and Posner interviewed, Karen Twaronite, the global diversity and inclusiveness officer of Ernst and Young. Her firm's survey of approximately 9,800 full time workers in Brazil, China, Germany, Mexico, India, Japan, the United Kingdom and the United States concluded that "trust is the cornerstone for creating a workplace where employees are engaged, productive, and continually innovative."[235]

And trust emanates from leaders. According to Kouzes and Posner,

> When you create a climate of trust, you create an environment that allows people to contribute freely and to innovate. You nurture an open exchange of ideas … You motivate people to go beyond compliance and inspire them to reach for the best in themselves … To get these kinds of results, you have to ante up first in the gamed of trust, you have to listen and learn from others, and you have to share information and resources with others. Trust comes first, following comes second.[236]

In a well-regarded business book, written in the form of a parable, author Patrick Lencioni identified the five major dysfunctions of a team, based on his years of observing organizational teams. It is notable that the "absence of trust" is at the base, or foundation of all other dysfunctions (Figure 4.1).

Pyramid of Dysfunctional Teamwork

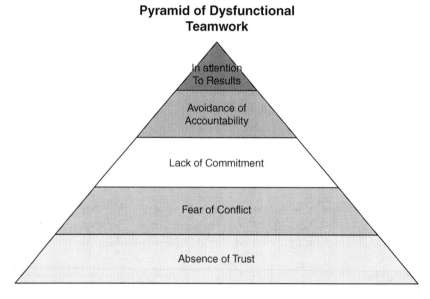

FIGURE 4.1

Source: Patrick Lencioni. *The Five Dysfunctions of a Team: A Leadership Fable*. San Francisco: Jossey-Bass, 2002.

Notes

1 See Chris Whipple. *The Gatekeepers: How the White House Chiefs of Staff Define Every Presidency*. New York, NY: Crown, 2017.
2 The White House. "The Cabinet," *The White House*, US Government, 9 June 2021. https://www.whitehouse.gov/administration/cabinet
3 Eizenstat, *President Carter*, 65.
4 Ibid., 71.
5 Ibid., 74.
6 Ibid.
7 Ibid., 75.
8 Ibid., 76.
9 Ibid.
10 Ibid.
11 Siegel, *The President as Leader*, 2nd ed., 57.
12 Hargrove, *Jimmy Carter as President*, 5–6.
13 Eizenstat, *President Carter*, 102.
14 Hargrove, *Jimmy Carter as President*, 5–6.
15 Eizenstat, *President Carter*, 77.
16 Eizenstat, *President Carter*, 134.
17 Glad, *Jimmy Carter in Search of the Great White House*, 440.
18 Bureton L. Kaufman and Scott Kaufman. *The Presidency of James Earl Carter, Jr.* Lawrence, KS: University of Kansas Press, 2006, 184.
19 Eizenstat, *President Carter*, 668.
20 Ibid., 669.

21 Ibid., 672.
22 Ibid., 684.
23 Ibid., 686.
24 Ibid., 691.
25 Ibid.
26 Ibid., 702.
27 Ibid., 700.
28 Miller Center. "Interview with Hamilton Jordan." University of Virginia, November 6, 1981. MillerCenter.org/thepresidency/presidential-oral-histories/hamilton-jordan-oral-history
29 Cannon, *President Reagan*, 182.
30 Robert Hershey. "Politics, Not Business as a Model for Government." *The New York Times*, October 18, 1983.
31 Reagan quote from PBS's *The American Experience*. www.pbs.org/ughh/americanexpereince
32 Barrett, *Gambling with History*, 72.
33 Ibid.
34 Ibid., 72–73.
35 Siegel, *The President as Leader*, 2nd ed., 87.
36 Cannon, *President Reagan*, 428 and 526.
37 Cannon, *President Reagan*, 564.
38 Siegel, *The President as Leader*, 2nd ed., 90.
39 Cannon, *President Reagan*, 573.
40 Ibid.
41 Ibid., 589.
42 Woodward, *Shadow: Five Presidents and the Legacy of Watergate*, 120.
43 Tower Commission, *President's Special Review Board Report*. New York, NY: Bantam Books, 1987, 79–80.
44 Cannon, *President Reagan*, 593–594.
45 James P. Pfiffner. "Establishing the Bush Presidency." *Public Administration Review*, January/February 1990, 69.
46 Siegel, *The President as Leader*, 2nd ed., 127.
47 Andrew Card. "The Bush White House and the Presidency," in Thompson, ed., *The Bush Presidency*, 46.
48 Michael Duffy and Dan Goodgame, *Marching in Place: The Status Quo Presidency of George Bush*.
49 Ibid., 113.
50 Ibid., 115.
51 Ibid.
52 Meacham, *Destiny and Power*, 394.
53 Ibid.
54 Ibid., 395.
55 Duffy and Goodgame, *Marching in Place*, 12.
56 Meacham, *Destiny and Power*, 527.
57 Siegel, *The President as Leader*, 1.
58 Fred I. Greenstein. "The Two Leadership Styles of William Jefferson Clinton," *Political Psychology*, 15, No. 2, 1999, 351–352.
59 Ibid., 356.
60 Clinton, *My Life*, 467.
61 Michael Waldman. *POTUS SPEAKS: Finding the Words that Defined the Clinton Presidency*. New York, NY: Simon and Schuster, 2000, 125.
62 Clinton, *My Life*, 451.
63 Ibid., 452–455.
64 Ibid.

65 Chris Whipple. *The Gatekeepers: How the White House Chiefs of Staff Define Every Presidency.* New York, NY: Crown, 2017, 187.

66 Ibid., 188.

67 Clinton, *My Life*, 521.

68 Ibid.

69 Gergen, *Eyewitness to Power*, 291.

70 Ibid.

71 Ibid., 293.

72 Ibid.

73 Whipple, *The Gatekeepers*, 191.

74 Bob Woodward, *The Agenda: Inside the Clinton White House.* New York, NY: Simon and Schuster, 1994, 254.

75 Whipple, *The Gatekeepers*, 192.

76 Ibid., 197.

77 Ibid., 198–199.

78 Ibid., 199.

79 William Jefferson Clinton. Inaugural Address, January 20, 1997, in *Public Papers of the Presidents of the United States.* Book I, January 1 to June 30, 1997. Washington, DC: Government Printing Office, 1997, 44.

80 Ibid.

81 Al Gore. *Creating a government that Works Better and Costs Less.* New York, NY: Plume, 1993, 5.

82 Ibid.

83 Clinton, *My Life*, 488.

84 Pfiffner, "The First MBA President," 6.

85 Ibid.

86 Ibid., 7.

87 Warshaw, *The Co-Presidency of Bush and Cheney.*

88 Peter Baker. *Days of Fire: Bush and Cheney in the White House.* New York, NY: Doubleday, 2013, 8.

89 Ibid.

90 Whipple, *The Gatekeepers*, 222.

91 Ibid., 223.

92 Scott McClellan. *What Happened? Inside the Bush White House and Washington's Culture of Deception.* New York, NY: Public Affairs, 2008, 82–83.

93 Kettle, *Team Bush,* 43–45.

94 Kettle, *Team Bush*, 248.

95 Ibid.

96 Jonathan D. Bruel. "Three Bush Management Reform Initiatives: the President's Management Agenda, Freedom to Manage Leadership Proposals, and the Program Assessment Rating System." Public Administration Review, January/February 2007, 21.

97 Ibid.

98 Ibid., 22.

99 Ibid.

100 Ibid.

101 Ibid.

102 Ibid., 23.

103 Ibid.

104 Ibid., 23–24.

105 Ibid., 25.

106 Ibid.

107 *The President as Leader*, 2nd ed., 225–226.

108 Homeland Security Act of November 25, 2002. PL 107–296.

109 George W. Bush, "Statement on Congressional Action on Homeland Security, November 19, 2002," in *Public Papers of the Presidents, Bush. 2002: Book II: July–December 31, 2002.* Washington, DC: Government Printing Office, 2006, 2095.

110 Siegel, *The President as Leader*, 225.

111 Shirley Anne Warshaw, "Mastering Presidential Government," in John Kraus, Kevin McMahon, and David M. Rankin, eds. *Transformed by Crisis: The Presidency of George W. Bush and American Politics.* New York, NY: Palgrave Macmillan, 2004, 105–106.

112 Ibid., 103.

113 Dan Eggen and Paul K. Jane. "Gonzales: Mistakes Were Made." *The Washington Post,* November 19, 2002, A1.

114 Gellman, *Days of Fire*, 30.

115 Chuck Todd. *The Stranger: Barack Obama in the White House.* Boston, MA: Little Brown and Company, 2014, 272.

116 Jonathan Alter. "Failure to Launch: How Obama Fumbled HealthCare.Gov." *Foreign Affairs.* March/April 2014, 45.

117 Whipple, *The Gatekeepers*, 260.

118 Obama, *A Promised Land,* 209.

119 Whipple, The Gatekeepers, 259.

120 David Corn *Showdown: The Inside Story of How Obama Fought Back Against Boehner, Cantor, and the Tea Party.* New York, NY: Harper and Collins, 2012, 124.

121 Andrew Rudalevige, "Rivals or a Team: Staffing and Issue Management in the Obama Administration," in Bert Rockman, Andrew Rudalevige and Colin Campbell. The Obama Presidency: Appraisals and Prospects. Washington, DC: Congressional Quarterly Press, 2012, 178–180.

122 Obama, *A Promised Land*, 215.

123 Ibid., 216.

124 Grunwald, *The New New Deal,* 225–226.

125 Ibid., 256.

126 Ibid., 259.

127 Ibid., 262.

128 Alter, "Failure to Launch," 46.

129 Elaine C. Kamarck. *Why President Fail and How They Can Succeed Again.* Washington, DC: The Brookings Institution, 2016, 95.

130 Ibid., 96–99.

131 Alter, "Failure to Launch," 46.

132 Ibid.

133 Ibid.

134 Ibid.

135 Ibid.

136 Kamarck, *Why Presidents Fail, 103.*

137 Ben Rangel. "Too little, too late for veterans under Obama," *The Hill,* 9/27/16. https://thehill.com/blogs/pundits-blog/healthcare/298065-too-little-too-late-for-veterans-under-obama/

138 Carolyn Y. Johnson. "Health Exchange Sign-Ups Fall Short," *The Washington Post.* August 28, 2016, A1+A8.

139 Kamarck, *Why Presidents Fail*, 96.

140 Alter, *The Promise,* 210.

141 *See Larry Bossidy, Ram Charan, and Charles Burch. Execution: The Disciple of Getting Things Done.* New York, NY: Currency, 2002.

142 Nazaryan, *The Best People*, Introduction, xxix.

143 Ibid.

144 Michael Lewis. *The Fifth Risk.* New York, NY: WW Norton and Company, 2018, 18.

145 Ibid.

146 Ibid., 18–19.

147 Lewis, *The Fifth Risk*, 19.

148 Ibid., 21.

149 Nazaryan, *The Best People*, 47.

150 Lewis, *The Fifth Risk*, 30–31.

151 Ibid., 31–32.

152 Nazaryna, *The Best People*, 45.

153 Ibid., 53 and 206–207, and "Department of Commerce, et al., v. New York et al.," supremecourt.gov/ opinions/188df/18-966_bq7c.pdf.

154 Nazaryan, *The Best People*, 53.

155 Ibid., 156.

156 Ibid., 54.

157 Ibid., 202.

158 Ibid., 203.

159 Ibid., 127.

160 Ibid., 128.

161 Ibid., 132–133.

162 Ibid., 175.

163 Ibid., 177.

164 Ibid., 177.

165 Ibid., 190.

166 Ibid., 191.

167 Ibid., 195.

168 Ibid., 215.

169 Ibid., 215.

170 Woodward, *Rage,* 2.

171 Ibid.

172 Ibid., 2–3.

173 Nancy A. Youssef and Gordon Lubold, "Mattis Blindsided by Trump's Syria Decision, Resigned Days Later." *Wall Street Journal*, December 21, 2018.

174 Woodward, *Rage,* 5.

175 Ibid., 11.

176 Ibid., 11.

177 John Cassidy. Rex Tillerson Gets Fired the Day After He Criticized Russia. *The New Yorker,* March 13, 2018. https://www.newyorker.com/news/our-columnists/rex-tillerson-gets-fired-the-day-after-he-criticized-russia/

178 Nazaryan, *The Best People*, 152–153.

179 Ibid., 153–154.

180 Ibid., 159.

181 Ibid., 160.

182 Ibid., 168.

183 Lewis, *The Fifth Risk*, 26.

184 Ibid., 36–37.

185 Ibid., 37.

186 Ibid., 37.

187 Ibid.

188 Ibid.

189 Ibid.

190 Ibid.

191 Ibid., 40–41.

192 Ibid., 42–43.

193 Ibid., 43.

194 Ibid., 45.

195 Ibid., 42–43.

196 Woodward, *Rage,* Prologue.

197 Ibid. Prologue, xiv–xv.

198 Eric Lipton, David E. Sanger, Maggie Haberman, Michael D. Shear, and Julian E. Barnes. "Despite Timely Alerts, Trump Was Slow to Act," *The New York Times,* April 12, 2020, A1 and A13.

199 Woodward, *Rage,* Prologue, xvii.

200 Ibid., Prologue, xviii.

201 Ibid.

202 Ibid., Prologue, xix.

203 Lipton et al., "Despite Timely Alerts," A13.

204 Ibid.

205 Ibid. A14.

206 Ibid.

207 Ibid.

208 Ibid.

209 Ibid., A15.

210 Ibid.

211 "Biden Offers Rare Praise of Trump during Covid Speech." https://www.cnn.com/2021/12/21/politics/biden-trump-covid-vaccine-booster/index.html/

212 Sharon La Franiere, Katie Thomas, Noah Wiland, David Gelles, Gary Stolberg, and Denise Grady, "Politics, Science and the Remarkable Pace for a Coronavirus Vaccine." *The New York Times,* November 21, 2020, and updated on November 30, 2020.

213 "Trump Administration Announces Framework and Leadership for 'Operation Warp Speed'" Department of Defense, May 15, 2020. https://www.defense.gov/News/Releases/Release/Article/2310750/trump-administration-announces-framework-and-leadership-for-operation-warp-speed/

214 La Franiere, et al., "Politics, Science and the Remarkable Pace for a Coronavirus Vaccine."

215 "Brutally optimistic" means honest about the challenges but optimistic about outcomes.

216 NBC News, First Presidential Debate of 2020, September 29, 2020. www.youtube.com/watch?v=5cafhanZFexs

217 Matt Viser, "Life and destiny have converged to deliver a new challenge for Biden," *The Washington Post,* "The 46th President: The Inauguration of Joseph R. Biden, Jr.," January 20, 2021, F3.

218 Chelsea James, "As Veep, Harris breaks the door open for women after a mere 232 years." *The Washington Post,* "Madam Vice President: The Inauguration of Kamala D. Harris," January 20, 2021, G3.

219 Kate Rabinowitz, "More Diversity in Biden's Cabinet Choices than Trump's or Obama's." *The Washington Post.* "The 46th President: The Inauguration of Joseph R. Biden, Jr.," January 20, 2021, F14.

220 Ibid.

221 Ibid.

222 Kevin Liptak, "Biden Announces American Troops Will Leave Afghanistan by September 11: 'It's Time to End America's Longest War.'" https://www.cnn.com/2021/04/14/politics/joe-biden-afghanistan-announcement/index.html/

223 Zeke Miller and Aamer Madhai. "'Overdue': Biden Sets Aug 31 for US Exit from Afghanistan." https://apnews.com/article/joe-biden-afghanistan-government-and-politics-86f939c746c7bc56bb9f11f095a95366/

224 Congressional Research Service, "US Military Withdrawal and Taliban Takeover in Afghanistan: Frequently Asked Question," https://crsreports.congress.gov/product/pdf/R/R46879

225 Rebecca Shabad. "Contradicting Biden, top general say they recommended a small force stay in Afghanistan." NBC News, September 28, 2021. https://www.nbcnews.com/politics/congress/pentagon-leaders-austin-milley-face-questions-chaotic-afghanistan-withdrawal-n1280230/

226 Partnership for Public Service. "Biden's Political Appointments Tracker," www.ourpublicservice.org/political/-appointee-tracker/

227 Larry Bossidy and Ram Charan. *Execution: The Discipline of Getting Things Done.* New York, NY: Crown Publishers, 2002.

228 Ibid., 3.

229 Ibid., 15.

230 Jeffrey Pfeffer. *Managing With Power: Politics and Influence in Organizations.* Cambridge: Harvard Business School Press, 1992, 17.

231 Bossidy and Charan, *Execution,* 22.

232 Jim Collins. *Good to Great: Why Some Companies Make the Leap and Others Don't.* New York, NY: Harper Collins, 2001.

233 Ibid.

234 Kouzes and Posner, *The Leadership Challenge,* 6th ed., 2017, 198.

235 Ibid.

236 Ibid., 200.

5

PROCESS, DECISION-MAKING

Importance to Presidents and All Other Leaders

Decision-making is vital to presidential leadership; presidents, like all other leaders, need to develop processes, techniques, and strategies that contribute to effectiveness in this skill. In the spring of 2005, President George W. Bush described the office he held as follows: "It is a decision-making job; when you're dealing with a future president, you ought to say, 'How do you intend to make decisions? What is the process by which you will make large decisions and small decisions? How do you decide?'"[1] A year later, he described himself as the "decider,"[2] and when he published his autobiography in 2010, he titled it *Decision Points*.[3]

Questions a president might ask about decision-making include:

- How will I make and announce decisions?
- Who will I include in the decision-making process?
- Will I deliberately encourage dissenting views?
- How will I manage strong disagreements among my advisers?
- How will I keep track of the consequences of my decisions?
- How will I apply "damage control" when needed?

There are several conditions that contribute to effective leadership decision-making. Being decisive, as President Bush averred, is certainly one of them. Research and experience indicate that citizens and followers grow frustrated with leaders who have trouble making clear decisions. But, as Stanford University management professor Jeffrey Pfeffer suggested, the most important leadership skill may be "in managing the consequences of decisions."[4] And since it is almost impossible to flawlessly predict the consequences of decisions, leaders need to obtain the very best information available, seriously consider

DOI: 10.4324/9781003285229-5

contingencies, aggressively solicit dissenting views, and think carefully about the best venue for decision-making. The venue element is frequently ignored.

Regarding the White House in particular, the president must hear diverse views before reaching a decision. Research on "group-think," how groups tend to quickly form the illusion of consensus and block out any dissenting opinions, has been applied to presidential decision-making by psychologist Irving Janis.[5] Using the 1961 US operation in the Bay of Pigs (Cuba) as a case study, Janis analyzed the flawed decision-making process that led to a disastrous outcome for President Kennedy. In that situation, Janis argues, Kennedy's advisers were far too quick to support the president's ill-conceived plan that the United States could "liberate" Cuba from the Communist regime of Fidel Castro by fomenting a "revolution," which would be ignited by the arrival of US troops. The mission failed, and Kennedy learned an important lesson: that most presidential advisers will give the president the advice he *wants*, instead of the advice he *needs*. On the other hand, a president, or any other leader, can actively solicit a diverse set of views, consider each one seriously and analytically, and then make a clear decision—as President Kennedy subsequently did in the Cuban Missile Crisis—with superior results. The intentional seeking out of diverse views was also a hallmark of President Lincoln's leadership during the civil war.[6]

There is a familiar dialectic underpinning the relationships between a powerful leader and those who report to him or her, and the normal course of events suggests deference and diplomacy on the part of the less powerful participants in the decision-making process. Nevertheless, critical decisions require an honest and open exchange of ideas. Dean Acheson served as secretary of state under President Harry Truman, and he described the relationship needed as follows:

> It is important that the relations between the President and the Secretary of State be quite frank, sometimes to the point of being blunt. And you just have to be deferential. He is the President of the United States, and you don't say rude things to him—you say blunt things to him. Sometimes he doesn't like it. That's natural, but he comes back, and you argue the thing out. But that's your duty. You don't tell him only what he wants to hear. That would be bad for him and everyone else.[7]

James Earl Carter

As described earlier in this book, President Carter was a detail person, an engineer by training, and he brought those habits of mind to the presidency. When it came to making decisions, Carter tried to understand each argument that came before him in detail. As Carter explained to his domestic policy adviser, Stuart Eizenstat, "I want to make a judgment based on what I know, and much of what I know was what I was told by you and by Harold Brown (secretary of defense) and others."[8] Carter elaborated further, "I didn't want to run at the negotiating table and say, 'Harold explain to me what the characteristic of this or that missile is.' I knew the missile."[9] In this and other areas, Carter was, according to Eizenstat, "intrigued" by issues and had to understand them "when I was the one who had to make the ultimate judgement."[10] We can hear the "decider" theme again!

Stuart Eizenstat correctly observed that "Each president brings a unique style of leadership to the Oval Office."[11] Carter was well-versed in public policy, as were Presidents Bush (41), Clinton, and Obama. These presidents developed an expertise in various policy areas, and when the time came to decide, they could weigh the options being presented by others against what they themselves knew to be true. Presidents like Reagan and Bush 43, on the other hand, were guided more by general principles in making decisions, and were willing to defer to experts on matters of policy (or politics). President Trump is an outlier in this area, and so many others, as he was clearly not an expert in public policy and frequently disdained the expertise of intelligence officers, scientists, and medical professionals.

Focusing specifically on President Carter, it is fair to say that he liked to be prepared for decision-making and leadership responsibilities. For example, in the preparation for the Camp David Peace Process that Carter initiated in September 1978 between Israel and Egypt, he voraciously reviewed CIA profiles of Egyptian President Anwar Sadat and Israeli Prime Minister Menachem Begin.[12] Throughout the 13 days of mediation at Camp David, Carter proved to be very well-versed about the issues that needed to be addressed and about the details of the proposals and counterproposals of both sides of the conflict.[13] On the other hand, Carter's expertise in policy did not always lead him to being decisive. It is fair to say that on personnel matters in the White House and cabinet, he was notably indecisive. Nowhere is this issue more clearly illustrated than in Carter's foreign policy team.

President Carter staffed the top tier of his foreign policy team with two individuals who were almost total opposites. He appointed Cyrus Vance as his secretary of state. Vance was an accomplished Wall Street lawyer, a calm conciliator and negotiator, temperate, and measured in almost all his interactions with others. As his national security adviser, he named Zbigniew Brzezinski, an erudite, academically accomplished Polish emigree, who was irascible and emotional, especially regarding the Soviet Union.[14] On almost all foreign policy issues requiring a presidential decision during the Carter years, Vance and Brzezinski took diametrically different positions and offered Carter dramatically different advice. Typically, Vance favored negotiating with the Soviets to resolve conflicts, seeking compromises where possible, and enlisting the United Nations and other international organizations to resolve regional disputes. Vance placed great emphasis, for example, on strengthening the

Strategic Arms Limitations Treaty (SALT).[15] Brzezinski, on the other hand, favored a tougher, more muscular approach to the Soviet Union, and believed the United States could negotiate with them from a "position of strength."[16] Vance and Brzezinski also disagreed about what President Carter should do about the faltering regime of the Shah of Iran. By the later part of 1978, it was becoming clear that the Shah was losing his grip on power, and that the revolutionary Islamic forces, led by the Ayatollah Khomeini, were gaining strength. Khomeini was living in exile but exerting a great deal of influence over radical students and others in Iran, who sought to depose the Shah, and the US influence that they perceived reinforced his rule. As Stuart Eizenstat wrote,

> The decisions facing Carter on Iran were among the toughest any president would face in peacetime: How to support an increasingly unpopular autocratic leader but a strategically vital ally; whether to block his radical successor and then navigate a new relationship with the unique reality of an Islamic republic; whether to allow the Shah to enter the United States for medical treatment, knowing the risks of inflaming the Iranian pubic; and finally the worst dilemma of dealing with the unprecedented capture of the American diplomats serving in what was then the largest embassy on the world.[17]

As the forces of revolution gained strength in Iran, and as US support for the Shah became increasingly problematic, Vance and Brzezinski offered divergent advice to President Carter: Brzezinski believed that restoring order was of paramount importance and only a show of force by the Shah could save the day. Vance, whose attention was more focused on SALT and Middle East negotiations, continued to emphasize negotiations with the opposition and progress to implement the Shah's reform; however, he was not ready to abandon the Shah.[18]

Meanwhile at a breakfast meeting with reporters on December 7, Carter seemed to ignore both of his advisers by answering a question about whether the Shah could survive. Carter said, "This is something that is in the hands of the people of Iran. We have never had any intention and don't have any intention of trying to intercede in the internal political affairs of Iran. We primarily want an absence of violence and bloodshed."[19] He added that "We personally prefer that the Shah maintain a major role in the government, but that is a decision for the Iranian people to make."[20]

As Eizenstat said, "This sent an unintended signal that Washington was distancing itself from the Shah and leaving decisions not to him but to the 'people of Iran'—the ones who were already in the streets demonstrating against the Shah."[21]

Carter clarified his position in subsequent statements, emphasizing that the United States still backed the Shah; however, Vance and Brzezinski were still at loggerheads, with Vance arguing that Brzezinski's tough language was a prescription for mass violence in Iran, and Carter was "caught in the middle," with Vance endlessly seeking diplomatic solutions and Brzezinski encouraging the use of military might to pursue diplomatic ends.[22] In the end, the situation deteriorated, with the Iranian capture of 66 US diplomats from the embassy and holding them for 444 days; Carter tried to rescue them in April 1980 through Operation Eagle Claw, which failed miserably and probably contributed to Carter's losing his bid for a second term to Ronald Reagan.[23] Vance resigned shortly before the operation was launched.

During the Iranian hostage crisis, and throughout his presidency, Carter showed strengths and weaknesses as a decision maker. As Eizenstat and others indicate, President Carter showed strong moral rectitude which prevented him from initiating any kind of military action that would endanger the lives of the hostages, despite Brzezinski's entreaties for him to do so.[24] He also showed great courage in accepting responsibility if anything were to go wrong with the hostage rescue operation (which it did). In a White House meeting, Carter told his advisers, "This operation will be conducted by the military ... If it is successful, it will redound to the benefit of the military. And if it is a failure, it would be my failure."[25]

But as a decision maker, President Carter frequently displayed an inability to make clear choices: instead, he tried to please everyone in his orbit. In a speech he gave at the US Naval Academy in June 1978, Carter sought to define US policy toward the Soviet Union in the midst of differing statements from Vance and Brzezinski on the issue. In his speech, Carter tried to blend both of their positions into one composite statement.[26] Only when the Soviets invaded Afghanistan did Carter throw his full weight behind Brzezinski.[27]

TAKEAWAYS FOR ALL LEADERS

- A leader who has strong ethical, even religious, convictions will be aided by those in making tough decisions.
- A leader must encourage members of his or her executive team to furiously debate issues, but the leader must clearly decide his or her own course.
- It does not serve the leader, or anyone else, when top deputies conduct their strong disagreements publicly.

Ronald Wilson Reagan

As I have written elsewhere, "Like President Franklin Delano Roosevelt," Reagan believed "that the decisive aspect of presidential leadership was inspirational rather than programmatic."[28] In this view of decision-making, the president's major responsibility when making important decisions is to frame these decisions in ways that create hope and optimism. Clearly, Reagan as a decision maker was less guided by policy expertise than he was by general principles and values. According to his biographer Lou Cannon:

> The paradox of the Reagan presidency was that it depended totally on Reagan for its ideological inspiration while he depended totally on others for all aspects of governance except for his core ideas and his powerful performances He left to others what he called the "details" of government, a category that included the preparation for a budget, the formulation of foreign policy, the translation of ideas into legislative proposals, and the resolution of conflicts among his principal advisers.[29]

One of the details of governing as a leader, as seen in the Carter administration, is deciding what advice to take from the many presidential advisers, and sometimes how to resolve conflicts among them. But Reagan's approach was to steer clear of conflicts, to step aside and hope the principals would work things out on their own. According to author Laurence Barrett, "Reagan so despised turmoil in the ranks that he tended to deny, even to himself, that it even existed, so that he might have to impose order."[30]

On the other hand, when President Reagan cared deeply about an issue he became quite decisive and used a range of talents, including negotiation skills, to accomplish his goals. He had to exercise negotiation skills as president of the Screen Actors Guild earlier in his life, and as a two-term governor of California, the largest state in the union.

Meg Greenfield, the late editor of the Washington Post editorial page, and a great reporter as well, took note of Reagan's negotiation skill in a 1982 *Newsweek* essay titled "How Does Reagan Decide?" Greenfield compared Reagan's decision-making process to that of a labor leader:

> .... the long waiting out of an adversary, the immobility meanwhile, the refusal to give anything until the last moment, the willingness— nonetheless—finally to yield to supreme personal force or particular circumstances on almost everything, but only with something to show in return and only if the final deal can be interpreted as furthering the original Reagan objective.[31]

President Reagan's decision to appoint Jim Baker as his first chief of staff, instead of the presumptive candidate, Ed Meese, was an example of how Reagan was clear-eyed decision maker, who understood that for his agenda to be adopted, he would need support from at least some of the Washington establishment; and Baker was the best way to achieve that.[32] Naming Baker set off fire alarms among Reagan's true believers, because they correctly perceived that Baker was a political pragmatist.[33] Displaying a keen sense of how this decision would fall hard on his longtime political associate Ed Meese, President Reagan said to Baker, "I want you to make this right with Ed."[34] And Baker did so by proposing that the two men agree on a division of duties and responsibilities—the agreement they developed ostensibly favored Meese but left Baker holding more power.[35]

On the other hand, Reagan could be naïve and, at times, duped by his advisers, as was evident during the Iran–Contra situation. President Reagan believed the September–October 1985 briefings of two of his national security advisers, Bud Mcfarlane and later Admiral John Poindexter, reassuring the president that the United States had done nothing illegal in swapping arms for hostages with Iran. The president knew the United States had shipped anti-tank and anti-aircraft missiles to Tehran and that certain Iranians could exert influence over terrorists in Lebanon to arrange for the release of US hostages. "In Reagan's mind," said his second chief of staff, Donald Reagan, "that did not constitute arms for hostages."[36] President Reagan according to Reagan, thought about the matter this way:

> ... If there is a kidnapping, and if one of the kidnapped person's relatives—say a father or husband or wife—is contacted by an intermediary who says that he might be able to secure the release of the victim through that intermediary, and in the end the intermediary is rewarded for his services, then you haven't dealt with the kidnappers or paid them ransom.[37]

With this kind of reasoning as a foundation, Reagan decided, against the strong advice of some of his advisers, to go on national television on November 13, to explain to the American people what had transpired. Reagan noted that the "raw material" for the speech came from the NSC staff, who were not prepared to tell the president the truth.[38] John Poindexter allowed President Reagan to make the following statement: "I authorized the transfer of small amounts of defensive weapons and spare parts for defensive systems to Iran. These modest deliveries, taken together, could easily fit into a single cargo plane. We did not, repeat not, trade weapons or anything else for hostages, nor will we."[39]

In one of the few times in his political career, Reagan's speech failed to move public opinion in his favor. *The Los Angeles Times* published the results of a poll indicating that only 14 percent of the public believed the president when he said he had not traded arms for Hostages. White House polls showed the same results.[40]

Another surprising feature of Reagan's decision-making was revealed after he left office. While it was widely known that First Lady Nancy Reagan exerted a great deal of influence on her husband's decisions, especially regarding personnel decisions in the White House, what was not so well known was that Nancy Reagan relied a good deal on a San Francisco astrologer to guide her own decisions, and consequently those of the president at times. Nancy consulted the astrologer on matters like scheduling meetings and foreign travel for her husband, and specifically, Nancy's communication with her "friend," even influenced the scheduling of President Reagan's June 1985 surgery to remove a large polyp in his intestinal tract.[41]

A fuller picture of Nancy Reagan's influence on her husband's decision-making emerges from a recent book by Washington Post reporter Karen Tumulty, titled, *The Triumph of Nancy Reagan*.[42] In an excerpt from the book published in *The Washington Post*, Tumulty explains that Nancy Reagan persistently and deftly toward a more conciliatory posture toward the USSR, especially in Reagan's second term. Nancy Reagan developed a close relationship with President Reagan's second secretary of State, George Schultz, and the two of them convinced the president to explore negotiations with the Soviets, especially in the area of arms control. According to Karen Tumulty, "Of all the things that Nancy wanted to see her husband achieve as president, ending the Cold War, she believed, would stand as an accomplishment that secured his legacy as a giant among US presidents."[43]

Together, Nancy Reagan and Secretary Schultz helped convince President Reagan to enter three direct discussions/negotiations with the new Soviet leader, Mikhail Gorbachev. The first meeting took place in Geneva in November 1985. In this case, the president prepared thoroughly for the meeting, having spent the previous six months poring over two dozen briefing papers on topics from Russian history and culture to Soviet objectives and negotiating tactics. "For once," an aide noted, the president didn't express annoyance about being loaded down with paperwork and information."[44]

Nancy Reagan, in cahoots with presidential advance man William Henkel, took the perceptive step of identifying a charming boathouse, 100 yards away from the primary summit venue, as a place where Reagan and Gorbachev could get to know one another as human beings. The boathouse had a fireplace and a spectacular view of the water.

The talks between Gorbachev and Reagan began with a "disappointingly conventional script, talking past each other and arguing over their countries' long-standing differences. In the afternoon, the atmosphere got 'heavy,' as Reagan vigorously defended his Strategic Defense Initiative ('Star Wars') and Gorbachev angrily dismissed it as 'emotional' and only a 'dream.'"[45] At that point in the discussion, President Reagan suggested that the two men and their interpreters take a walk and breathe the crisp outdoor air. The small group walked over to the boathouse, where a fire had already been started by aids in the fireplace. Away from the formal discussion, President Reagan offered a dramatic observation to Gorbachev:

> Mr. General Secretary, here we are, two men born in obscure rural ham-
> lets, both poor and from humble beginnings. Now we are the leaders of
> our countries, and probably the only two men who can start Word War
> III, and possibly the only two men …. who can bring peace to the world.[46]

Reagan's heartfelt communication with Gorbachev made an impression, and the two agreed to two additional meetings.[47] The common ground that was established by Reagan and Gorbachev about nuclear de-escalation was most likely more important than the relatively few concrete results of the November 1985 Geneva summit, which included agreements on cultural exchanges, civil air safety procedures, and new consulates.[48]

At the October 1986 Reykjavik summit, Gorbachev surprised state department officials by handing Reagan a printed summary of Soviet proposals in the format of actual instructions to Soviet ministries:

- An agreement on a 50 percent reduction in the strategic offensive weapons of the Soviet Union and the United States
- An agreement on the complete elimination of US and Soviet medium-
  range missiles in Europe
- An agreement pledging not to use their right to withdraw from the anti-
  ballistic missile (ABM) systems for ten years[49]

It was the third provision that gave Reagan pause, because it directly threatened his cherished SDI. Reagan reiterated his belief that the SDI was defensive in nature and even proposed to share its operational details with the Soviets. Gorbachev reacted coolly, sarcastically saying that the Americans would not even share agricultural secrets with the Soviets. Gorbachev insisted that the proposals were meant to be a package and refused any alteration of the defense provision. The two men went home without an agreement.[50]

Reagan and Gorbachev met again in December 1985 in Washington and signed the Intermediate-Range-Nuclear Forces Treaty, a landmark agreement prohibiting land-based cruise missiles with ranges between 311 miles and 3,429 miles.[51] According to Karen Tumulty, "For the first time, the two superpowers had agreed to eliminate an entire category of nuclear weapons."[52] The INF Treaty helped set the stage for the Strategic Arms Control Treaty (SALT), that was signed in 1991 and cut Soviet strategic missiles in almost the exact ration that Reagan had proposed.[53]

TAKEAWAYS FOR ALL LEADERS

- A leader who combines strong passion for an issue with adequate preparation will be able to make clear and informed decisions.
- Even powerful leaders can be duped by their advisers when those advisers try to shield the leader from bad news or provide incomplete information.
- The sources of influence on a leader's decision-making are varied, and sometimes surprising.

George Herbert Walker Bush

The key to understanding President George H.W. Bush's decision-making style is the realization that Bush was not an ideologue, and that he believed the work of government was less about radical reform and more about careful stewardship. Where Reagan saw politics as a "clash of convictions," Bush was more apt to see politics as a "search for common ground."[54]

Furthermore, while President Bush was a man of principle (duty, honor, country"),[55] he was not driven by emotion in pursuit of principle but by reason and logic. For example, his decision to drop out of the 1980 presidential race, after winning the Iowa caucus and losing the New Hampshire primary to Ronal Reagan, was driven by a calculated analysis, offered by his associate Jim Baker. The reality was that if Bush were to remain in the race and ultimately lose the delegate count to Ronald Reagan, which seemed likely, Bush would not be in a strong position to become Reagan's choice for vice president. According to historian Jon Meacham, Bush's decision, which he described as the "toughest decision of my entire life,"[56] was made easier by the Bush worldview of looking ahead.[57]

When Bush ran for president in the 1988 race, he surprised several politicians and pundits when he chose Dan Quayle, a young Indiana US Senator (R), as his running mate. Quayle, who had defeated liberal icon, Indiana US Senator Birch Bayh (D) in 1980, had less name recognition and party standing than other potential candidates, including US Senator Bob Dole (R, KS), US Representative Jack Kemp (R, NY), US Senator John Danforth (R, MO), US Senator Alan Simpson (R, WY), and US Senator John McCain (R, AZ).[58] But Bush chose Dan Quayle, because he reasoned, the young Indiana senator was conservative and a new face, and because he represented generational change and the Midwest.[59]

We can also see President Bush's reason-based, non-emotional decision-making in the realm of foreign policy. During the summer of 1989, he proposed a reduction by 25 percent in the deployment of US troops in Europe, and reduced the suggestion to 20 percent after negotiations with the Pentagon.

His aim was "to show that we were serious and committed to responding to the positive changes that we were seeing in the policies of the Soviet Union."[60] Bush also calculated that the reduction of US troops would also reduce the levels of concern, especially in Germany, over short-range nuclear weapons.[61]

In addition, when on June 3, 1989, the Chinese army attacked anti-regime peaceful student demonstrators in Beijing's Tiananmen Square, killing several hundred of them in the process, Bush resisted the temptation to impose a full embargo on China, as some were advocating; he chose instead to suspend military sales and prohibit visits between Chinese and US military officers. Bush met with his national security adviser, Brent Scowcroft, and secretary of state, Jim Baker, to lay out his objectives, telling them "I want a measured response, one aimed at those who had pushed for and implemented the use of force ... I did not want to punish the Chinese people."[62]

Historian Jon Meacham characterized Bush's reduction in military forces in Europe idea and his reaction to Tiananmen Square as examples of "steadiness, realism, and the search to further peace and stability."[63] And these traits were, again, on full display when President Bush decided how to react to the fall of the Berlin Wall, which happened on November 9, 1989.

While this development was ostensibly a cause for elation in the West, and possibly some US gloating, Bush demurred. The president understood that a visible and emotional response by the United States would create difficulty for Soviet General Secretary Mikhail Gorbachev. When asked CBS reporter Lesley Stahl if he was "excited" about the fall of the Berlin wall, Bush responded, "I'm not an emotional kind of guy."[64]

When President Bush subsequently met with Gorbachev at a summit in Malta, he told Soviet leader, "I hope you have noticed that as dynamic change has accelerated in recent months, we have not responded with flamboyance or arrogance that would complicate Soviet relations .... I have not jumped up and down on the Berlin Wall." Gorbachev replied, "Yes, we have seen that, and appreciate that."[65]

In the words of Jon Meacham:

> As the wall fell, Bush was pragmatic. He kept his options open and resisted alienating rhetoric or sweeping declaration. He led by checking here and balancing there, understanding that a world in convulsion was inherently unstable, and everything in him was about bringing stability, or a semblance of stability, to the unruliness of reality.[66]

In the US–Israel relationship, Bush also demonstrated the non-emotional pragmatic decision-making style. Bush was far less effusive toward Israeli leaders than Reagan had been. While he was in actuality a strong supporter of the Jewish state, and provided Israel with a host of military and economic resources and agreements, he was also quite blunt with Prime Minister Yitzhak

Shamir about the problems he was creating by continuing to build settlements in Palestinian occupied territory.

According to Middle East Envoy and presidential adviser Dennis Ross, Bush perceived that expanding settlement activity gave the appearance that the Israelis had no intention of withdrawing from the West Bank and Gaza, and this ruled out the land for peace ideas of UN Security Council Resolutions 242 and 338.[67]

In an April 1989 discussion with Shamir, President Bush, referring to the settlements, said, "This is an issue of great concern to us." Shamir responded by saying that "settlements ought not to be such a problem." Shamir probably thought he was telling the president that he should not be so concerned about the issue; however, Bush believed that Shamir was saying he would stop the settlements, thereby alleviating the "concern."[68] The upshot was that Bush believed Shamir lied to him, as settlements continued to be built, and their relationship would be strained in the future.[69]

President Bush showed his decisiveness and resolve again in his willingness to deploy US troops to help depose Panamanian strongman and dictator, Manuel Noriega. While Noriega had been a US ally in the Latin American theater of the cold war, he was also a drug trafficker who stole a presidential election. Noriega had declared war on the United States on December 15, 1989 but Bush paid little attention to this—until he learned that Panamanian troops were harassing and brutalizing US troops stationed there.[70]

After conferring with Secretary of State, Colin Powell, and Secretary of Defense, Dick Cheney, Bush ordered an operation against Noriega's Panama Defense Forces. Operation Just Cause, Bush's invasion of Panama, was, at that time, the largest US military deployment Since the Vietnam War. The 26,000 US troops quickly deposed Noriega, who took refuge for 10 days in the Vatican Embassy in Panama City before surrendering to US troops. He was brought to the United States for a federal trial on drug trafficking charges.[71]

As I have written elsewhere, "Bush was certainly an active president who fulfilled his job with energy and enthusiasm."[72] But the range of his contacts was limited to the circle of professional men and women with whom he could communicate freely and easily. The discussions among professional politicians, federal officials, and even foreign leaders were drawn from many years of accumulated wisdom, and "inside" information. This was the playbook of President George H.W. Bush, and it was a viable one as long as there was not an urgent need for change. Toward the end of Bush's term of office, however, with a deepening economic recession causing misery among millions of Americans, proceduralism was no longer an adequate leadership strategy.

As a decision maker and as a leader, President Bush was more interested in results; he believed that results were the only real measurement of success for political leaders. And he had a tendency, as explained by Jon Meacham, "to assume that other people were living inside his head with him and understood what he was doing and why he was doing it."[73] He governed by making decisions he felt were right and then moving on to the next order of business.[74] But this behavior is more fitting of a judge than it is a leader. According to Meacham:

> Bush's discomfort with the rhetorical requirements of his office was one of his cardinal weaknesses as president. He had worked hard, devilishly hard, to manage the affairs of the age, but then he wanted to go back to work, no to deliver a grand address or present a consistent message.[75]

TAKEAWAYS FOR ALL LEADERS

- An exemplary leader will be guided by reason, logic, and data in making decisions, not by emotion or instinct.
- A leader with deep knowledge and experience, surrounded by equally capable associates, will frequently make sound decisions and win support from followers.
- In leadership, making decisions is not the end of a process, but instead, it is the beginning.

William Jefferson Clinton

As I have written elsewhere, "The early Clinton White House was not hospitable environment for orderly or rapid decision-making."[76] President Clinton was impressively knowledgeable about the details of public policy and could easily see the complexity and nuances of proposals brought to him. He enjoyed the analysis and the debate. According to Clinton's biographer, *Washington Post* reporter John Harris, "Clinton found rivalries among his subordinates liberating. He found his ideas and opinions, he once acknowledged, 'in the seams' between the clashing ideas of others."[77]

But the "clashing ideas of others" could also lead President Clinton to a state of paralysis or delay. If George W. Bush easily earned the moniker of "the decider," perhaps Clinton's title should have been "the procrastinator" or "the contemplator."

President Clinton possessed a flexible, penetrating mind but lacked discipline. In preparing for the 1996 presidential campaign against Republican candidate, Senator Bob Dole (R, KS), Vice President Al Gore suggested to Clinton that he should "elevate self-discipline as the hallmark of this strategy—in his remarks, ideas, and behavior."[78] Gore was expressing a widely held view that Clinton's notorious lack of self-discipline was contributing to a chaotic White House, characterized by inconsistent decision-making and the tendency for gaffes, scandals, and political failures among White House staff. Many saw the Clinton White House as the embodiment of indecision, uncertainty, and delay.[79]

Part of the problem of the new Clinton presidency, as indicated in the last chapter, was Clinton's selection of Thomas F. "Mack" McLarty as the White House chief of staff. McLarty, Bill Clinton's boyhood friend, was CEO of Arkla, a Fortune 500 natural gas concern. He had also been elected as one of the youngest men ever, at age 23, to the Arkansas House of Representatives and during the mid-1970s had been chairman of the state Democratic Party. But he was neither known in Washington, DC, nor did he have any experience working in the nation's capital.[80]

McLarty did not understand what Bill Clinton needed in a chief of staff, as became obvious during the transition. Addressing a group of people headed for White House jobs, McLarty said he would run the operation as a "confederation." He said that he knew everyone was talented and had the president's best interests at heart, making his job one of a "facilitator." This idea may have been what Clinton wanted, but not what he needed. Because even if Clinton's staff had his best interests in their hearts, they would have conflicting ideas of what those interests were, and only a powerful chief of staff could keep those conflicts from spiraling into chaos.[81]

As John Harris noted, the people who had succeeded in Clinton's orbit in the past did so "not by deferring to his instincts but by pressing aggressively against them. In the Arkansas years, these had included people like former chief of staff Betsey Wright or political consultant Dick Morris."[82]

Betsey Wright had counseled Clinton against entering the 1988 presidential race, after Democratic candidate Gary Hart's withdrawal due to newspaper revelations of marital infidelity. Wright bluntly told Clinton he would face the same problem as Hart did, and Clinton decided not to run to protect his family, especially his 8-year-old daughter, Chelsea.[83] Dick Morris, Clinton's longtime political adviser, rescued him after the 1994 healthcare debacle by bluntly telling Clinton that if he wanted to win a second term, he would have to move back to the center, which Morris called "triangulation." Clinton took his advice, actively pursued welfare reform, and won a second term.[84]

In the early months of his presidency, Clinton displayed a decision-making pattern of reversing earlier decisions, as can be seen in the issue of the Haitian refugees. A fledging Haitian democracy had been defied in 1991, when elected President Jean Bernard Aristide—a leftist priest and advocate for the poor—was ousted in a military coup by the nation's wealthy elite.[85]

As a presidential candidate, Clinton attacked the Bush administration policy of refusing to allow refugees from Haiti to enter the United States. But in early January 1993, CIA officers visited Clinton in Little Rock and showed him satellite photographs of tens of thousands of Haitians hacking down trees, and even their own homes, to build makeshift boats. The Haitians were aware of Clinton's campaign promises. By the time of his swearing in on January 20, some 100,000 Haitians were heading toward the United States. It was estimated that 10,000 would most likely die at sea, and that those who made it would swamp the Gulf Coast in desperate need of food, shelter, and medical aid.[86]

Sadly, Clinton had to revoke his campaign promise before he was inaugurated. At a subsequent news conference, President Clinton insisted that he was not reversing himself on Haiti, but that his earlier comments about offering asylum hinged on a distinction between political refugees, who were entitled to stay in the United States, and economic refugees, who were not.[87] As biographer John Harris commented, "Reporters covering Clinton were learning to listen for the escape hatches and qualifiers incorporated, as if by subconscious instinct, into his language—placed there as insurance to preserve flexibility for later."[88]

On the issue of indecisiveness, the situation in Bosnia demonstrated that characteristic in a compelling manner. Bosnia was a Muslim enclave that became an independent nation after the break-up of Yugoslavia in the early 1990s. Bosnia was surrounded by Bosnian Serbs, who were rich in resources and weapons from their benefactors in Belgrade and were attacking Bosnia with unrelenting brute force. The Muslims were especially endangered because of a UN-imposed arms embargo, an embargo that the European allies wanted kept in place.[89] French and British troops on the ground in Bosnia were serving in a UN humanitarian mission effort to keep food and medical lines to Bosnia open, but they were not preventing attacks on the Bosnian Muslims. Clinton had the option of lifting the ban unilaterally, as some of his advisers recommended; but if he did, and the Europeans made good on their threat to withdraw, there would be a period when the Bosnian Muslims would be particularly vulnerable. The Bosnian Serbs would exploit the window of time to crush their opposition.

The alternative to simply lifting the embargo was what came to be called "lift and strike." In this scenario, the arms embargo would be lifted, ideally in concurrence with European allies, and if the Bosnian Serbs tried to exploit the situation, NATO warplanes would strike.[90]

At around the same time, on April 22, 1993, President Clinton attended the dedication of the US Holocaust Memorial Museum in Washington DC. On that occasion, Elie Wiesel, the Nobel prize-winning author, activist, and survivor of the Holocaust, looked directly into President Clinton's eyes and said, "As a Jew, I'm saying that we must do something to stop the bloodshed in that country." According to John Harris, "Clinton sat back in his chair with a notable jolt."[91]

Clinton leaned in to the more aggressive "lift and strike" option, but he did so, according to Harris, "in the most tentative way."[92] He dispatched Secretary of State Warren Christopher to Europe to sell the president's policy decision. At each stop, Christopher met stiff resistance, which Harris explained was exacerbated by two factors:

- Christopher's dry and understated style did little to convey any sense of the administration's urgency about the war. According to a British diplomat, Christopher offered the American proposal "with all the verve of a solicitor going over a conveyance deed."[93]
- Christopher himself was ambivalent about the ideas he was selling. In internal debates he was skeptical about intervening.[94]

According to John Harris:

> The core problem was that he was not really selling a policy, nor had he been instructed to do so. Clinton had sent Christopher to Europe to "consult" with allies and get their response. This was quite different proposition than making clear in emphatic terms that lift and strike was what the United States wanted and that the US president expected their support.[95]

Christopher came home with nothing, and the trip was seen as a symbol of the "timidity of American power during the early Clinton years.[96] What Clinton needed in this case was someone who could quiet his doubts, as Lloyd Bentsen had done on the economic program. Clinton eventually authorized the bombing of Serbia, in coordination with NATO in 1999, but a lot of time, and a lot of lives had been lost.

In terms of a poorly thought-out decision, President Clinton's nomination of Zoe Baird to be the Attorney General of the United States comes to mind. Baird was a strongly credentialed and experienced attorney, who had served as general counsel at Aetna Insurance. Bill and Hillary Clinton thought it was time for a female Attorney General, and the nomination was strongly endorsed by Warren Christopher, who had worked with Baird in the Carter administration.[97] As the confirmation process evolved, however, it was revealed that Baird and her husband had hired undocumented immigrants to work in their home and care for their three-year-old child. But Baird, like many other people in this situation, did not pay social security taxes on her employees. *The New York Times* detailed the problem in a front page story on January 16, 1993, three weeks after Baird was selected by Clinton and only six days before the president's swearing in.[98] People were outraged that a person nominated to be the nation's chief law enforcement officer was breaking the law in her personal life. Most of Clinton's advisers, especially George Stephanopoulos and legislative liaison Howard Paster, advised the president to pull the nomination, while White House counsel Bernard Nussbaum urged Clinton "to fight."[99]

Clinton pulled the nomination when the chairman of the Senate Judiciary Committee, Delaware Democratic Senator Joe Biden called him to let him know that Baird would not be able to get enough votes to secure her nomination. Finally, Baird wrote to Clinton asking that he withdraw her nomination, which he did.[100] Later, Baird maintained that she had informed the Clinton transition staff of her child-care arrangements; Christopher said that he had told Clinton, but could not recall the exact details, and Clinton said he was never told about this.[101]

But Clinton showed a capacity to learn and grow as a decision maker and as a leader. According to political scientist Paul Quirk, "By 1996, Clinton had learned a good deal from his mistakes. He had strengthened the White House staff and submitted himself to orderly processes of decision-making."[102]

He became more comfortable with the decisional aspects of the commander-in-chief role. For example, on October 2, 1996, when Anthony Lake, Clinton's national security adviser, made a secret trip to Little Rock to bring the president options for a cruise missile attack on Iraq, Clinton appeared confident and animated as he peppered Lake with technical questions about "target site" and BDA's (bomb damage assessments). In the summer of 1993, on the other hand, when Clinton had to order a missile attack on Iraq for the first time, he seemed "tense and wobbly." At the last minute he asked Lake, "Are you sure this is the right thing to do?"[103]

And while he became tougher about deciding to use military might, Clinton also demonstrated a capacity to make decisions to pursue peace, especially in the Middle East. According to Ambassador Dennis Ross, Clinton strongly encouraged Prime Minister Yitzhak.

Rabin in order to pursue negotiations with the Palestinians and decided that an appropriate role for the US "would be to make it easier for Israel to take risks for peace."[104] Clinton's efforts helped the Palestinians and Israelis achieve the Oslo Accords, which enunciated a "Declaration of Principles," setting the stage for the Palestinians to recognize the legitimacy and permanence of the Jewish state, and Israel to recognize the Palestinian Authority as the formal representative of the Palestinians people with whom Israel would subsequently negotiate for a permanent solution to the conflict.[105] Clinton's determination and sound decision-making also led to a peace treaty between Israel and Jordan in October 1994.[106] In 2000, Clinton attempted to mediate a treaty between Israel and the Palestinians at Camp David, but he could not bring this about. Nevertheless, most observers gave the president high marks for the effort.[107]

TAKEAWAYS FOR ALL LEADERS

- A leader cannot escape the ultimate loneliness and burdens of making tough decisions.
- Deliberation and debate are absolute requirements for making tough calls, but they cannot go on interminably.
- Leaders can grow in the decision-making skill and confidence.

George Walker Bush

In his 2010 autobiography, titled *Decision Points*, President George W. Bush explained that his book "focused on the most important part of the job: making decisions."[108] It is clear that Bush favored a "business" approach to managing and leading: listening carefully to advisers, permitting a free flow of information, and declaring a clear and concise verdict. He followed a clearly different decision-making model than did President Clinton, especially in the early days of Clinton's presidency. Bush's second secretary of state, Condoleezza Rice, once described how President Bush frowned on statements that began with "This is complicated."[109]

In the early days of his presidency, George Bush seemed to encourage the expression of a wide variety of opinions on urgent policy matters. He extended "walk-in" access to the oval office (entry with no appointment) to a greater number of presidential aides than Reagan did, and certainly, more than Nixon had.[110] In addition, Bush sought a diverse group of professionals to join his administration. He acknowledged the dangers of groupthink in policy-making in a 2002 interview with *Washington Post* reporter Bob Woodward: "If everyone had the same opinion and the same prejudices and the same belief structure, I would not get the best advice."[111] Finally, as late as 2004, he commented about the dangers of his staff trying to please the boss, instead of telling him the truth: "They walk in here and they just get overwhelmed by the oval office, and they say, 'Man, you're looking good, Mr. President.' So I need people walking in here saying, 'You're not looking so good.'"[112]

But as the Bush presidency advanced, the "open-mind" approach changed. Bush's Treasury Secretary, Paul O'Neill, described cabinet meetings as entirely "scripted," where the participants were assigned the order and substance of their comments in advance.[113] When National Economic Council Chairman, Lawrence Lindsey, suggested the coast of the war in Iraq might approach $200 billion (it ended up costing $500 billion), he was dismissed. When General Shinseki told Congress that several hundred thousand soldiers would be needed to provide post-war security in Iraq, he was publicly chided by Deputy Secretary of State Paul Wolfowitz, and some believe that his planned retirement as the Army chief of staff was advanced as a result of his congressional testimony.[114]

Bush's March 2003 decision to go to war in Iraq reveals some of the closed-mindedness of his decision-making style. It also revealed the president's weakness in examining the consequences of his decisions. Based on his research on decision-making, management scholar Jeffrey Pfeffer concluded that "we almost invariably spend more time living with the consequences of our decisions than we do in making them."[115] This was not the case with President Bush. Once he made a decision, he was unlikely to doubt himself and even less likely to change course, even in the face of data showing that the goals of the decision were not being reached. In the first presidential debate during the 2004 presidential campaign, Bush's challenger, Massachusetts Democratic Senator John Kerry said to the president: "It's one thing to be certain, but you can be certain and wrong."[116]

Regarding the Iraq war, many foreign policy experts, notably Brent Scowcroft, Jim Baker, and Colin Powell, advised him not to do it. But Vice President Cheney, Defense Secretary Rumsfeld, and several other close advisers supported the invasion. Here is how Bush described his decision to go to war in his autobiography.

> For months I had solicited advice, listened to a variety of opinions, and considered counterarguments. .... Years of intelligence pointed overwhelmingly to the conclusion that Saddam had WMD. He had used them in the past. He had not met his responsibility to prove their destruction. He had refused to cooperate with the inspectors .... I knew the cost would be high.
>
> But inaction had a cost too Given everything we knew, allowing Saddam to stay in power would have amounted to an enormous gamble. I would have had to bet that every major intelligence agency was wrong or that Saddam would have a change of heart. After seeing the horror of 9/11, that was not a chance I was willing to take ....[117]

Once Bush decided on war, his mind was no longer open to doubts or disagreements. He went into a "marketing" campaign to gain support for his decision, as discussed earlier in the book, and he enlisted the assistance of his deputies, including Vice President Cheney, Secretary of Defense Rumsfeld, and several others. Cheney worked especially hard to convince House Majority Leader Richard Armey (R, TX), who had expressed doubts about the incipient invasion. In a private meeting in the vice president's temporary Capitol hideaway, Cheney presented maps and blood-curdling graphics depicting Saddam's aluminum tubes (allegedly being used in the process of enriching uranium for a bomb), and adding the unproven assertion that Saddam had developed the ability to miniaturize WMD's (weapons of mass destruction).[118]

Of course, the weapons of mass destruction were never found. As well, it is clear that Bush and his team did not closely examine the consequences of their decision to invade, as previously described by Jeffrey Pfeffer. As described by the Iraq Study Group and in many other places,[119] Bush and his team under-estimated the number of troops that would be needed to not only overthrow Saddam, but stabilize the country afterwards; under-estimated the lingering deep animosities between Shia and Sunni communities; neglected the need to quickly revitalize the infrastructures of the country, including the provision of security and governance institutions. Accordingly, after the rapid and success-ful removal of Saddam Hussein, there was extreme chaos and anarchy in Iraq. Overall, this was not an effective decision by President Bush.

On the other hand, according to political scientist Stephen Benedict Dyson, Bush's later decision in late 2006 to add 20,000 troops to the US effort in Iraq, in a "surge" action, seems to have had more positive results.[120] Ironically, Dyson noted that Bush's "surge" decision was characterized by three traits of his general leadership repertoire: closed mindedness, stub-bornness, and risk acceptance.[121] While these traits are usually not associated with effective decision-making, in the Bush surge decision they led to an effective outcome.

At the time Bush made this decision, the situation in Iraq had significantly deteriorated in terms of reduced security and increased rates of sectarian vio-lence. Bush was faced with an almost unanimous set of recommendations to accept a scaled back definition of success in Iraq and to initiate a troop withdrawal. The advice from the military, from Congress (with the exception of Arizona Republican US Senator John McCain), and from public opinion polls all pointed in the same direction—a withdrawal or a scaled back effort. But Bush identified a few advisers in the National Security Council and in academia or think tanks (Fred Kagan of the American Enterprise Institute, Eliot Cohen of Johns Hopkins University, and Stephen Biddle of the Council on Foreign Relations) who advised him to consider a change in the military leadership on Iraq and an increase in troops.

As well, Bush was privately approached by US Senator Chuck Robb (D, VA), who had been part of the Iraq Study Group, but expressed the dissenting view of increasing the troops.[122] When Bush added this dissident advice to his own convictions, and his own stubbornness, he came up with a formula on winning the war and justifying the sacrifices that had already been made by so many. Reflecting on the decision later in a television interview, Bush, in response to a question about compromising on his principles, said,

> The pullout of Iraq … would have compromised the principle that when you put kids into harm's way, you go in to win. And it was a tough call, particularly since a lot of people were advising me to get out of Iraq .... I listened to a lot of voices, but ultimately, I listened to this voice: I'm not

going to let your son die in vain. I believe we can win. I'm going to do what it takes to win in Iraq.[123]

While the final outcome of the war in Iraq is still uncertain in 2022, by September October 2008, violence in Iraq was down by 80 percent since the 2006 surge, and ethno-sectarian violence—which threated civil war in 2006—was down by over 90 percent. US military deaths had in Iraq dropped from 70 a month in 2007 to 25 a month in 2008.[124]

TAKEAWAYS FOR ALL LEADERS

- Leaders need to be decisive, and they also need to closely examine the consequences of their decisions.
- Leaders should actively seek out dissenting viewpoints and guard against the tendency of groups to drift toward groupthink.
- Sometimes, strong convictions, even stubbornness, in decision-making can lead to positive outcomes.

Barack Hussein Obama

In November 2009, President Obama told The Washington Post that he favored a decision-making style "based on information, not emotion."[125] Political scientists Rockman, Waltenberg, and Campbell found that Obama's decision-making style was characterized as "cool, cerebral, and resolute."[126] Journalist David Maraniss confirmed the cool, deliberative, and somewhat detached elements of Obama's style and noted how some were disappointed by those traits:

> …. At various times in his presidency, there were calls from all sides for him to be hotter. He was criticized by liberals for not expressing more anger at Republicans who were stifling his agenda, or at Wall Street financiers and mortgage lenders whose dealing helped drag the country into recession. He was criticized by conservatives for not being more vociferous in denouncing Islamic terrorists, or belligerent in standing up to Russian President Vladimir Putin.[127]

There is widespread consensus in the academic and journalistic communities that Obama's decision-making style was also characterized by careful preparation and focus, manifested on how he constantly drove meetings in the direction of outcomes that produced operational choices.[128] Obama was more intellectually curious than was George W. Bush, and more analytically structured than Bill Clinton was. According to Rockman, Waltenberg, and

Campbell, "Obama's decisions are deliberate and marked by careful consideration of logic and **consequences** (emphasis by author), but a conclusion is reached …. In this sense he is quite different from his immediate Democratic predecessor, Bill Clinton."[129] According to journalist Jonathan Alter,

> …. Clinton liked to ruminate; Obama liked to delegate. Clinton, especially at the beginning, would sometimes do the math himself on complex budget issues, Obama thought this was what his smart staff was for. Clinton was habitually late and let himself get fatigued from too much work; Obama was always punctual and well rested, with a sensibly paced daily routine reminiscent of Reagan's without the naps …[130]

Obama's proclivity to consider an issue from several perspectives, and to hold his own counsel in abeyance, can be traced back to his days as chief editor of the *Harvard Law Review*. In that capacity, Obama was heralded for his impressive listening skills and for his remarkable ability to cogently synthesize the arguments of two sides of a discussion and to find common ground between warring parties.[131] In an author interview with Ambassador Dennis Ross, who served as special assistant to President Obama for Iran policy, Ross described the difference between advising Presidents Clinton and Obama. With Obama, said Ambassador Ross, it was all business-cordial but clearly focused. With Clinton, on the other hand, said Ross, there was a sense that a friendship was being developed in addition to the business at hand.[132] This profile of the two presidents was reinforced by Jonathan Alter's discussion of Clinton and Obama:

> Clinton was an inductive thinker with a horizontal mind. He talked to people in wide-ranging bull sessions (or late at night on the phone) to establish a broad array of policy and political options, then looked at them in context and fashioned a synthetic and often brilliant political approach out of the tangled strands of his analysis. Aides were not surprised to learn that he had cut most of his classes at Yale Law School in the 1970's to work on political campaigns. His connective intelligence seemed untouched by narrow legal reasoning. When making policy he favored decision memos with a range of options to be discussed and often second-guessed his final choices … The result was often positive, but the process was invariable messy and wasted energy of staff.
>
> Obama was a deductive thinker with a vertical mind. He thought deeply about a subject, organized it lucidly into point-by point arguments for a set of policies or a speech, and then said, Here are my principles and here are some suggestions for fleshing out the details. He favored option memos that included options but contained clear policy

recommendations that would then be rigorously tested to make sure they met his policy goals. He placed more faith in logic and insisted on a process that was tidy without being inflexible.[133]

Unlike Bush's decision to go to war in Iraq, Obama's 2009 decision to send an additional 30,000 US troops to Afghanistan was preceded by months of intense debate and prodigious information gathering: there were ten formal meetings of Obama's advisers following the receipt of General Stanley McChrystal's August 30 report suggesting a build-up of between 10,000 and 40,000 troops to help implement a counterinsurgency strategy. There were several months of deliberation and debate among Obama's senior advisers where positions ranged from strong support for as many as 40,000 troops by Secretaries of defense and state (Robert Gates and Hillary Clinton); to a challenge launched against the surge by the then United States to Afghanistan Karl Eikenberry, based on his opinion that the Afghan government led by Hamid Karzai was unreliable and ill-suited to be a strategic military partner with the United States, to a devil's advocate role played by Vice President Biden.[134]

In late November 2009, Obama decided on a 30,000-troop surge, an official NSC review of progress in December, and the beginning of a withdrawal of the troops in July 2011. The president was sufficiently frustrated by the continuing debate and the military's persistence in advocating for more troops that he wrote his decision down on paper, declaring, "Maybe I am getting too far down in the weeds on this, but I feel like I have to."[135]

Another example of Obama's careful, cerebral, methodical, and rational decision-making can be seen in the planning of the May 2011 US raid in Pakistan that led to the execution of terrorist mastermind Osama bin Laden. The process leading to Operation Neptune Spear began with an April 2010 meeting that Obama had with the director of the CIA, Leon Panetta, and the deputy director, Mike Morell.[136] The two men told Obama that they were fairly confident that they had located Osama bin Laden, living in a large compound in a Pakistani town called Abbottabad, in an affluent neighborhood 35 miles north of Islamabad.[137] Through extensive surveillance conducted by the CIA, Panetta and Morell were able to give President Obama information that led to the conclusion that the intelligence was accurate: The number of women and children living in the compound paralleled the size of bin Laden's family, the residents went to great lengths to conceal their identities, they had no phone lines or Internet connections, and they burned their trash. There was a large man who constantly walked around the compound in circles, whom the called "the Pacer" and strongly believed to be OBL. Obama probed deeply and aggressively and wanted additional confirmation; but in a relatively short time concluded that there was enough information to begin the development of options for attacking the compound.[138]

By March 2011, Obama was presented with two options:

a. An air strike on the compound
b. A special ops mission on the compound to kidnap or kill bin Laden[139]

In his autobiography, Obama described how he narrowed the SCOPE of the decision by dismissing the air strike or drone strike option because it could kill as many as 30 people in addition to bin Laden, and because there would be no definitive way to prove that he was dead.[140] He continued to reject it when the military told him the strike could be "surgical" and kill only the designated target.

President Obama chose the special ops idea, and he quickly determined that the operation would be led by Vice Admiral William McRaven, head of the military's Joint Special Operations Command, who had commanded or helped carry out 1,000 previous complicated operations.[141] McRaven organized extensive aerial photography of the city and built a full-scale model of the Abbottabad compound at Fort Bragg, North Carolina. He selected a group of SEALS to train and rehearsals.[142]

On March 29, 2011, in a meeting in the Situation Room in the White House, McRaven gave Obama assurance that the mission would succeed. Obama carefully surveyed his team and found Leon Panetta, John Brennan (then Assistant to the President for Homeland Security, and later CIA director), and Mike Mullen (chairman of the joint chiefs of staff) to be strongly in favor of the raid; Hillary Clinton (secretary of state), lukewarm but generally supportive; and Robert Gates (secretary of Defense), along with Vice President Joe Biden opposed.[143] President Biden had to go ahead for the operation on April 29, and left the exact timing and other operational details in the capable hands of Admiral McRaven.[144] The mission was successfully completed, including bin Laden's elimination, on May 2, 2011.[145]

There was jubilation in the streets of Washington, DC when Obama announced the success of the mission, and even Pakistan's President, Asif Ali Zardari expressed congratulations and support. According to Obama, Zardari showed genuine emotion, recalling how his wife had been executed by extremists with reported ties to al-Qaeda.[146]

There were many other events and developments demanding President Obama's attention during this time, including the whole "birther" incident that featured Donald Trump challenging Obama's citizenship and claiming that he was not eligible to be president.[147] Yet Obama focused and probed, asked high level officials to complete "homework," deliberated, challenged, and listened to his experts in the planning and execution of Operation Neptune Spear. He considered dissident voices, allowed their full expression, and came to his own decision clearly and firmly. In short, President Obama, according to political scientist James Pfiffner, "conducted the type of decision-making process often advocated by political scientists."[148] His style also reflected the strengths of a great lawyer, as described by one of Obama's Harvard law professors, Christopher Edley:

> For law students it's very important to understand the other side of an argument. If you are a litigator, a critical skill is trying to anticipate and dissect the argument your opponent is going to make, so you drill down and understand his argument as well as your own. That gives you a certain humility because it forces you to face the weaknesses in your own position and to appreciate that any difficult problem has, by definition, good arguments on both sides. That's where Barack was so strong. Now why did he seem to hate debates in the Presidential race, and wasn't particularly good at them at first? Because the difference between someone who is a great lawyer and merely a great debater is that the lawyer appreciates nuance and only subsequently focuses on how to communicate. His talent … was also evident in his openness in engaging people with whom he disagrees. It's antithetical for a good lawyer to have a self-righteous conviction that he has a monopoly on truth. You are trained to have an appreciation for complexity.[149]

TAKEAWAYS FOR ALL LEADERS

- Reason and logic will help a leader make sound decisions; emotion and impulse will not.
- A leader must reserve enough time for an exploration of diverse opinions before making a critical decision.
- With adequate preparation and due diligence, a risky decision can succeed.

Donald John Trump

President Trump's decision-making reflected many of the traits of his overall leadership style: impulsive, emotional, generally ill-informed, and chaotic. As he entered the White House, with "minimal planning and preparation,"[150] he could have attempted to build his chances for successful leadership the way previous presidents did—either through prodigious personal effort, wholesale delegation to qualified associates, or a calculated combinations of these approaches, described as "strategic competence" by political scientist Paul Quirk.[151] Instead, in the estimation of Professor Quirk, "Trump in effect rejected the basic assumption—never before challenged in the modern era—of the need for specialized skills and highly informed **decisions** (emphasis by author) for a successful presidency."[152]

As indicated in Quirk's analysis, decision-making is a sophisticated skill that needs to be honed and developed by a president. Instead, Trump's presidency, according to Quirk, "was an experiment in substituting the skills and methods that he had learned during his business and entertainment career and in the 2016 presidential campaign for those normally associated with presidential leadership."[153]

This critical view of Trump's decision is reinforced by presidential scholar George Edwards who listed Trump's leadership and decision-making traits as follows:

- Lack of preparation
- Routine use of hyperbole, distortion, and fabrication
- Intellectual incoherence and disarray
- Ignorance of policy and functions of government
- Uninformed, impulsive, and capricious decision-making
- Rejection of inconvenient information
- Narcissistic certitude[154]

> Edwards added, "No president in modern times had adopted a decision-making style less reliant on information and more dependent on instinct."[155] The flaws in Trump's decisional style were visible within the first few days of his presidency. A poignant illustration was the evolution of his executive orders restricting travel from several majority Muslim countries.[156]

During the 2016 presidential campaign, Trump announced his intention to ban travel from Muslim countries. On January 27, 2017, he issued an executive order banning entry into the United States for 90 days by citizens from Syria, Iraq, Iran, Libya, Somalia, Sudan, and Yemen.[157] The order was not drafted by policy professionals with clear knowledge of potential policy and legal ramifications. It was, instead, drafted by Trump's chief strategist, Steve Bannon, and policy adviser Stephen Miller, neither of whom had deep experience with US immigration policy. Senior officials in the Department of Homeland Security, the agency to be responsible for implementing the order, were not consulted. Indeed, the HHS Secretary, John Kelly, was not consulted, and was on a plane when the ban went into effect, which meant that his deputy had to organize an emergency conference call to explain to department officials how it would be enforced.[158] Chaos ensued at airports all over the world, and at the White House staffers working through the weekend were shocked by footage of dark-skinned people being rounded up in foreign airports and escorted away from boarding lines for the United States.[159]

Advocates and lawyers quickly introduced several lawsuits against the ban, and several US district courts stopped the ban on constitutional grounds.

Trump issued a revised ban in March 2017; the new ban showed evidence of vetting and review by Justice Department and national security officials and attempted to address several issues that defeated the original ban. The revised ban applied to six, not seven, countries; it also detailed a specific category of people who would be able to apply for case-by-case waivers to the order, including those previously admitted to the United States for "a continuous period of work, study, or other long-term activity."[160]

Nevertheless, the revised order was once again successfully challenged on constitutional grounds, and in June 2017, after a terror attack in London, Trump resorted to an emotional outburst on Twitter to condemn the revised order and those who crafted it.

> "The Justice Dept. should ask for an expedited hearing of the watered down Travel Ban before the Supreme Court – & seek much tougher version."
>
> "People, the lawyers, and the courts can call it whatever they want. But I am calling it what we need and what it is, a TRAVEL BAN!"[161]

Within days of the tweets, the Ninth Circuit Court of Appeals upheld a lower court ruling to block the order. In its decision, the court cited Trump's tweets as evidence that that ban constituted a blanket ban on travel based on nationality—illegal under federal immigration law.[162] The US Supreme Court reinstated key parts of the ban in late June 2017, pending further review.[163]

The travel ban experience was an early indication that Trump "stepped into the presidency so certain that his knowledge was the most complete and his facts supreme that he turned away the expertise of career professionals upon who previous presidents had relied," according to *Washington Post* journalists Rucker and Leonnig.[164] The two journalists quoted a senior administration official as saying, "Instead of his pride being built on making a good decision, it's built on knowing the right answer from the onset."[165]

As a decision maker, then, President Trump was not inclined to coordinate with policy professionals in advance of making or announcing significant policy initiatives. Instead, he tended to make decisions on the spur of the moment, without extensive information or qualified advice, even on sensitive issues of national security. For example, in a July 2017 NATO (North Atlantic Treaty Alliance) meeting, Trump caught his national security team off guard by omitting the expected affirmation of the alliance's mutual defense commitments, an omission that deeply offended USA allies. Defense Secretary Mattis rushed to publicly affirm the American commitment, but the "damage had already been done to both the United States' and NATO's credibility."[166]

In another surprise for national security officials, in the summer of 2017, Trump tweeted a declaration that the US military would no longer permit service by transgender personnel, even though an estimated several thousand transgender individuals had been providing valued service for many years with no reported problems. The legal status of an order conveyed by Tweet from POTUS with no accompanying formal document was unclear. The message gave no guidelines on the handling of transgender people who were currently serving. The Defense Department, openly annoyed, essentially nullified the order, at least temporarily and announced there would be no change on policy until further review.[167]

Another problematic aspect of President Trump's decision-making was his surpassing confidence on his negotiation and persuasion capabilities. The belief in an elevated ability to persuade is true of many of the other presidents covered in this book; however, few of them came into office or campaigned on the negotiation ability with the same vigor and bluster as Trump demonstrated. To illustrate, we shift our attention to Trump's third year on office and his fight for the construction of a US–Mexico border wall. Once again, the origin of this policy initiative came from Trump's campaign promise to build a wall and have Mexico pay for it.

When it became clear that Mexico was not going to pay for the wall, President Trump had to turn to Congress and its appropriations responsibilities. In a December 11, 2018 meeting with Senate Minority Leader Chuck Schumer and soon-to-be Speaker of the House Nancy Pelosi (after the Democrats had gained 41 seats in the House in the 2018 elections), Trump implored the Democratic leaders to appropriate funds for wall construction, or he would shut down the federal government.[168] Trump told Schumer and Pelosi that he would be "proud to shut down the government for border security." He added that "I will take the mantle … I will be the one to shut it down. I'm not going to blame you for it."[169] Pelosi and Schumer were surprised, because Trump no longer had control of both houses of Congress, which he had had a year earlier.

Subsequently, after changing his mind twice, Trump rejected a compromise funding bill. At midnight, December 22, a partial government shutdown began. Trump canceled his trip to Mar-a-Lago, and then during the last few days of January, while the shutdown remained in effect, he demanded the resignations of Defense Secretary Mattis and (by then) Chief of Staff John Kelly. According to political scientist Lara Brown, "The timing appeared designed to change the subject."[170]

A few days later, Trump threatened to declare a national emergency and redirect appropriated funds to the southern border to begin wall construction. The president used tweets, a national address, and a visit to the border to persuade Congress and the public to the urgency of building a border wall. But public opinion polls showed most Americans blamed Trump for the government shutdown and the budgetary impasse. Trump stood firm, refusing to sign legislation to open the government without funding for a wall; however, he could not mobilize adequate support for the idea.[171] Meanwhile, Speaker

Pelosi increased the pressure on President Trump by threatening to withdraw his invitation to deliver the State of the Union address. When she withdrew the invitation, Trump agreed that he would deliver the speech later. And after a total of 35 days, Trump finally agreed to sign a short-term funding bill that reopened the government though it did not contain additional funding for a border wall.[172]

Even after this development, Trump reissued his threat to declare a national emergency to begin construction of a border wall if the longer-term budget did not include the necessary funds.[173] But too many Republicans opposed him and prevailed on Trump to relinquish the threat. He did not repeat the threat in his State of the Union address, but ten days after the speech, and one day after his nominee for Attorney General, William Barr was confirmed by the Senate, Trump declared a national emergency and began to reallocate funds to build the wall on the southern border. A month later, Congress passed a resolution rescinding his national emergency declaration; Trump vetoed the congressional resolution, and Congress could not override the veto. Subsequently, 16 states, whose appropriations funding from Congress was jeopardized, sued the Trump administration. Other groups also filed suits, while Trump argued that he would prevail in the Supreme Court.[174]

Two federal courts (US district courts) issued nationwide orders blocking the Trump administration's use of $3.6 billion in military construction funds to build a wall along the US–Mexico border, saying the repurposing of funds was unlawful.[175] In October 2021, the US Supreme Court repudiated a lower court ruling that found that the House had a right to file a lawsuit against the Trump administration for the use of funds to construct a wall on the southern border. The Court also ordered a lower court to declare that the case was now moot and the courts didn't need to consider additional substantive issues, since President Joe Biden stopped the spending on wall construction that Trump had ordered.[176]

Finally, as discussed in the last chapter, in Trump's decisions regarding the COVID-19 calamity, he was more animated by ideological faith than by empirical evidence.[177] Trump wanted to believe that the virus would not cause serious damage to his "beautiful economy," or to the stable, predictable social environment that made it flourish. He embraced all kinds of strange theories, saying, variously, that it was "no big deal," that we "can easily manage it," that "when the weather gets warmer it will recede," among others. (Meanwhile, he told Bob Woodward that he understood how serious a disease it was.) The president overlooked the hundreds of thousands of deaths in this country alone, and the millions worldwide, routinely dismissed the advice of experts in the medical and scientific community, and gave platforms to charlatans who espoused nonsense and dangerous theories to the public.

TAKEAWAYS FOR ALL LEADERS

- Decisions need to be made after adequate deliberation and discussion, and they must be carefully and strategically announced.
- Confidence is a positive force for making tough decisions, but it must be balanced with a modicum of humility because we live in an uncertain world.
- Impulse, emotion, and whim are poor foundations for sound decisions.

Joseph Robinette Biden

The motivation behind Joe Biden's decision to enter 2020 presidential race provides insight into his decision-making style. Biden said that his decision to run for president one more time was sealed in August 2017, after learning of President Trump's response to the tragic events in Charlottesville that month when Trump said that there were "some very fine people on both sides,"[178] Biden said, "In that moment, I knew the threat to this nation was unlike anything I had ever seen in my lifetime."[179]

Washington Post reporter Marc Fisher described Biden as an unusual combination of ambition and empathy. His ambition was revealed by the many times he considered running or actually ran for president, including in the 1980, 1984, 2004, 2016, and 2020 elections.[180] His decisions have always had a political calculus behind them.

But another equally powerful motivation behind Joe Biden's presidential decision-making is his empathy for people. Born of the tragedies of his own life, his upbringing, and his strong religious beliefs, Biden makes decisions knowing that political decisions will profoundly affect the lives of millions of ordinary people. As he expressed during the 2020 presidential campaign. "I trust people who start with the gut … People who arrive at it purely from an intellectual standpoint, they're not always ones that can be counted on at the very end when it gets really tough."[181]

Biden presented himself as a serious, experienced political leader who had been "in the room" when important decisions were made, during his 36 years in the US Senate and 8 years as President Obama's vice president. Nevertheless, when he became president, Biden acknowledged that the decision-making and leadership responsibilities changed also. In a January 19, 2022, press conference, he gave direct expression to this matter in response to a reporter's question:

> One of the things that I think has been made clear to me … is the public doesn't want me to be President Senator. "They want me to be the President and let senators be senators …. I'm used to negotiating, to get

things done, and I've been, in the past, relatively successful at it in the United States Senate, even as Vice President. But I think that role as President is a different role."[182]

Biden showed courage and clarity in decision-making when he decided to withdraw US troops from Afghanistan in August 2021. Biden chose to frame the decision as either complete withdrawal or endless escalation.[183] Biden had been telling the public that there was no other choice, because he knew that people had grown disenchanted with the "forever" war and favored getting out. Biden's predecessor, President Donald Trump, had been moving in the same direction.[184]

In fact, Biden felt obligated to honor a February 2020 deal that President Trump negotiated with the Taliban. Under that agreement, Trump agreed to withdraw all US troops by May 2021, lift sanctions, and approve the release of 5,000 prisoners held by the Afghan government. (The Afghan government was not party to the negotiation.) The Taliban committed to not attacking US troops on the way out or allowing terrorist groups to use Afghanistan as a staging ground for attacks on the United States. Following the signing of the deal, Trump reduced the US troop's presence on Afghanistan from 13,000 to 4,500.[185]

Biden was the third president in a row dedicated to end the war in Afghanistan, which cost the United States more than 2,400 troops and $2 trillion in resources. There were also 240,000 Afghans killed during the two-decades war.[186] Still, other voices in the Biden administration, notably Defense Secretary Lloyd Austin and Chairman of the Joint Chiefs of Staff, General Mark Milley, argued for keeping a modest force of some 3,000 to 4,500 troops, augmented by an extensive use of drones and close air support, to continue to hold off the Taliban.[187]

But Biden rejected the middle ground strategy, contending that it amounted to continued war. *New York Times* White House correspondent Peter Baker argued that President Biden's views were shaped by his experience as vice president in 2009, when he argued against President Obama's temporary troop surge to Afghanistan. According to Baker, Biden emerged from that experience "soured on the military" and convinced that they had "rolled Mr. Obama by making it politically difficult to resist the troop increase."[188] In the August 2021 withdrawal decisions, Biden was also influenced by a series of intelligence assessments he requested about Afghanistan's neighbors and near neighbors; the intelligence was that Russia and China wanted the United States to be bogged down in Afghanistan.[189]

While Biden came into the White House with strong views on withdrawing troops from Afghanistan, he took a necessary step in making the decision by asking his national security adviser, Jake Sullivan, to conduct an interagency examination of Afghan policy that resulted in ten meetings of departmental deputies, three cabinet-level meetings, and four meetings in the Situation Room that included President Biden.[190] The withdrawal itself, however, was ineffective, and resulted in considerable chaos and destruction in Afghanistan, including the death of 13 US service members and an estimated 170 Afghan civilians in an attack just outside the airport.[191] One major Democratic party donor expressed a more widespread disappointment with the Biden Administration when he told *Time Magazine,* "When the f...d up in Afghanistan, they obliterated the competency thesis, and I don't know how he comes back from that."[192] Biden's approval ratings fell to about 42 percent by the end of January 2022.[193]

Biden made another significant decision on February 1, 2022, when he ordered a raid on a terrorist target on Syria, which led to the death of the leader of the Islamic state, Abu Ibrahim al Hashimi al-Qurashi.[194] In a February 1, 2022, meeting with Secretary of Defense Lloyd Austen and Chairman of the Joint Chiefs of Staff, Mark Milley, Biden decided to order the raid. The final authorization was the culmination of months of behind-the-scenes work by US intelligence and military personnel. After operatives located al Qurashi in the fall of 2021, Biden was briefed in "really exquisite detail" by a small group of senior advisers on December 20. Biden and his team saw an opportunity to deal a major setback to the Islamic State, a militant terrorist group that some analysts worried could make a comeback. In the words of a senior administration official, Qurashi was one of the few remaining "legacy leaders," and his death would be a serious blow to the organization.[195]

The operation was unusually complex, because in the same building that housed al-Qurashi, lived several families with small children. The fact that children were there led Biden to quickly abandon the idea of an airstrike, in favor of a special force operation that was used to take down President Obama.[196]

According to *Washington Post* reporter Matt Viser, the debates that unfolded inside The Situation Room were not entirely different from the ones that occurred in 2011, when Obama was contemplating a Navy SEAL raid on Pakistan to go after bin Laden. In the previous situation, as discussed earlier, Biden was skeptical. But in this current case, he was in favor of the operation. According to former CIA Director Leon Panetta, "In many ways that's the difference between being president and being vice president …. The vice president can give thoughts and opinions. But in this situation, he's the president. He's got to make the final decision."[197] The operation succeeded, though not exactly as planned. Upon arrival at the complex, US troops used a bullhorn to announce their presence, and some of the families, including eight children, from the first floor evacuated the building and were led to safety. Moments later there was a massive explosion, as al-Qurashi had detonated a bomb on the third floor killing himself and his family.[198]

Application to Other Sectors

Decision-making is a critical leadership skill required of leaders in all sectors. We have learned a great deal about decision-making through research in many disciplines, including economics, psychology, political science, public and business administration, organizational behavior, law, and ethics.

Stanford University organizational behavior professor Jeffrey Pfeffer offered important insight into leadership decision-making realities. Pfeffer's research led him to the conclusion that one of the most important aspects of competent decision-making is the leader's skill in the management of the consequences of decisions.[199] He elaborated three components of the central argument as follows:

- A decision by itself changes nothing. A leader, for instance, can decide to launch a new product, change the organization's performance appraisal system, or adopt new technology; but the decision will have little meaning or consequence until it is implemented. How many people have decided to quit smoking, lose weight, or spend more time with their family—and failed to implement their decision?[200]
- At the moment a decision is made, we cannot possibly know whether it is a good or bad decision; there are always risks involved in a decision.[201] In this regard, author and professional poker player Annie Duke, argued that decision-making is more similar to poker than it is to chess. According to Duke, the game of poker has a tremendous amount of uncertainty due to hidden information, while, in the game of chess there is widely shared information and some degree of predictability.[202]
- We almost invariably spend more time living with the consequences of our decisions than we do making them. Whether leaders are deciding whether to acquire a company, change the compensation system, or allow telecommuting, it is likely that the "effect of the decision will be with us longer than it took us to make the decision, regardless of how much time and effort we invested."[203]

In summary, Pfeffer wonders, if the aforementioned propositions are true—decisions themselves change nothing, at the time of decision-making we cannot know the consequences, and if we spend more time living with the consequences of decisions than we do in making them—than it seems evident that the emphasis in much management training and practice has been misplaced. Rather than spending inordinate amounts of time and effort in the decision-making process, it would seem at least as useful to spend more time on implementing decisions and dealing with their ramifications. "In this sense," says Pfeffer, "good managers are not only good analytic decision-makers, more important, they are skilled in managing of the consequences of their decisions."[204]

Nevertheless, leaders do need to make decisions, and we have accumulated a good deal of evidence to challenge Pfeffer's assumption that leaders are "good analytic decision-makers." The research comes from many disciplines, and one of the more interesting and influential streams of evidence comes from the work of Nobel-prize winning author and emeritus Princeton University economics professor Daniel Kahneman. In his pioneering and widely acclaimed book, *Thinking Fast and Slow,*[205] Kahneman explained two "systems" that human beings use to make decisions:

- **System 1** operates automatically and quickly with little or no effort and no sense of voluntary control.[206] System 1 is fast, instinctive, and emotional. It is a way for us to take cognitive shortcuts, and to categorize people and events in a world of information overload. According to Stanford University psychology professor, Jennifer Eberhardt, System1 thinking can lead to bias, because of its tendency to categorize. Eberhardt avers that categorization is a "universal function of the brain that allows us to organize and manage the overload of stimuli that constantly bombard us. It's a system that brings coherence to a chaotic world, it helps our brains make judgments more quickly and efficiently by instinctively relying on patterns that seem predictable."[207]
- **System 2**, according to Daniel Kahneman, allocates to the effortful mental activities that demand it, including complex calculations. The operations of System 2 are frequently "associated with the subjective experience of agency, choice, and concentration."[208] System 2 is conscious, deliberative, methodical, and logical.

The previous analysis of US presidents would identify President Trump as a System 1 decision maker and President Obama as a System 2 decision maker. Bush 43 would lean more toward System 1, and Bush 41 and Clinton toward System 2.

Author Michael Lewis, in his fascinating study of Daniel Kahneman and his equally talented collaborator, Amos Tversky, provided additional insight into how the human mind works or fails to work when forming judgments or making decisions. In his best-selling book, *The Undoing Project: A Friendship That Changed Our Minds,* Lewis explained how Kahneman and Tversky's research collaboration challenged the model of the leader as rational decision maker.[209] When leaders approach a decision, Kahneman and Tversky found that they take two shortcuts to help them reach closure:

a. *Availability.* What information is readily available to the decision maker? People driving on an uncrowded highway might be tempted to speed; however, when they come upon an accident they will slow down, and continue to drive at a slower pace for some time, because the available information influences them.[210] In launching the Iraq War, President George Bush claimed that the available intelligence indicated that Saddam Hussein possessed weapons of mass destruction.

b. *Similarity.* Lewis indicates that people make judgments about people or events based on their similarity to other people or events. For instance, as described earlier, US presidents may decide on launching or not launching a special operation depending on its similarity to a previous one. But, as Kahneman and Tversky found in their research, similarity may not be the right framework for a decision maker to use.

As Lewis explains, things are grouped together for a reason, but once they are grouped together the grouping itself causes them to seem more like each other than they otherwise would be. In an April 2, 2021, podcast with the Federal Judicial Center, Lewis used the world of sports to illustrate the limitations of using similarity to make decisions. He described how basketball scouts, for instance, would judge the potential of a college athlete by assessing that person's similarity to Michael Jordan, or Larry Byrd, or Magic Johnson—all world-class players. But the comparisons were not accurate, and the results were poor. Team owners and managers decided that they would have a better chance of predicting the potential of a player through a statistical analysis of their performance than by similarity assessments through observation.[211]

Fascinating research by author Daniel Pink shed further light on the impact of TIMING on decision-making. Based on hundreds of research studies from diverse organizational settings, Pink concluded that our cognitive abilities do not remain static over the course of a day.[212] During the approximately 16 hours we are awake, those abilities change in a generally predictable way. According to Pink, "We're smarter, faster, dimmer, slower, more creative and less creative in some parts of the day than others."[213]

For most people (around 80 percent) mood and cognitive ability follow a common pattern—a peak in the early part of the day, a tough in the middle of the day, and a rebound toward the end of each day. Most people are more likely to excel at analytical work, which includes sharpness, vigilance, and focus, in the morning. During the trough, which occurs about 7 hours after people wake up, we become less focused and more prone to error. In the United Kingdom, for example, sleep-related vehicular accidents peak twice every 24 hours: between 2 a.m. and 6 a.m., and between 2 p.m. and 4 p.m. Researchers have found the same patterns of traffic accidents in the United States, Israel, France, and Finland.[214] A separate British survey got even more precise and found that the typical worker reaches the most unproductive moment of the day at precisely 2:55 p.m.[215]

In Israel, two judicial boards process about 40 percent of the country's parole requests. At the head of the process are individual judges who hear prisoners' cases and render decisions about the facts—release after time served with adequate signs of rehabilitation, or denial of release and continued prison time. Of course, the judges aspire to be rational, deliberative, and wise in meting out justice based on facts and law. In a social science study based on parole board data, however, researchers found that the judges were more likely to issue a favorable ruling—granting the prisoner parole or allowing him to remove an ankle monitor—in the morning than they were in the afternoon. The researchers also found that early in the day, judges ruled in favor of prisoners about 65 percent of the time. But as the day wore on, the percentage declined, and by late morning the favorable rulings dropped to almost zero. Yet, after they took a lunch break, judges became more forgiving and willing to grant parole, only to slip back to the tougher stance a few hours later.[216] As Pink says, "If you happen to appear before a parole board just before a break rather than just after one, you'll likely spend a few more years in jail—not because of the facts of the case but because of the time of day."[217]

Finally, University of Pennsylvania's organizational psychologist Adam Grant has advanced the research on decision-making in his widely acclaimed book, *Think Again: The Power of Knowing What We Don't Know.*[218] Grant argues that intelligence is frequently thought to be our ability to learn and to think, but he argues, in a turbulent world, there's another set of cognitive skills that might matter more: "the ability rethink and unlearn."[219] As Grant says, there is a human tendency to equate our opinions without identity, and reconsidering something can deeply threaten our identity, making it seem as if we are losing part of our identity. But we must proceed anyway!

In the realm of decision-making, the tendency to rely on previously held assumptions and beliefs can be a hindrance to reaching sound decisions in a rapidly changing environment. Grant argues that decision makers and leaders frequently lapse into three unhelpful mindsets: the "preacher" (who delivers sermons to protect and defend decisions), the "prosecutor" (who finds flaws in the arguments of opponents), and the "politician" (who seeks to win over her audience). Perhaps a more useful mindset for a leader or decision maker, says Grant, is that of a "scientist" (who seeks the truth and runs experiments to test hypotheses).[220]

Grant shares a study of European researchers who ran an experiment with more than a hundred founders of Italian startups in technology, retail, furniture, food, health care, leisure, and machinery. Most of the founders' businesses had yet to earn any revenue, making this an ideal experimental study of how scientific thinking could influence the bottom line.[221]

The entrepreneurs participated in a Milan-based training program in entrepreneurship. Over the course of four weeks, they learned how to create a business strategy, interview customers, build a minimum viable product, and then refine a prototype. The entrepreneurs did not know that they had been randomly assigned to either a "scientific thinking" group or to a control group. The training for both groups was identical, except one group was encouraged to view the startups from the perspective of a scientist. From that vantage point, their business strategy is a theory, tested through customer interviews, and the minimum viable product and prototype are used as experiments to test hypotheses. Their task is to measure results and make decisions based on validation or refutation of the hypotheses.[222]

Over the following year, the startups in the control group earned $300 in revenue. The startups in the scientific group averaged around $12,000 in revenue.[223] The explanation is that the startups in the control group remained wedded to their original strategies and products. They preached the virtues of past decisions, prosecuted the vices of alternative options, and politicked to advisers who favored their current direction. The entrepreneurs who had been taught to think like scientists, on the other hand, pivoted more than twice as often. When their hypotheses were not validated, they knew it was time to rethink their business models.[224]

It is hard to sustain the scientific perspective in decision-making, as Grant avers:

> Scientists morph into preachers when they present their pet theories as gospel and treat thoughtful critiques as sacrilege. They veer into politician terrain when they allow their views to be swayed by popularity rather than accuracy. They enter prosecutor mode when they're hellbent on debunking or discrediting rather than discovering.[225]

Relating back to our study of US presidents, Grant opines that what set the great presidents apart was their intellectual curiosity and openness. They read widely and were eager to learn about developments in biology, philosophy, architecture, and music, in addition to foreign and domestic affairs. They were interested in hearing new ideas and revising old ones. He adds, "They saw many of their policies as experiments to run, not points to score. Although they might have been politicians by profession, they often solved problems like scientists."[226]

Notes

1 Alexis Simendinger, "Bush's 'Aha' Moments," *National Journal*, July 23, 2005, 2358.
2 Sheryl Gay Stolberg, "The Decider," *The New York Times*, Week in Review, December 21, 2006.
3 George W. Bush. *Decision Points*. New York, NY: Crown, 2010.
4 Pfeffer, *Managing with Power*, 23.
5 Irving Janis. *Groupthink: Psychological Studies of Group Discussions and Fiascoes*. Boston, MA: Houghton-Mifflin, 1982.
6 Doris Kearns Goodwin. *Team of Rivals: The Political Genius of Abraham Lincoln*. New York, NY: Simon and Schuster, 2005.
7 Haas, *The Power to Persuade*, 80.

8 Eizenstat, *President Carter*, 86–87.

9 Ibid., 87.

10 Ibid.

11 Ibid.

12 Lawrence Wright. *Thirteen Days in September: The Dramatic Story of the Struggle for Peace.* New York, NY: Vintage Books, 2014, 11–49.

13 Ibid., 211–257. And Eizenstat, *President Carter,* 498–530.

14 These insights were shared with the author by Dr. Mark A. Siegel, who served as President Carter's liaison to the American Jewish Community, Washington, DC, October 1982.

15 Fallows, "The Passionless Presidency," 25.

16 Kaufman and Kaufman, *The Presidency of James Earl Carter, Jr.*, 213.

17 Eizenstat, *President Carter*, 720.

18 Ibid., 735.

19 Ibid., 738.

20 Ibid.

21 Ibid.

22 Ibid., 739.

23 Ibid., 784–801.

24 Ibid., 775.

25 Ibid., 798.

26 Fallows, "The Passionless Presidency," 26.

27 Siegel, *The President as Leader*, 2nd ed., 63.

28 Siegel, *The President as Leader*, 2nd ed., 87.

29 Cannon, *President Reagan*, 94.

30 Barrett, *Gambling with History*, 37.

31 Quoted on Reeves, *President Reagan*, 333.

32 Whipple, *The Gatekeepers*, 107–108.

33 Ibid., 108.

34 Ibid.

35 Ibid., 109.

36 Donald T. Reagan, *For the Record: From Wall Street to Washington.* New York, NY: Harcourt Brace and Jovanovich Publishers, 1988, 31.

37 Ibid.

38 Ibid., 32.

39 Ibid.

40 Ibid.

41 Ibid., 3.

42 Karen Tumulty. *The Triumph of Nancy Reagan.* New York, NY: Simon and Schuster, 2021.

43 Karen Tumulty, "How Nancy Reagan helped end the cold war." *The Washington Post*, April 4, 2021, A26.

44 Ibid., A27.

45 Ibid.

46 Reeves, *President Reagan*, 289, and Tumulty, "How Nancy Reagan helped," A27.

47 Tumulty, "How Nancy Reagan helped," A27.

48 Reeves, *President Reagan*, 294.

49 Ibid., 343.

50 Siegel, *The President as Leader*, 2nd ed., 93.

51 Tumulty, "How Nancy Reagan helped," A28.

52 Ibid.

53 Siegel, *The President as Leader*, 2nd ed., 94.

54 Meacham, *Destiny and Power*, 211.
55 Ibid., 418.
56 Ibid., 238.
57 Ibid., 25.
58 Ibid., 337.
59 Ibid.
60 Ibid., 370.
61 Ibid.
62 Ibid., 374.
63 Ibid., 375.
64 George H.W. Bush and Brent Scowcroft. *A World Transformed*. New York, NY: Vintage Books, 1999, 149.
65 Meacham, *Destiny and Power*, 385–386.
66 Ibid., 3.
67 Dennis Ross. *Doomed to Success: The U.S.-Israeli Relationship from Truman to Obama*. New York, NY: Farrar, Strauss and Giroux, 2015, 220.
68 Ibid., 221.
69 Ibid.
70 Meacham, *Destiny and Power*, 388.
71 Ibid., 389.
72 Siegel, *The President as Leader*, 2nd ed., 229.
73 Meacham, *Destiny and Power*, 417.
74 Ibid.
75 Ibid.
76 Siegel, *The President as Leader*, 2nd ed., 173.
77 John F. Harris. *The Survivor: Bill Clinton in the White House*. New York, NY: Random House, 2005, Prologue, X.
78 Bob Woodward. *The Choice*. New York, NY: Simon and Schuster, 1996, 14.
79 Bert A. Rockman, "Leadership Styles and the Clinton Presidency," in Colin Campbell and Bert A. Rockman, eds., The Clinton Presidency: First Appraisals. Chatham, NJ: Chatham House, 1995, 352–362.
80 Harris, *The Survivor*, 27–28.
81 Ibid., 28.
82 Ibid.
83 Siegel, *The President as Leader*, 2nd ed., 147–148.
84 Ibid., 168–169.
85 Harris, *The Survivor*, 6.
86 Ibid.
87 Ibid., 7.
88 Ibid.
89 Ibid., 44.
90 Ibid., 44–45.
91 Ibid., 43.
92 Ibid., 45.
93 Ibid., 46.
94 Ibid.
95 Ibid.
96 Ibid.
97 Ibid., 14.
98 Ibid.
99 Ibid.
100 Ibid., 16.

101 Ibid., 15.
102 Paul J. Quirk and Sean Matheson. "The Presidency: Elections and Professional Governance," in Michael Nelson, ed. *The Election of 1996*. Washington, DC: Congressional Quarterly Press, 1997, 127.
103 Karen Breslau, Debra Rosenberg, Leslie Kaufman, Andrew Miller, and Evan Thomas. *Back from the Dead: How Clinton Survived the Republican Revolution*. New York, NY: Atlantic Monthly Press, 1997, 1.
104 Ross, *Doomed to Success*, 257.
105 Ibid., 266–268.
106 Ibid., 272.
107 Ibid., 294–296.
108 Bush, *Decision Points*, Introduction, xi.
109 Siegel, *The President as Leader*, 2nd ed., 227.
110 Draper, *Dead Certain*, 54.
111 Bob Woodward. "A Course of Confident Action." *The Washington Post*, November 19, 2002, A1.
112 Andrew Rudalevige, "The Decider," in Colin Campbell, Bert A. Rockman, and Andrew Rudalevige, The George W. Bush Legacy. Washington, DC: Congressional Quarterly Press, 2004, 152.
113 Ibid.
114 Ibid.
115 Pfeffer, *Managing with Power*, 19.
116 Commission on Presidential Debates. "Debate Transcripts: The First Bush-Kerry Presidential Debate." September 30, 2004. Cphemp.smu.edu/2004election/bush-kerry-debates/
117 Bush, *Decision Points*, 252–253.
118 Gellman, *The Angler*, 216–217.
119 See Michael R. Gordon and General Raymond Tanter. *Cobra II: The Inside Story of the Invasion and Occupation of Iraq*. New York, NY: Pantheon Books, 2006.
120 Stephen Benedict Dyson. "George W. Bush, the Surge, and Presidential Leadership." *Political Science Quarterly*. Winter 2010–2011, 557–585.
121 Ibid., 559–560.
122 Ibid., 572–573.
123 Ibid., 578.
124 Stephen Biddle, Michael O'Hanlon, and Kenneth M. Pollack. "How to Leave a Stable Iraq: Building on Progress." *Foreign Affairs*. September/October 2008, 41.
125 Joel Achenbach. "Obama Goes With Head, Not Gut," The Washington Post, November 25, 2009, A1.
126 Bert A. Rockman, Eric Waltenberg, and Colin Campbell, "Presidential Style in the Obama Presidency." In Bert A. Rockman, Andrew Rudalevige, and Colin Campbell. eds., *The Obama Presidency: Appraisals and Prospects*. Washington, DC: Congressional Quarterly Press, 2012, 339.
127 David Maraniss, "The Content of His Presidency." *The Washington Post*, April 24, 2016, A8.
128 Rockman, Waltenberg and Campbell, "Presidential Style," 339.
129 Ibid., 340.
130 Alter, *The Promise*, 46.
131 Siegel, *The President as Leader*, 2nd ed., 296.
132 Author interview with Ambassador Dennis Ross, July 25, 2016, Washington, DC.
133 Alter, *The Promise*, 212.
134 James P. Pfiffner. "Decision Making in the Obama White House," *Presidential Studies Quarterly*, 41, No. 2 (June 2011), 260.

135 Bob Woodward. *Obama's Wars*. New York, NY: Simon and Schuster, 2010, 315.
136 Obama, *A Promised Land*, 677.
137 Ibid., 678.
138 Ibid., 678–679.
139 Ibid., 680.
140 Ibid., 687.
141 Ibid., 681.
142 Ibid., 683.
143 Ibid., 686.
144 Ibid., 688.
145 Ibid., 695.
146 Ibid., 696.
147 Ibid., 672–673.
148 Pfiffner, "Decision Making in the Obama White House," 261.
149 David Remnick. The Bridge: *The Life and Rise of Barack Obama*. New York, NY: Vintage, reprint ed., 2011, 205–206.
150 Paul Quirk, "Presidential Competence," in Michael Nelson, ed., *The Presidency and the Political System*, 11th ed. Washington, DC: Congressional Quarterly Press, 2018, 154.
151 Ibid., 152.
152 Ibid.
153 Ibid.
154 George C. Edwards. *Changing Their Minds? Donald Trump and Presidential Leadership*. Chicago, IL: University of Chicago Press, 2021, 8.
155 Ibid.
156 Steven E. Schier and Todd E. Eberly. *The Trump Presidency: Outsider in the Oval Office*. New York, NY: Rowman and Littlefield, 2017, 96.
157 Ibid.
158 Philip Rucker and Carol Leonnig. *A Very Stable Genius: Donald J. Trump's Testing of America*. New York, NY: Penguin Press, 2020, 29.
159 Ibid.
160 David Nakamara, Matt Zopotosky, and Abigail Hauslohner, "Revised Executive Order Bans Travel from Six Muslim-Majority Countries from Getting Visas." *The Washington Post*, March 6, 2017.
161 Schier and Eberly. The Trump Presidency, 9.
162 Ibid., 98.
163 Ibid.
164 Rucker and Leonig, *A Very Stable Genius*, Prologue, 4.
165 Ibid.
166 Quirk, "Presidential Competence," 156.
167 Ibid.
168 Lara M. Brown. *Amateur Hour: Presidential Character and the Question of Leadership*. New York, NY: Routledge, 2021, 180.
169 Ibid.
170 Ibid.
171 Ibid., 181.
172 Ibid.
173 Ibid.
174 Ibid.
175 Ibid.
176 Todd Reyer. "Supreme Court Ends Legal Clash Over Border Wall Spending." *Roll Call*. October 12, 2021 https://rollcall.com/2021/10/12/supreme-court-ends-legal-clash-over-border-wall-spending/

177 Quirk, "Presidential Competence," 138.

178 See Vision Chapter of this book.

179 Marc Fisher, "Ambition Combined with Empathy Yields Uncommon Politician." *The Washington Post.* "The 46th President," January 20, 2021, F6.

180 Ibid.

181 Ibid.

182 The White House. "Remarks by President Biden in Press Conference." January 19, 2022. https://www.whitehouse.gov/briefing-room/speeches-remarks/2022/01/19/remarks-by-president-biden-in-press-conference-6/

183 Peter Baker, "Biden Saw Afghanistan Choice as Either All In, or All Out." *The New York Times,* August 29, 2021, 10.

184 Ibid.

185 Ibid.

186 Ibid.

187 Ibid.

188 Ibid.

189 Ibid.

190 Ibid.

191 Dan Lamothe and Alex Horton, "Military's Kabul Exit Was Resisted." *The Washington Post,* February 9, 2022, A1.

192 Molly Ball and Brian Bennett, "Big Promises, Bad Outcomes," *Time,* January 31/February 7, 30.

193 Ibid.

194 Matt Viser. "Inside Biden's First Major Counterterrorism Operation." *The Washington Post,* February 4, 2022,

195 Ibid.

196 Ibid.

197 Ibid.

198 Ibid.

199 Pfeffer, *Managing with Power,* 23.

200 Ibid.

201 Ibid.

202 Annie Duke. *Thinking in Bets: Making Smarter Decisions When You Don't Have all the Facts.* Portfolio Reprint Edition, May 7, 2019. And *In Session: Leading the Judiciary.* Episode 8: "Making Smarter Decisions Under Pressure. Federal Judicial Center, April 13, 2019. Podcasts.apple.com/us/podcasts/in-session-leading the judiciary/id 1399122541.

203 Pfeffer, *Managing with Power,* 19.

204 Pfeffer, Ibid., 19–20.

205 Daniel Kahneman. *Thinking Fast and Slow.* New York, NY: Farrar, Straus and Giroux, 2011.

206 Ibid., 20.

207 Jennifer L. Eberhardt. *Biased: Discovering the Hidden Prejudice That Shapes What We See, Think, and Do.* New York, NY: Penguin Books, 2020, 24.

208 Kahneman, *Thinking Fast and Slow,* 21.

209 Michael Lewis. *The Undoing Project: A Friendship That Changed Our Minds.* New York, NY: W.W. Norton and Company, 2017.

210 Ibid., 114.

211 FJC: In-Session Podcasts. Michael Lewis, "Decision-Making, Collaborating and Coaching." April 2, 2001. Podcasts/apple.com/us/podcasts/in-session-leading-the-judiciary-/id 399122541.

212 Daniel Pink. *When: The Scientific Secrets of Perfect Timing.* New York, NY: Penguin, 2018, 33.

213 Ibid.
214 Ibid., 77.
215 Ibid., 79.
216 Ibid., 85.
217 Ibid., 86.
218 Adam Grant. *Think Again: The Power of Knowing What We Don't Know.* New York, NY: Viking, 2021.
219 Ibid., 2.
220 Ibid., 18–19.
221 Ibid., 20.
222 Ibid.
223 Ibid., 21.
224 Ibid.
225 Ibid., 22.
226 Ibid., 27.

CONCLUSION

What Have We Learned about Presidential and Executive Leadership?

What have we learned about presidential leadership, and leadership generally, from the review of the eight US presidents, and the insights of other leaders, in previous chapters of this book?

We learned that leadership is more difficult and complicated than it might appear from the outside. According to leadership scholar Joseph Rost, in his article on leadership in the "new millennium," "Yes, leadership is hard. To use influence is hard; to promote real change is hard; to collaborate is hard; to achieve mutual purpose is hard. Changing paradigms is hard. The whole thing is fraught with difficulties."[1] And presidential leadership is not only hard, but also, according to journalist John Dickerson, "the hardest job in the world."[2]

It is doubtful that any president enters the White House with the thought of making things worse, just as it is doubtful that any CEO, university president, or any other leader begins his or her tenure with the idea of creating problems instead of solving them. Leaders are ambitious, dedicated, and flawed human beings who invest great energy, take considerable risk, and pursue ambitious goals as they enter the "arena."[3] And all leaders have strengths and weaknesses, wins and losses.

Consider the major achievements and defeats of the presidents in this book.

Achievements:

Jimmy Carter helped Israel and Egypt achieve the Camp David Accords, a peace treaty that has stood for over 40 years in a region of tremendous strife and ongoing conflict. Carter appointed more woman and minorities to the federal bench than any president before him, and he fought vigorously for environmental protections and to improve the federal student loan program.

DOI: 10.4324/9781003285229-6

Ronald Reagan revitalized the conservative movement in the United States and achieved substantial economic and tax reform, social welfare cutbacks, and defense increases, all with a Democratic House of Representatives. In his second term, Reagan reached significant nuclear arms control agreements with the Soviets.

George H.W. Bush displayed competent management of the activities leading to the end of the cold war as well as the reunification of Germany. Bush achieved a significant military and political victory in the Persian Gulf War against Saddam Hussein. And he fought for the passage of the American with Disabilities Act.

Bill Clinton revitalized the Democratic Party and promoted policies and legislation that led to substantial reductions in the nation's deficits, unemployment, and crime rates. He came close to achieving a peace agreement between the Israelis and Palestinians with the "Clinton Parameters" presented at Camp David.

George W. Bush achieved the first meaningful education reform legislation in decades, and effectively, if only temporarily, competently led the US response to the terrorist attacks of September 11. Bush provided effective political, moral, and strategic leadership for several months.

Barack Obama helped rescue the imperiled US economy through a massive stimulus package. He also achieved substantial healthcare reform, which provided healthcare coverage to millions of Americans who were previously uninsured. Obama also successfully negotiated nuclear arms deal with Iran to prevent Iran from achieving nuclear weapons capability. He also initiated and oversaw the operation that led to the execution of Osama-bin-Laden.

Donald J. Trump successfully facilitated the Abraham Accords, that opened diplomatic and commercial relations between Israel and several Gulf states. Moreover, he directed the rapid development of COVID-19 vaccines on "Operation Warp Speed."

Joe Biden led the effort to substantially increase the number of Americans who received the COVIDS-19 vaccinations. He lobbied for and achieved passage of the American Recovery Act, which provided over a trillion dollars to states, communities, and individuals for COVID relief. He was also able to get Congress to pass (with some bipartisanship) the $1 trillion Infrastructure Investment and Jobs Act.

Defeats/disappointments:

Jimmy Carter was unable to free the US hostages in Iran, and he did not achieve passage of a comprehensive energy program. President Carter's relations with a Democratic-controlled Congress were poor, and he took on far too many issues at the same time.

Ronald Reagan was either duped by his own staff or failed to grasp the seriousness of the Iran-Contra scandal on his own. He projected a feeling of indifference to growing budget deficits, to AIDS victims, and to welfare recipients.

George H.W. Bush was unable to deliver on his "no new taxes" promise, and never truly explained the legitimate reasons for doing so to the American public. His domestic policy initiatives were insufficient to address deep-seated problems of inequality in the United States.

Bill Clinton was slow to act to forestall genocide in Rwanda and ethnic cleansing in the Balkans, and showed poor judgment in having a sexual affair with a White House intern.

George W. Bush became obsessed with preempting the terrorists and drove the country into lengthy and exorbitant military commitments in Iraq and Afghanistan. He did not respond quickly or effectively to Hurricane Katrina.

Barack Obama failed to develop an effective US response to the civil war in Syria, to achieve compressional passage of background checks on firearms or meaningful immigration reform.

Donald J. Trump dodged his leadership responsibilities around the COVID-19 pandemic, obfuscated the facts about medical realities, and presided over a poorly managed federal response to the crisis. He also flagrantly and consistently ignored or violated constitutional norms regarding the office of the presidency.

Joe Biden led a chaotic and flawed withdrawal of US troops from Afghanistan, and was unable (as of this writing) to achieve passage of a major $1.6 trillion "build back better" legislative initiative.

Almost all other leaders experience wins and losses on policies, personnel, programs, or products; no one bats a thousand! The book's purpose, then, has not been to thoroughly analyze any one policy success or failure, but instead to search for the deeper qualities or components of leadership that presidents and other leaders need to perfect. The author has attempted to introduce a systemic approach to leadership effectiveness in the White House or any other leadership "house."

The central analysis of the book revolves around the four elements of leadership. Considering the eight presidents that have held office for a full term since Watergate, here is a summary of how they performed along the four dimensions of leadership:

Policy: Vision/Purpose

Jimmy Carter was not a visionary leader. He was forceful in his critique of the status quo and fierce in his denunciation of Nixon's "imperial" presidency; he offered himself to the American people as an "outsider" who would govern in a purser fashion than conventional politicians. Carter emphasized that he was not beholden to interest groups or even the strictures of a strong party man. President Carter emphasized that he was a man of honesty and integrity who would attack problems with an engineer's objectivity and a scientist's rigor. His proclaimed strength was the mastery of detail of governance, not a grand strategy or poignant vision.

There was a visionary aspect of his presidential campaign; it was Carter's personal story. Jimmy Carter emphasized who he was, not what he would do! He was a good, honest, decent man with strong religious convictions and a belief in social and racial equality. He believed in the power of moral suasion and on the peaceful resolution of conflict in areas like the Middle East.

Ronald Reagan was a visionary president. Like Carter he was a DC "outsider," and not wedded to conventional wisdom on foreign or domestic policies. Unlike Carter, however, Reagan did not try to govern as an outsider. Reagan had what his biographer, Lou Cannon, called "bedrock convictions"[4]: that the federal government was bloated and its proliferating regulations were sapping vitality and energy from the US economy; that taxes were too high leading to a decrease in motivation of people to be highly productive; that social welfare programs had become lavish and were seen by their recipients as "entitlements," rather than as temporary measures of relief. Reagan believed in "supply side" economics, holding the view that people relieved from paying high taxes would invest on productive enterprises and everyone would benefit. (He quoted JFK, that "a rising tide lifts all boats.") Reagan fought hard to change federal budget and taxation policies, and with the dexterity of his lobbying effort and clarity of his vision, he largely succeeded.

In foreign policy, Reagan also showed a proclivity for nonconventional thinking. He entered the White House as a confirmed "cold warrior," describing the USSR as an "evil empire" and detested their economic system and their mistreatment of religious minorities; however, his ultimate goal (vision) was a more peaceful world with fewer nuclear weapons. In the second term, President Reagan's view became more conciliatory and more focused on diplomatic overtures to Mikhail Gorbachev in the pursuit of arms control agreement.[5] President Reagan expressed very strong doubts about the viability of the doctrine of "mutual assured destruction" (MAD), which had oriented US and Soviet foreign policy since the late 1940s and strove to negotiate a reduction in nuclear weapons by both sides.[6]

George H.W. Bush was skeptical and even cynical about what he called the "vision thing." To Bush, success in leadership and politics meant building and sustaining friendships and relationships. President Bush had held almost every important position in the US government, and among all the presidents considered here, except for Joe Biden, the only one who chose to—or even could—campaign as an "insider." Based on the depth of his political experience and vast network of professional contacts he had cultivated, George

H.W. Bush offered the nation a sense of trusted competence and a reservoir of impressive experiences, especially in foreign policy.

President Bush expressed the view that leadership is not always grandiose and does not always occur "with trumpets blaring," but lurches forward in small steps as "history unfolds one page at a time." The world, during Bush's tenure, was undergoing profound, transformational change, and Bush believed the role required of the US president was that of a manager, someone who could help maintain some semblance of stability in the face of the massive changes in Eastern Europe and elsewhere, unleashed by the fall of the Berlin Wall and dissolution of the Soviet empire.

Bush was not as talented in the domestic policy arena, either in terms of comprehending the needs or in developing policy initiatives to address them. He shared Reagan's idea of "laissez-faire" economics and tax cuts; however, his expressed hope that a surge of voluntarism—"a thousand points of lights"—would significantly help to address the serious domestic problems of poverty, drug use, and crime was facile and devoid of merit. Bush believed that government was not always the answer to social and economic problems because it was not always capable and because of the deficit ("our will is bigger than our wallet"). Bush did his best, in a slow, plodding way, to continue the Reagan Revolution; however, he did not aspire toward dramatic change in domestic policy.

Nevertheless, President Bush did champion legislative initiatives in the areas of protecting the rights of disabled US citizens and the environment.

Bill Clinton called himself a "New Democrat" and demonstrated a clear willingness to challenge previous orthodoxies of the Democratic Party. Through his long involvement in political campaigns, activity in the Democratic Leadership Conference, and experiences as governor of Arkansas, Clinton believed that the Democratic Party needed to revitalize itself. Clinton urged his colleagues to embrace business perspectives, global awareness, a passion for healthcare and education reform, and a political philosophy of "personal responsibility." He embraced fiscal discipline, fending off supplications of his liberal allies inside and outside the administration. When he veered off course and retreated into a more liberal posture (as he did with healthcare reform), he was willing to acknowledge the error and need to find his way back to the center.

In foreign policy, Clinton embraced globalism and an interest in advancing trade and business policies to enhance the US role as a global leader. Though he described himself as a humanitarian, Clinton was slow to act in Bosnia and Rwanda, where humanitarian crises called for US intervention, but he also displayed a tremendous acumen ion grasping the details of diplomacy when he waded into an attempted settlement of the Israeli-Palestinian conflict.

Geore W. Bush defends himself as a "compassionate conservative." Influenced by scholars like Marvin Olasky, Bush believed that private agencies and faith-based groups could be more effective than government agencies in administering social welfare programs. Bush pushed to release the restrictions on faith-based groups' active participation in social welfare programs, and it was not a surprise when he created an Office of Faith Based Initiatives in the White House. Like Reagan and Bush 41, Bush 43 firmly opposed tax increases and doggedly favored tax cuts, with considerable success. In addition, Bush took great pride in being the first MBA in the White House and was determined to apply business principles to government. He encouraged government agencies to improve their managerial performance and demanded that they be held accountable for their results; the accountability aspect of his vision was clearly reflected in his major education reform initiative, No Child Left Behind.

In foreign policy, as a presidential candidate Bush decried the Democratic Party's proclivity for nation-building and promised a more modest foreign policy agenda. But when the United States was attacked by Islamic terrorists on September 11, 2001, Bush developed a notably stronger and more militaristic foreign policy vision to guide US policy in a globalized world threatened by terrorists and weapons of mass destruction in the hands of people like Saddam Hussein. President Bush quickly enunciated a national security vision based on preemption and prevention instead of containment and deterrence. Like Reagan's rejection of MAD, Bush's rejection of containment and deterrence surprised many conservatives and delighted the "Vulcans" in his advisory orbit.[7] But the use of preemption led to a highly militaristic foreign policy and to elongated US military commitments in Iraq and Afghanistan.

Barack Obama's domestic vision focused on the need for a powerful federal government, and a powerful chief executive within the government, to assure equal opportunities and fairness for US citizens. Obama did not attack big government, but emphasized that government should be effective. President Obama believed that government should play a leadership role reducing inequality by adopting a progressive tax policy where the wealthy would pay their fair share. He also believed that federal government should protect vulnerable individuals, including undocumented immigrants and uninsured US citizens. Obama reached for the goal of being a transformational leader, not only because he was the first African-American elected to the White House, but because he intended to reduce the level of partisan rancor and animosity extant in the political process.

In foreign policy, Obama wanted to move away from the bellicosity and aggressiveness of the Bush 43 foreign policy orientation and toward the realism and restraint of the Bush 41 team. Obama's vision of an effective foreign policy was one that was balanced, restrained, precise, and sustainable. President Obama also believed on engagement with adversaries like Iran and a "re-set" of relations with Russia.

Donald Trump, a total "outsider" to political leadership, campaigned for president on a promise to "Make American Great Again," by restoring economic prosperity, repairing a deteriorating infrastructure; keeping Americans safe from domestic criminals, international terrorists, and untrustworthy immigrants; and by achieving more favorable trade deals for the United States. Trump's ideas did not amount to a coherent vision, nor did they reflect strong philosophical beliefs. He was not a traditional conservative, and promised to preserve social security and Medicare, as well as to sustain access to healthcare for all Americans with reduced costs and superior service than provided for by Obamacare. Over the course of his lifetime, and as president, Trump always chose "strength" over weakness or perceived weakness. Leaders, he believed must always project strength and must never appear to be weak.

In foreign policy, Trump clung to an "America First" vision and said his administration would be preoccupied with the well-being of US citizens, not the denizens of the globe. His foreign policy vision was predicated on replacing the costly mantle of moral leadership, which Trump claimed characterized past administrations, with consideration of America's most immediate economic and security needs. There was considerably less focus in Trump's foreign policy on the US role in preserving the "liberal world order," and there were considerable tensions and strains in relations between the United States and its NATO allies during Trump's presidency.

Joe Biden, throughout his long political career in the US Senate and in the Obama White House, reflected the proclivities of a moderate politician, not an ideologue. Nevertheless, when he campaigned for president against Donald Trump, Biden sounded a more visionary message. In the 2020 presidential campaign, Biden advocated for an activist federal government that would protect US citizens from the COVID-19 pandemic. Biden also promised relief to states and localities who had experienced considerable hardships during COVID and a massive infusion of federal funds to upgrade America's infrastructure, including deteriorating roads and bridges, as well as social "infrastructure," including unemployment and poverty relief and enhanced programs for childcare. Several analysts and historians detected a streak of FDR in the Biden vision.

Candidate and President Biden also emphasized the restoration of unity in US society, including its politics. He emphasized that only through unity could the nation defeat COVID-19, improve infrastructure and play a leadership role again on the global stage. President Biden's foreign policy vision included repairing our relations with our allies and rededicating our commitments to international institutions, such as NATO and agreements, such as the Paris Climate Accords. Little did he know that by March 2022, the NATO alliance would face an existential test, with the Russian invasion of Ukraine.

TAKEAWAYS FOR ALL LEADERS

- It is fine to campaign against the status quo or the past when seeking office, but the real creativity of leadership lies in the articulation of goals to be achieved in the future.
- A leader must be as clear about what he or she is FOR as he or she is about what they are AGAINST.
- Research in all sectors indicates that followers are inspired by leaders who are forward-looking and inspirational. Visionary leaders give people hope and strength.
- When leaders have a strong vision or purpose it helps define them and gives people a reason to follow that goes beyond personal characteristics.
- At times, a leader must challenge established, even revered, institutions, when they have not kept pace with significant changes in the environment.
- A vision can shift over time, as conditions change. A strong vision does not have to be rigid. Core ideology can remain constant, but strategies can change.
- A vision can become an obsession, as a leader clings to strong beliefs in the face of a rapidly shifting environment.
- A leader must encourage challenges and criticisms of his or her vision.
- A vision that is developed in consultation with elites alone will not resonate with entire organizations or endure for long periods of time. (The US Constitution may be an exception.)
- When the vision a leader enunciates seems consistent with the way they have lived their life, this is a powerful combination.
- A leader must consistently show strong conviction for his vision, even when it seems tedious or undignified to do so.
- A vision based primarily on grievances aimed at the status quo or the establishment is not sufficient for long-term viability.
- A vision of transformational leadership is a high benchmark, and a vision for effective transactional leadership should not be disparaged.

Politics: Strategy/Execution

Jimmy Carter disdained retail politics, except when he was on the campaign trail. He believed that people should do the right thing and that the president should encourage them in that direction; however he resisted playing the "insider's" game of relationship-building and influence peddling.

As a Democrat, President Carter had an unusually strong political situation, because his party controlled both houses of Congress. But Carter was reluctant to engage in transactional leadership with people like Tip O'Neill, the Speaker of the House. For President Carter there was a higher level of conversation than that provided by routine political exchange, and in that regarded he saw himself as a "transformational" leader, instead of a "transactional" one.[8]

President Carter did not prioritize his legislative agenda and offered so many legislative proposals at one time that he literally overloaded the legislative process. He never spelled out his top 3–5 political/legislative priorities, and his aides were left in the difficult position of pushing forward on multiple fronts without clear direction or focus.

Finally, Carter surrounded himself almost exclusively with DC "outsiders." His closest advisers were from Georgia, and they aimed to interact with Congress the way they had interacted with the Georgia legislature when Carter was governor. They were ignorant of the ways of Congress and its increasingly active posture in the wake of Watergate.

Ronald Reagan, by contrast, was especially agile in the political world. President Reagan was a great communicator and had an easy-going manner paired with a sunny upbeat personality. Reagan moved expeditiously to build a highly effective White House staff that combined California ideologues with Washington political professionals, resulting in what journalist and former White House adviser David Gergen called "one of the strongest teams in the past forty years."[9] According to Gergen, "The conservatives liked to ensure that Reagan carried bold colors onto battle, the moderates said fine, but let's make sure that when the smoke clears he still has a victory."[10]

Reagan's legislative strategy emerged from a team effort that allowed the policy experts to have wide berth, and saved the president for what he did well—delivering speeches and persuading members of Congress one-on-one. Reagan and his team negotiated with House Democrats, who still held the majority. And since they had clear priorities, and a limited agenda, the Reagan team was able to focus their efforts on the attainment of the president's three major goals: tax cuts, social welfare spending cuts, and defense spending increases.

Reagan's legislative effectiveness declined slightly in his second term, due, in part to the enormous accomplishments of his first term, and because the president blithely approved a personnel switch that allowed first term chief of staff Jim Baker to trade jobs with first term treasury secretary Donald Regan. President Reagan lost a courageous follower who was also a great negotiator, and gained an arrogant sycophant in the chief of staff position.

George H.W. Bush, the ultimate "insider," achieved political and leadership success through the art of relationship building and insider negotiations. Facing a Democratic Congress and a growing deficit, President Bush moved cautiously on the domestic front, settling for a tactical, not strategic orientation.

Bush's proficiency in building relationships as a form of political influence played out in spectacular fashion on the international arena. President Bush and his team competently helped manage the dissolution of the Soviet empire after the fall of the Berlin Wall, as well as the reunification of Germany and the launching of democratic regimes among former Soviet satellite countries. Bush displayed considerable political and leadership acumen in building and sustaining an international coalition against Iraqi dictator Saddam Hussein's invasion of Kuwait.

Nevertheless, President Bush's political skills were found wanting in his failure to uphold a bold campaign promise of "read my lips, no new taxes!" Forced by circumstance to raise taxes as president, Bush proved inept at explaining his behavior to a disappointed public. He played the insider's game of compromise and negotiation, but he failed to educate the public about what he had done, a critical aspect of presidential leadership. As well, Bush seemed to be out of touch with the concerns of ordinary Americans who were suffering from a growing recession in 1991, and he lost his bid for reelection to Bill Clinton.

Bill Clinton was a "natural" politician who decided on a political career at the age of 16 and never looked back. Clinton was poised for leadership in 1992, as he ascended to the White House as the first Democrat to do so since 1980. But Clinton floundered in his early days as president due to a series of mishaps and lack of discipline in his White House. He made a policy stumble when he attempted to convince the military to allow gays to serve, while the political facts on the ground were not ready for this initiative. He recovered from early mistakes and achieved a substantial win on his economic reform package, which included tax increases. Resisting pressure from the left wing of his party and staff, Clinton proudly wore the moniker of a deficit hawk and helped the country achieve surplus budgets for several years of his administration. Like Reagan, Clinton mounted an intense lobbying effort to gain buy-in for his economic package; in the end, however, he succeeded only with the Democrats. President Clinton also succeeded in gaining (bipartisan) passage of the North American Free Trade Agreement (NFTA) and a major overhaul of the nation's welfare system.

Clinton stumbled badly on healthcare reform. He appointed the First Lady, Hillary Clinton, to lead the effort and champion the legislation for healthcare reform. Unfortunately, Hillary violated almost every known principle of persuasion and change management in her approach. Favoring a comprehensive, complex legislative proposal produced by healthcare "experts," with almost no congressional input, the first lady pushed forward and eschewed any attempt at compromise or modification. The effort failed miserably, and President Clinton suffered an enormous political setback, which led to the Republican takeover of the House of Representatives for the first time in 40 years. They quickly elected Newt Gingrich as the Speaker of the House, foreshadowing more challenges for President Clinton.

Clinton demonstrated his resiliency and moved back to the center after consultations with his long-time political adviser, Dick Morris. President Clinton rebuilt his political capital and showed considerable resolve in federal budget negotiations with Speaker Gingrich. Clinton refused to accept the Republican budget that included deep cuts in social welfare spending; the standoff resulted in a government shutdown, and Clinton emerged the winner when people could see the importance of federal programs when they stopped operating. It was during the shutdown that Clinton began an inappropriate sexual relationship with a White House intern named Monica Lewinsky. The affair led to impeachment hearings and the near destruction of the Clinton presidency.

George W. Bush had achieved political success in Texas politics by pursuing a bipartisan governing approach when he served as governor. He promised to continue that approach in the White House, and at first, he did. In an early legislative win, No Child Left Behind, President Bush reached across the aisle and gained strong support from Senator Edward (Teddy) Kennedy (D, MA). But the president experienced a serious challenge when Senator James Jeffords (R, VT) left the Republican Party because of policy differences with President Bush, and because of a slight the senator had experienced by being left off the White House guest list for an event honoring the teacher of the year, who happened to be from Jeffords' home state of Vermont!

The terrorist attacks of September 11, 2001, strengthened Bush's resolve as a leader and clarified his vision. His leadership excellence during the weeks and months following 9/11 gave him an unprecedented boost in popularity in public opinion polls (a 91 percent approval rating in October 2001), and a strong ability to influence Congress. Given the unity that existed on the country, Congress went into a highly bipartisan mode and gave President Bush almost all he asked for, including the Authorization for Use of Military Force (AUMF) to authorize a military operation Afghanistan, the USA Patriot Act, and a financial aid package for New York City. But the terrorists continued to weigh heavily on Bush's mind, and he decided, abruptly and without lots of debate, that there was a fundamental shift needed in the vision of US foreign policy—away from deterrence and containment and toward preemption and prevention.

Furthermore, Bush and his closest advisers decided that the first place to put this philosophy into operation was Iraq, part of the "axis of evil" in the world. It was at this point, that Bush's vision became an obsession, and he dragged the United States into a costly unsuccessful war in Iraq. He lost popularity due to the war's unpopularity at home, and the Democrats achieved a significant win in the 2006 congressional elections.

Barack Obama's political trajectory can be compared to the saying about what happens "when an irresistible force meets an unmovable object." In many respects, Obama was the "irresistible force"—he was young, charismatic, smart, energetic, and the first African-American to make it to the White House. The "immovable" object, however, proved to be the Republican Party, whose leadership expressed that their major goal was to prevent Obama from having a second term. Nevertheless, in the first two years of his presidency, Obama's Democratic Party was in the majority in both houses of Congress, and with the help of insiders like Vice President Joe Biden and Chief of Staff Rahm Emmanuel, President Obama was able to see his massive economic stimulus bill and ambitious healthcare reform bill to passage—both with little, if any, Republican support.

Obama was not strong on the art of "retail politics." Cerebral and introverted by nature, he was not effective at selling his ideas with alacrity and clarity, or at explaining the enormity of what he had accomplished to the public. Despite the substantial legislative victories achieved during Obama's first two years, the Democrats suffered a "shellacking" (Obama's word) in the 2010 congressional elections, and he subsequently struggled for legislative wins.

Donald Trump happily campaigned as an "outsider." During the campaign and even in office, Trump showed great disdain for the political establishment and promised to "drain the swamp" of Washington DC, meaning the established dynamics of political transactions in the nation's capital. He claimed that "he alone" could clean up the mess because he was a man of fabulous personal wealth who could not be controlled by DC lobbyists or power brokers.

Trump entered the White House with an auspicious political condition, as his Republican party held the majority in the House and Senate. One of his fist legislative priorities was to "repeal and replace" Obamacare; however, President Trump's input into the legislative process was inconsistent and incoherent, and ultimately, the Republicans failed to accomplish their goal, which they had also attempted on many precious occasions. President Trump was more successful in his attempt to cut taxes for wealthier Americans, which he accomplished with the passage of the Tax Cut and Jobs Act of 2017. However, the Republican Party suffered a significant defeat on the 2018 congressional elections, as the Democrats won back the House.

A good part of the remainder of Trump's presidency was consumed by legal and political challenges. Trump had to contend with the Muller Report and two impeachment proceedings, one of which took place after he had left office.

Joe Biden was elected with former US Senator Kamala Harris (D, CA) as his vice president. Harris was the first African-American and first woman of South Asian descent to be elected as vice president. Biden inherited a challenging situation, especially with the persistence of the COVID-19 pandemic in the United States. President Biden and his team acted quickly to expand the number of injected vaccinations, from 770,000 a day when he assumed office to 3 million a day by his hundredth day in office. Biden addressed the economic hardships created by COVID-19, and the need for recovery, with March 2021 passage of the $1.9 trillion American Rescue Act. Among other provisions, the bill sent $363 billion to states and localities that had been devastated by the pandemic. The bill passed along party lines, but Biden's next legislative success, a $1.2 trillion infrastructure bill, called the Infrastructure Investment and Jobs Act. In the infrastructure bill, Biden gained the support of several GOP members on the Senate and the House. As of this writing President Biden has not been able to attract enough votes to pass his "build back better" plan.

TAKEAWAYS FOR ALL LEADERS

- While part of leadership is conceptual in nature, a large part is all about the leader's ability to build and sustain relationships to help reach his or her goals.
- A leader needs to be clear about his or her goals and objectives and pursue only a limited number of them at any one time.
- A leader with focused agenda must still be willing to compromise on goals and objectives, and even on strongly held beliefs.
- When a leader is fully engaged in a cause and uses the full range of persuasion and influence tools, he or she can make great headway in introducing change.
- Leaders who pursue fundamental change in their countries or organizations will succeed if they mobilize a coalition for change, listen to dissenting voices, and compromise.
- Leaders who can achieve a significant change to the status quo need to EXPLAIN the changes to all stakeholders.
- Ideologues or purists will provide the intellectual and emotional passion for change, but the leader will also need practitioners and negotiators on the team.
- A leader who is an "insider" gains great leverage for making deals or introducing change from established relationships and friendships; however, that leader must also be aware of the dangers of over-relying on closed-door negotiations.
- A leader needs to surround himself/herself with strong, capable professionals, not with friends.
- A leader needs to preserve his physical energy and exert the necessary personal and organizational discipline for the most important issues at hand.
- A leader who asks for help when he needs it is a wise leader.

- Leaders must confront a crisis with confidence, composure, competency, and compassion. Followers are particularly attuned to leader behaviors during a crisis.
- Leaders can grow in office; they can mature and develop new skills.
- A leader can influence a great number of people through charisma and showmanship, but there are also dangers in relying on these assets alone.
- A leader will lose persuasive power when he or she lacks knowledge about critical issues and enunciates confusing and contradictory messages.
- A leader will lose influence if he or she becomes obsessed with a single idea or policy and sops paying attention to a changing environment or a variety of policy experts.
- It is dangerous for a leader to encourage his or her followers to resort to violence, or even extremism in pursuit of an agenda.

Structure/Management

Jimmy Carter surrounded himself with friends and associates from Georgia. Like Carter, they were mostly DC outsiders, and they had a great deal to learn about the culture of the nation's capital. Carter managed them closely, as his engineering and technical background inclined him to do, and encouraged them to focus on the accomplishment of multiple highly complex policy proposals that were not organized in priority order.

As well, President Carter was eager to break away from the tendency of the White House, especially under presidents like Nixon, to dominate the executive branch and to assure that cabinet agencies were always on alignment with the president's agenda. Carter relaxed the strict controls that White House staff had previously exerted over cabinet agencies and sought to manage the executive branch in the fashion of "collective collegiality," professionals who enjoyed the mutual respect of their colleagues and could enjoy a needed dose of autonomy in running their departments and agencies.

Carter's loose supervision of the executive branch, compounded by the absence of a chief of staff and by the lack of insiders in his administration, created significant management challenges for his administration. Cabinet members were assuming that the autonomy that Carter promised them meant they could develop their own policy directions and initiatives without close coordination with the White House. The president became aware of the problems and organized an unprecedented "retreat" to glean insights and idea son moving his administration productively forward. Following the retreat, President Carter asked his entire cabinet to submit their resignations and apply for reinstatement into his administration.

Ronald Reagan was, once again, almost totally Carter's opposite on the managerial aspect of leadership. Unlike Carter, President Reagan was largely ignorant of the details of policy. Accordingly, Reagan appointed Washington insiders and policy experts and truly delegated power for them to formulate and execute policy. As President Reagan had been quite clear about the nature and order of his policy priorities, his staff easily understood what the boss wanted to do and appreciated the room he gave them to operate. Reagan was essentially a 9–5 president who enjoyed spending quality time with his wife. Reagan's staff performed remarkably well in implementing his vision.

But Regan's "macro" management had its limitations, which became increasingly apparent in his second term. His ease in making important and ill-advised top personnel changes, his lack of substantiating information from his staff about Iran-Contra, and his growing distance from the details of governance became problematic. Even the Tower Commission, set up to investigate Iran-Contra, criticized President Reagan's management style and its over-reliance on delegation.

George H.W. Bush was a deeply experienced political leader who had asked an impressive group of credentialed policy and political professionals to join his administration. President Bush proudly considered himself a public servant and a manager, and one of the earliest speeches he gave as president was to a group of federal managers. The consummate insider, Bush surrounded himself with other insiders and led them in a tactical, not strategic direction, jointly focused on careful, incremental change in domestic policy. He occasionally took big steps on domestic issues, such as his championing of the Americans with Disabilities Act, but was generally regarded as a "guardian" president presiding over a status quo government.

The competency of President Bush's foreign policy team proved to be a substantial resource in German reunification, the Persian Gulf War, and several other monumental foreign policy events and developments during his tenure. Bush's professional staff, augmented by the president's vast experience and extensive network of personal relationships with foreign leaders, helped the US play the role of global leader with effectiveness and credibility.

Bill Clinton was notably uninterested in management. He was slow to staff his administration during the transition period, and was still filling vacancies during the inauguration. Clinton selected a cabinet and White House staff composed of insiders and outsiders. There was a decidedly youthful cast to the White House staff, and the atmosphere in the White House was more casual than it was in almost any recent previous administration. President Clinton erred by appointing several campaign staff to White House positions, as governing requires a different skill set than campaigning does. The president gave wide berth to First Lady Hillary Clinton, and entrusted Vice President Gore with several high profile projects, including "reinventing government."

President Clinton's lack of discipline or organizational savvy was reflected in the wider White House culture. Meetings never started on time and ran interminably long. The administration was slow to make decisions, and there was a lack of coordination between the White House and the agencies. Mac McLarty, Clinton's boyhood friend, was not an effective chief of staff. President Clinton recognized that he needed help, and he called on David Gergen to increase order and efficiency into the White House.

George W. Bush took great pride in his MBA training and believed he could instill business principles into the White House and a sense of accountability into the executive branch. President Bush's White House was populated by people with great experience and a surprising degree of diversity (at least on the "optics" level). He ran a more buttoned-down White House than Clinton did, and Bush insisted that his team place great emphasis on efficiency, clear decision-making and a strong "no leaks" policy. He developed a "grading" system to assess the performance of cabinet agencies by business criteria, like effective use of IT and cutting out waste.

Nevertheless, the record shows that President Bush was not always an exemplar of professional public administration. As the administration became more entrenched in its decision to go to war in Iraq, Bush and his team relied on a marketing campaign, not a reasoned policy debate, to browbeat their opponents into submission, as described by Bush's former press secretary Scott McClellan.[11] President Bush also showed more politics than public administration when he replaced nine US attorneys because they were not sufficiently loyal to the president's agenda.

Barack Obama entered the White House without significant executive experience. As President, his record as a public administrator was mixed. While President Obama took great care to carefully implement the economic stimulus program that Congress had passed, by appointing Vice President Joe Biden as the point man for implementation, he relied instead on delegation and subcontracting for the execution of his healthcare reform program. The mistake was reflected in the flawed launch of HealthCare.gov. Moreover, Obama's lack of scrupulous oversight of executive programs was also revealed in the serious managerial problems in the Department of Veterans Affairs and in the IRS.

Donald Trump's approach to management of the White House and executive branch was notably nonconventional. Trump did little to prepare himself for the awesome responsibility of managing the federal government and was apathetic, if not cynical, about absorbing the details of the vast government he would have to manage. President Trump was slow to fill the approximately 500 presidential appointment requiring Senate confirmation, and he filled several top leadership positions in cabinet agencies with corporate people whose professional experiences, in some cases, was antithetical to the agencies they would be heading.

Within the White House, Trump encouraged (or unwittingly allowed) the growth of two power centers, one dominated by the ideologically driven populist Trump political strategist, Steve Bannon, and a second camp consisting of more traditional conservatives, including chief of staff Reince Priebus and senior adviser Jared Kushner, who also was Trump's son-in-law.

Trump showed little deference to policy experts, and instructed his inner circle to write his flawed executive order banning travelers from Muslim countries from entering the United States. Trump's White House and cabinet staff experienced unusually high turnover, and many policy professionals found it difficult to work for a mercurial and impulsive boss who frequently changed his mind, resorted to tweets to announce important personnel decisions, and ignored or disdained scientific evidence concerning public policy issues.

The aforementioned qualities were evident in Trump's failure to adequately manage the government response to the COVID-19 pandemic. On the other hand, Trump showed managerial acumen in facilitating the development of a COVID-19 vaccine in record time.

Joe Biden's major challenge to incumbent President Donald Trump was over the issue of competence. Biden lashed into Trump's mishandling of the COVID-19 pandemic. In contrasting himself to Trump, Biden emphasized his own vast political experience in the US Senate and as a vice president. He also noted his widespread political connections and his ability to bring people together. President Biden chose an experienced hand, Ronald Klain, as his chief of staff and included a great deal of diversity on his cabinet.

President Biden moved quickly and expeditiously to deliver COVID vaccines to communities throughout the United States, and he secured passage of a massive relief bill for states, localities, and individuals. But the August 2021 US troop withdrawal, that Biden ordered, was a disaster.

TAKEAWAYS FOR ALL LEADERS

- While less glamorous than other aspects of leadership, execution is one of the leader's most important jobs.
- A leader must develop a strong management structure, and if he or she is not proficient in organizational skills, they must recruit a chief of staff or similar position to help.
- A busy executive, with an expansive agenda, will truly benefit from the assistance of a chief of staff or similar position to help control the flow of information and people.
- Focusing on management efficiency will help the leader move his agenda forward and will help reduce the need for micromanagement and the danger of burnout.

- Forming a capable executive team will greatly assist a leader in carrying out his or her agenda.
- Even when a leader has a highly experienced and talented executive team, he or she still needs to periodically revisit their shared vision or collective purpose.
- Members of an executive team will appreciate being trusted by the leader and will deeply resent being publicly undermined by him or her.
- Macro-management can be an effective leadership strategy, if the leader has carefully assembled his or her team and knows they are aligned with his or her agenda.
- Like micromanagement, macro-management can have pathologies, as the leader loses touch with important events or developments.
- During a crisis, a leader must fire on all cylinders and must be "brutally honest" (direct about the problems, optimistic about the outcome) with followers and stakeholders.
- Public sector leaders can incorporate cutting edge management ideas from the private sector.
- The skills of campaigning are significantly different from those of governing, and leaders need to be aware of this reality when staffing their organizations.

Process/Decision-Making

Jimmy Carter had the mind of an engineer. He studied problems carefully, comprehended the details and nuances or proposed solutions, and chose the one that was most logically correct. President Carter believed that he could put politics aside and make decisions for the good of the country and the people. Carter had an absorbent mind that could readily contemplate a multiplicity of policy proposals at once. But he failed to choose his policy priorities or objectives in a clear manner, nor did he pursue a focused agenda in a strategic manner, as discussed earlier.

Carter demonstrated an ability to admit to flaws in his decision-making, and he occasionally sought to diversify the sources of input into the decisions. On the other hand, President Carter evinced a great deal of confidence in his decision-making capability and strongly believed that he had righteous goals and purpose. Carter had profound religious convictions that influenced his to see the good in people, and he fought hard to bring the world to a better place, as evidenced in his spectacular work in the Camp David peace process. But he frequently seemed tone-deaf to staff concerns about the political dimensions of policy initiatives, and he antagonized important party and congressional leaders with what they perceived to be inappropriate self-righteousness bordering on arrogance.

Ronald Reagan's decision-making emanated from his values and principles. President Reagan used his vision to guide his decision-making, and favored policies and proposals that would advance his "bedrock" principles of smaller government, lower taxes, lower social welfare spending, and increased defense spending. Reagan moderated his ideological zeal by surrounding himself with political professionals who influenced the president's decisions by explaining the realities of Congress to him, and in some cases, protecting him from himself.

The clarity of Reagan's vision helped ease the decision-making process within his administration. His aides negotiated with congressional leaders with confidence and skill and armed Reagan with the knowledge he needed to conduct his own negotiations. He had enough humility to accept the assistance of his more knowledgeable staff. Toward the end of his White House years, we learned that some of Reagan's decisions were strongly influenced by First Lady Nancy Reagan, and that she was, at times, influenced by a California astrologer. As well, Reagan's decisions seemed blind to the impact they would have on welfare recipients and AIDS victims. His sunny personality was not enough to help struggling Americans in his time; his attempt to emulate FDR did not work all the time.

George H.W. Bush was the beneficiary of an Ivy League education and the tutelage of a successful political family. As president, Bush had an easy time with making decisions, because of his long, distinguished career in public service. When he needed advice, he consulted the highly credentialed, sophisticated network of advisers he assembled in the White House, and his larger network of professional contacts and friends that was global in nature. Bush was usually decisive, and highly confident that once a decision was made it would be expertly executed. President Bush had an unusually gifted foreign policy team that possessed the maturity and experience to help him manage the transformation of the Soviet empire and the end of the cold war, as well as the planning and execution of the Persian Gulf War against Saddam Hussein.

On the other hand, in domestic policy, Bush seemed to be devoid of fresh ideas and overly reliant on Reagan's policy, with slight modifications. He did make an occasional bold move, such as the legislation he pushed to protect the rights of disabled Americans and the environment. But he bowed to the pressures of a political campaign and decided to deliver a promise—no new taxes—that he could not keep. In making this promise, Bush repudiated the advice of his senior advisers who warned him about the magnitude of the federal budget deficit. He agreed to tax increases but never really explained himself to the public. Like Reagan, Bush seemed out of touch with a wide spectrum of the American public, his decision-making was competent, but not always inclusive.

Bill Clinton earned a reputation of having trouble with decision-making. He allowed his staff to engage him in lengthy policy debates and discussion, sometimes lasting until the wee hours of the night. President Clinton said he found his ideas and opinions in the "seams between the clashing ideas of others." Because he possessed a keen intellect and could see many sides of an issue, including their political dimensions, he could become paralyzed and overcome with "paralysis by analysis." Or he could enunciate policy initiatives that seemed inconsistent. During the 1992 presidential campaign, Republican candidate, President George H.W. Bush accused Clinton of being "spotted in more places on an issue than Elvis Presley."[12]

As president, Clinton showed an ability to learn from his mistakes and increase his confidence in making tough decisions, especially in the realm of foreign policy when he decided to launch military strikes to protect US interests. He also made bold decision when he tried to achieve a peace deal between the Israelis and Palestinians at Camp David.

George W. Bush described himself as "the decider" and exuded great confidence in his abilities as a decision-maker. In his early White House days, he was able to move his limited agenda forward and made clear, concise decisions on education reform and tax policy. Bush surrounded himself with competent professionals and with a vice president of unusually strong political credentials.

President Bush excelled in many decisions he made after the 9/11 terrorist attacks on the United States and earned a tremendous level of public support for his decisions to root out al-Qaeda from Afghanistan, to give law enforcement and intelligence agencies more freedom to operate, and to bail out New York City. But a president also faces issues that are not always clear-cut, and Bush's preference for clear and quick decisions interfered with his ability to determine the consequences of those decisions.

Barack Obama relied a great deal on evidence and facts, not emotion, to reach decisions, and he demonstrated a capacity to hear from all sides of an issue and structure a process to bring the matter forward and force a decision. He showed resolve and speed in decision-making around the economic stimulus and healthcare reform packages that his administration championed. President Obama showed tremendous decision-making acumen in planning and executing the special forces raid in Pakistan that led to the elimination of Osama bin-Laden.

Donald Trump's decision-making style reflected his personality; it was bold, inconsistent, often impetuous, and frequently not based on evidence. Trump often announced his decisions on social media, without the knowledge of White House staff. He made abrupt policy and personnel changes that took his own advisers by surprise. Because of the absence of proper vetting by competent staff, some of President Trump's decisions were ignored or deflected by his own staff, such as the policy banning transgender from military service. His abrupt decision to withdraw US troops from Syria led to the resignation of Secretary of Defense Jim Mattis.

President Trump decided to downplay the COVID-19 pandemic and the delay the sale of military hardware to Ukraine for political reasons. He decided to challenge the veracity of the 2020 presidential election outcome based on a "big lie" about election fraud, in spite of the fact that his own Attorney General and at least 60 state and federal courts rejected the claim.

On the other hand, Trump made a bold decision in helping to facilitate the Abraham Accords between Israel and several Gulf states, establishing diplomatic, business, cultural, and trade relationships between Israel and several of its Arab neighbors. And he showed effective leadership and decision-making when he facilitated the development of a COVID-19 vaccine in record time.

Joe Biden based his presidential decision-making on his 36 years of experience in the US Senate and his 8 years as vice president in the Obama administration. President Biden was able to draw on his knowledge and experience to make effective decisions in the White House. With the assistance of an experienced chief of staff, in addition to other policy professionals in the White House and agencies, Biden decided to launch a substantial federal effort to get Americans vaccinated, and won legislative support to provide federal relief to states, localities, and individuals who suffered during COVID-19.

At times, however, Biden's prior experience might have interfered with effective decision-making. For example, he overrode his chief military advisers when he ordered a complete, and abrupt, withdrawal of US troops from Afghanistan. Analysts suggested that Biden believed Obama had been "rolled" by the military when he ordered a significant increase in troops to Afghanistan. The withdrawal was quite flawed and cost Biden dearly in public support.

TAKEAWAYS FOR ALL LEADERS

- Leaders are more likely to make sound decisions when they are guided by analysis, logic, and evidence rather than impulse or emotion.
- Leaders must encourage a furious debate among their executive team before making a decision.
- A leader with a focused agenda.
- Even with the input of a team, the leader cannot escape the ultimate responsibility for a decision and the loneliness and burden that can result.
- Once a decision has been made, the leader must plan for the careful and strategic communication of that decision.
- It does not serve the leader, or anyone else, if members of the team publicly disagree about the decision.

- Even powerful leaders can be duped by their own advisers when those advisers try to shelter the leader from bad news or provide them with incomplete information.
- The sources of influence on a leader's decision-making are varied, and sometimes surprising.
- In leadership, decision-making is not the end of a process, but frequently the beginning of one.
- Confidence is a positive attribute for leadership decision-making, but it must be balanced with a modicum of humility because we live in uncertain times.
- A leader needs to monitor the consequences of his/her decision.
- Sometimes, strong conviction, even stubbornness by the leader can result in a positive outcome.
- Leaders can grow in decision-making capability and confidence.

It is not clear that we could have predicted the exact performance of the eight presidents by considering their family background, educational experiences, wealth, age, or even prior political experience. In their backgrounds, 3 had come from wealthy families, 2 from the middle class, and 3 from relatively poor families; 4 had been governors; 2 had been US Senators (one for only part of a term); 2 had attained an undergraduate degree, while 6 had achieved postgraduate degrees (mostly in law or business); they ranged in age (at the start of their presidencies) from 52 to 78; only two came from politically active and connected families, the others made it on their own; two campaigned as "insiders," all the rest as "outsiders" (of one kind or another).

None of the above factors seemed to have profoundly influenced the performance of the eight presidents in the White House. The conclusion of this book is that what matters more than family pedigree, formal education, social standing, prior political experience, and age is the leadership acumen of the president. Success seems to be tied to the president's ability to chart a clear vision, goal, or purpose that can energize his party and unify the country (policy); his capacity to select talented people around him, especially men and women who understand the nuances of developing effective relationships with Congress (politics); his attention to designing an effective management structure in the White House and cabinet agencies that will execute the president's agenda (structure); and his comfort and skill in making and announcing tough decisions, while understanding the need to actively encourage dissenting viewpoints in the deliberations phase (process).

These leadership criteria easily apply to leadership challenges on many other sectors of society, although there is no doubt that the White House environment is unique. The author has, nonetheless, tried to show the relevance of the four leadership variables to other sectors and important "takeaways" for all leaders.

All institutions need strong leaders, and the men and women who aspire to leadership need a road map or blueprint for success. The author hopes that he has provided this road map or blueprint that considers the leadership triumphs and failures of eight US presidents, and how the "lessons learned" might assist other leaders.

Notes

1 Joseph C. Rost, "Leadership Development in the New Millennium." *The Journal of Leadership Studies*, 1993, Vol. 1. No. 1, 93.
2 John Dickerson, *The Hardest Job in the World: The American Presidency.* New York, NY: Random House, 2020.
3 The "arena" is a term used by President Theodore Roosevelt to describe the space that courageous leaders enter to fulfill their dreams and redeem their promises. It also suggests that leaders must fight.
4 Cannon, *President Reagan*, 55.
5 Mann, *Reagan's Revolution.*
6 Siegel, *The President as Leader*, 2nd ed., 321.
7 The "Vulcans" were close advisers to Bush, like Dick Cheney, Paul Wolfowitz, and Condoleezza Rice who encouraged a very hard line against the terrorist threat. See, James Mann, *The Rise of the Vulcans: The History of Bush's War Cabinet.* New York, NY: Viking, 2004.
8 Burns, *Leadership.*
9 Gergen, *Eyewitness to Power*, 169.
10 Gergen, *Eyewitness to Power*, 183.
11 McClellan, *What Happened.*
12 R. Cutler and D.A. Pennebaker, "*The War Room.*" United States: Cyclone Films, 1993.

INDEX